HOME COOK

Also by Alastair Hendy:

Mushrooms
Cooking for Friends
Fresh in Spring
Fresh in Summer
Fresh in Autumn
Fresh in Winter

To Mum, Dad and Catherine. My Family.

Contents

introduction

I eat Big Macs. I love their fries. I eat junk doner kebabs, dialled-up pizzas and Kentucky Fried Chicken. I don't always feel brilliant afterwards – but I still do it. Twiglets, Hula Hoops and those cheap orange Wotsits I'll scoff. I put squirty chocolate sauce and that toffee stuff from the squeezy bottle on to ice-cream, and I'll put the tomato ketchup on the table with my fish pie. Yet I insist on only buying free-range everything, my chocolate has to be busting with cocoa solids, and I'll fuss over which virgin oil gets to handle my salad leaves. Don't we all? It's not some quasi-inverted snobbery, is it? Who cares anyway. I don't give a toss what others think. I just love my food, in all its guises – down 'n' dirty or exceptionally good.

A lot of us now cook rarely. And I'm not going to preach that you should. We're way too busy. Anyway, there are now so many routes for us to get to instant food. And that's fine. So, in this book I've taken the view that when we do want to cook, we want to do it properly. Why else buy a cookbook? Really – *why?* Methods may look long, not because things are in any way tricky or take time, or because I want to bore

the socks off you, but because some of us need to know exactly how to get something right. To get a result.

And when I say cook, I don't mean restaurant food. Go out to have that. You'll never achieve it at home. I mean cook the everyday stuff you can't get in restaurants. Not the stuff of clever-clog master chefs but home food. I've left out the cheats' shortcuts of cook-in sauces or ready-made dressings and things, for you might just as well go and buy a complete ready-made meal. And there's nothing wrong in that. No, I've devoted this book to proper home cooking. All the things I reckon we want today when we cook. Fast-and-furious and five-ingredient cooking may have instant appeal but this doesn't mean easy. The sling-it-in-the-pan stuff requires technical skill. A slow-cooked pot of gorgeousness may have a long list of ingredients and take time in the oven but will demand nil from you. Remember that.

Home food is all-round stuff now: it can be quick enough for last-minute things; big enough for the family Sunday lunch; and proper enough to do dinner with. You'll be loved and adored by all for a shepherd's pie or a spag bol. The ordinary is now special. And thanks to our love of Italian food, we've learnt to

get to grips with fresh ingredients again – and the simple ways in which things can be cooked to get the best out of them.

Not that long ago all posh cooking was done *à la française* – just think 70s – but it didn't stay; its flamboyant saucing went out with glam rock. And so we turned to Italy. Then we didn't know our bruschetta from our crostini or our tagliatelli from our linguini – let alone know what they were. Lasagne and Sophia Loren were equal exotics (Father still thinks so). We've gone AWOL on it now. So hell-bent on it that we think things like pasta are ours. We bodge it around a bit though, doing what we do best – gorgeous atrocities that would have Latino mamas' hands ringing in the air. Only Italians can cook proper Italian you know, but bless us, eh?

Our daily lives have changed – quotidian things like walking less, over-heating our homes – and we no longer need the fuel of the old-style food. And what with all this whizzing off to far-flung corners of the globe, we now hanker for the stuff from the East too. Yet although British food may now have its fingers in every pie, it still clings to its roots. The best carries some historical weight and mum's no-nonsense stuff is up there too. I reckon it's grabbed the best of all worlds – but without too much to master. We love the authentic, but then we also love it trashed to perfection. At home, we do world food our way, and that's by simplifying it. Much of which we were raised on. It's fabulous stuff, and I'm going to sing on endlessly about it in this book.

We cooks are now a mixed bunch. Some who may be excellent with a wok or – more worryingly – a dab-hand with the blow-torch, haven't a clue how to knuckle down to make a seriously good fish pie. There again, those brilliant at roasts, gravy and perfect roast potatoes are, when it comes to throwing together a Moroccan tagine or a mound of glorious couscous, as good as fish riding bicycles. So, with a mind firmly set on how to get the best out of our ingredients easily, I've covered it all – and spelt out the basics in detail, so that less confident cooks will not be left with a jigsaw of ingredients without a plot. 'Your instructions reminded me of the

ones you write for strangers to find their way to a wedding,' wrote reader Ian Hillary of my recipes in my column in the *Sunday Times*. Well, I learnt how to cook from books, so I know how important it is for a recipe to be clear and directional, and above all to end in something wonderful. (Not that weddings always do.)

I'm nearly done. Phew. But just one more thing. I know we cookery writers all bang on about using locally grown seasonal veg – yawn – but it does make a huge difference. The better the ingredient, the less work you need to do to it: less time at the hob, more time for you. The same goes for meat and eggs. Animals that have led a life – been allowed to graze, root and forage in fields and fresh air, interact with each other, build muscle without in-feed antibiotics and hormones – will taste good. This may cost a few pounds more but – wow! – you'll taste every decent bit of it.

And I don't want you to get hung up on measuring out. All

that precision. Slavishly measuring things to a tee can be a right turn-off in cooking. When I say a tablespoon of something, you can guess it when you tip the packet or jar. So, I've made this book for everyone: me, you, mums, dads, sisters, brothers, aunties, the lot – all non-cooks and cooks alike. Fish sauce and Worcestershire sauce, and lemongrass and asparagus is about as exotic as it gets. It's not poncy but straightforward stuff, and I hope you thumb, spatter, crease and mark the pages. Really use it.

Note – All recipes serve four, unless otherwise stated, and all tablespoon and teaspoon measures are level. I've kept many of the cake-type recipe ingredients in 5g denominations for those that like to convert back to ounces (not that it helps us metrics). Tea time we have no time for, so I take it that when we make a cake now it's either for a pud or for a birthday or something. Hence why there's more sponge and less proper cake on offer in here. Sense, I think. Hope you agree.

On toast, eggs and fry-ups

Come the weekend, I wake late and loll in front of the TV with something fried to eat. And usually it's on toast. This – quite happily – goes against the way I was brought up. My military father would turf me out of my duvet at an unjust hour on Sundays, and attach me to the mower. Why the grass couldn't be seen to later in the day still escapes me. Then came breakfast, an orderly and regimented affair: toast had to be meagrely buttered and cut into four neat squares; no elbows on table; naturally he disapproved of fried food; and telly was verboten till 6 pm. All this has got me to enjoying lying-in longer than I hope is good for me, eating large toast that drips butter, and taking fry-ups in bed – all washed down with kids' TV. His disapproval has made the whole bed-in-breakfast experience a truly rewarding one. Thanks, Dad.

Brunchy breakfasts are an invention for people like me. It's for those who stay up too late, get up too late, have missed breakfast but want something like it for lunch with perhaps something puddingy thrown in too. Like something I once ate at the Palace Café, New Orleans. In this temple to breakfast excess, grilled spicy sausages arrived piled on to fried eggy-bread with fried apple and pecan nuts heaped on top, and it didn't end there – as the lot was varnished in a drench of maple syrup. Pudding meets main course. Don't Americans always know how to over-do everything?

Some of the best all-day breakfasts or brunchy snacks come either on toast or sandwiched between it. Simple and pretty instant, they make supper too. Toast is a transformer, meagre stuff becomes a meal. Your average tomato, once sliced and popped on toast, then salted, peppered and splashed with fruity virgin olive oil, can make your holiday memories of grade one Vesuvius-reared toms pale into insignificance. The toast does something. Think cheese on toast, with a splash of Worcestershire sauce. Pips the post, always. Mum sprinkles garlic granules on hers – and I sometimes spread a layer of mustard on the toast first. Dad would do cans with toast – curried beans was his most creative: curry powder and some sultanas stirred into baked beans, and we'd eat it with a dab of butter on top. Sardines on toast was another favourite: a tin of the fishes mashed with Branston pickle, a splash of white wine vinegar and a few twists of pepper. Sounds dodgy, I know, but tastes the part – and made Sunday nights Sunday nights.

And mushrooms. Mushrooms on toast would be my last meal on earth. It's pure mushroominess; it's home; and it's the simplest dish I always want to know. Nothing fancy, mind. It either has to be those giant flat-cap field mushrooms or a host of perfect pearly little button mushrooms. The sort I grew up on: fried in a foam of hot butter, twisted with black pepper and mounded on doorstops of buttered toast. The toast acts as juice collector, making the prized final mouthful out of this world.

The perfect omelette

My prep-school art and pottery teacher, Pam McDonald – who hated cooking but loved throwing pots – would fluff-up her omelettes by whizzing the frying pan under a hot grill. The egg mixture would soufflé into a 15-tog duvet of eggy loveliness. There are many ways to make an omelette – and that was hers. And a good one. More fascinating than the making of pots.

What's the secret behind a good omelette? You need more eggs than you'd imagine to make an omelette for one. Too few and your average-sized frying pan will produce something thin and flannel-like. So use at least four eggs – you can always cut it in half and serve it up for two. Now, don't season the omelette mixture before cooking. Once I forgot to season the mix, only getting to salt 'n' pepper on dishing up, and it turned out drop-dead fluffy gorgeous. The reason being – and since learnt – that salt breaks down the enzymes in the egg mixture, thus sabotaging it. So, salt at the end. And don't thrash your eggs. Over-beating will kill them. They just need a good forking, if you get me. There are some omelettes that are made from egg yolks folded into foamy, whipped-up egg whites, which produce rather fancy souffléd hotel-type omelettes.

They don't have the true texture or flavour that omelette connoisseurs would lick lips on. So, manhandling of eggs is a definite no-no.

The eggs? It goes without saying that the best eggy things are made from the freshest of eggs. That means free-range eggs that have deep orange yolks from hens that have done henny things and clucked contentedly. Eggs have porous shells, so don't store them next to anything smelly because they'll soak it in. They also lose moisture and gain air the longer they're left, so if you're not sure how long yours have been lying around, here's a test: put an egg in water – if it sinks, it's fine; if it floats end up – it's turning but still okay; if it bobs on its side – chuck it.

And which pan? If you have one, use a good-old all-steel frying pan, preferably with a 20cm diameter base, for even heat distribution. It should be well seasoned. This means it's seen much cooking and has gained a natural fat-baked coating – which makes it pretty non stick. Or you can use a non-stick pan.

Filling your omelette If you want to tart it up a bit more add one of the following, but not an Aladdin's cave of the lot: some cooked asparagus; cheese, such as grated Gruyère or Parmesan, or Boursin for something retro; fried bacon bits; chopped soft herbs (parsley, basil, chives, chervil and tarragon) for *omelette fines herbes*; or blanched spinach. Wild garlic leaves are up for free grabs in spring if you reside in the country. In autumn some fried wild mushrooms could be added with Parmesan. For something Mexican – and now bordering on over-elaboration – throw in chopped avocado, tomato, coriander and a dash of Tabasco, or go Chinese and stuff it with some wok-fried beansprouts, garlic and prawns.

Omelette

An omelette is a great user-upper of things you have left lying around in always ridiculously small quantities. But don't crowd it. Keep it simple. It's how I like mine, and the following quantities make one omelette.

4 large eggs, at room temperature
large knob of butter, that's about 30g
small dash of oil, about 2 tsp (to prevent the
    butter from scorching)

Break the eggs into a mixing bowl, then using a fork, break up the yolks first, then gently mix them with the whites. The idea is to end up with a yolky looking mixture that still has strong trails of white running through it.

Set your frying pan with its butter and oil over a good heat and get the lot foaming. Plenty of butter makes a good omelette. Swirl the fat around the pan so that it washes the sides, then tip the egg mixture into it and turn up the heat. The pan should be hot to start, so that the omelette seals and browns. Immediately, using a table knife in one hand and tipping the pan at different angles in the other, draw in the setting egg, so that more of the loose mixture hits the pan. This will produce a lovely light rucked effect to the setting egg –

like a kicked-up bed. After about 30 seconds or so, turn down the heat and leave the pan flat. (There should still be plenty of runny egg on top.)

It will be done before you think it is, so catch it at the stage where the egg is still a little wobbly and runny on top. About a minute or so after the drawing-in bit, lift the edge to check it's golden. At this point you can fill it. But tread carefully. Omelettes shouldn't be fancified too much, otherwise you lose the textures and subtleties of the soft egg, and the filling will steal the show. Put any of the fillings specified overleaf on to the omelette before you roll it up. Then flip it over on to itself and roll it out of the pan on to a warmed plate, and the egg will continue to cook and remain seductively gooey inside. Now season it a little, and dig in. Never keep an omelette waiting. But if you like your omelette plain, leave as it is – just season before rolling over on to the warmed plate.

Spanish omelette

A Spanish omelette – a tortilla – is an omelette fattened with slices of delicious olive-oil-poached potato. It's my choice for when I'm in need of something delicate yet bold. If you're not keen to use your oil on poaching potatoes then use boiled spuds instead (a good way with leftovers), frying them first with the onion before adding the egg. You can – if you must – chuck other things into this one too, such as bits of chorizo, roast or grilled red pepper, chilli, artichoke, ham, bacon, prosciutto etc. So, a good one for hoovering-up the fridge hangers-on and all the bits and bobs left in packets or jars. Serves two or a very hungry one.

250ml olive oil
1 onion, chopped
1 clove garlic, finely chopped
350g small waxy potatoes, peeled and cut
   lengthways in half if long, or into thick
   slices if rounded
4-5 large eggs, lightly beaten

Heat the olive oil in a 25cm diameter frying pan and fry the onion with the garlic until translucent. Add the spuds and some salt, cover with a large saucepan lid, and gently stew, without frying, for about 20 minutes or until tender. Remove the potato and onion with a slotted spoon and drain on kitchen roll, then tip the oil out of the pan and keep for later use. Put about 3 tsp of the oil back in the pan and place on a medium heat, then scatter in the potatoes and onion and pour over the beaten egg. Once the mixture has begun to set, shake the pan gently but firmly at regular intervals, to prevent sticking and burning. Reduce the heat to medium-low and cook for a further 3 minutes.

Run a bendy knife around the edges of the omelette to free its edges. Place a large plate over the top, and – holding the two together – invert the tortilla on to the plate. Add a touch of oil again to the pan and slide the tortilla back in – uncooked side down – and cook for about 3 minutes on low, giving it a nudge to make sure it's not catching. Alternatively, to avoid breakage or a full-on collapse, don't invert the tortilla, just slip the pan under a preheated grill for a minute or two, rather than flip it over. The tortilla should end up with a softish centre and not be rock solid. Eat up – it's a good one.

Mum's scrambled egg and bacon toast

I reckon you need at least two large eggs per person for scrambled egg. You can omit the bacon and add grated Cheddar to the egg just before spilling it over the toast if you like – and a splash of Tabasco will Mexicanise it. Alternatively, fold the scrambled egg with fried chopped onion and mushrooms or herbs. Variations are endless. This one serves two.

4 large hen or duck eggs
30g butter
2 tbsp crème fraîche
2 rashers bacon, chopped, or a big handful of
   lardons, both fried until crisp
2 rounds hot buttered toast

Crack the eggs into a bowl and very lightly fork together. Melt the butter in a frying pan (preferably a non-stick one) or large saucepan over a gentle heat and swirl it around – but don't let it brown. Then tip in the eggs and stir every few seconds, making sure you scrape the base of the pan with a wooden spatula. When the egg looks like it's setting, stir in some salt and pepper, the crème fraîche, then the crisped bacon and remove from the heat. The egg should still be ever-so-slightly runny at this stage – for it will have cooked further by the time it reaches the plate. Pile on to buttered toast, and put some tomato sauce at the ready for those that feel naked without it.

A jumble of mushrooms on buttery toast

No set of toast recipes would be complete without it. I can eat this morning, noon and night. Here's a reminder.

button mushrooms (button chestnut or tiny
   pearl ones), or large flat caps, thickly sliced
butter, for frying and buttering
thick slices of white bread (tin loaf or
   farmhouse)

Fry the mushrooms in some butter until well browned – but don't lower the heat too much, otherwise they'll release all their delicious juices into the pan. Season with salt and plenty of black pepper when cooked. Toast the bread until golden brown and be generous with the butter. Top the toast with the mushrooms and scrape out any of the remaining juices in the pan on top. Twist over some more pepper and serve straightaway.

Variation Add roughly chopped marjoram, thyme or some sage leaves to the pan, and then you can go in a garlic direction too if you like. (The meaty flat-cap mushrooms are great with a dollop of horseradish cream on top: beat freshly grated horseradish into crème fraîche with finely chopped shallot, and a tsp of honey dissolved in a dash of wine vinegar, and some seasoning.) There again, forget about toast and turn it into salad: toss the fried mushrooms with fried bacon bits and garlic, then tip the pan contents over salad leaves, splash with balsamic vinegar, more of your best virgin, and then throw over some shavings of Parmesan. A classic with those ladies that lunch.

Roes on toast

Roes are totally underrated. For me, they're as gorgeous as sweetbreads or foie gras – for their textures and flavours are similar, yet are had for a fraction of the cost. Easy-peasy too.

500g herring roes (available from all
   fish counters)
plain flour
60g butter
drop of vegetable oil
2 shallots, chopped
2 tbsp capers, rinsed, or soaked if salted
   (optional)
4 thick slices buttered toast
juice of 1 lemon
handful of rocket leaves (optional)

Rinse the roes under cold water, drain and dab off excess moisture with kitchen roll. Season them all over, then roll in a plate of flour until coated. Fry them in the butter and oil until golden on all sides and tender, about 3 minutes. Then stir in the shallot and capers (if using), and cook for a further minute until the shallot loses its edge but hasn't completely softened. Pile on to the buttered toast. Add the lemon juice to the pan, whack up the heat and swirl it about a bit, then spoon the lemony butter over the top. Add a wodge of rocket (if using), and serve.

Quick tomato bruschetta

Use any tomatoes you have. Blob with a bit of goat's cheese too if you fancy. Great on barbecue-grilled bread. Another great way is to roast vines of cherry tomatoes in a hot oven with a spash of olive oil and sea salt for 8 minutes until they're at splitting point, then plonk these on the toast, squashing them into the toast as you eat – another deliciousness.

4 thick slices bread (any sort, but not that flimsy
   pre-sliced white)
extra virgin olive oil
4 large plum tomatoes or other toms
handful of basil leaves, ripped or chopped

Toast or grill the bread, then lay each slice on a plate and slosh with a little oil and sprinkle with a little sea salt. Slice up the tomatoes either into wedges, chunks or thick slices, and pile on to the toast with the basil. Sprinkle with sea salt, twist over some pepper, slosh generously with oil, and eat. (See image on page 10.)

The ultimate cheeseburger

A double cheeseburger that holds Cheddar in the mince mixture and Roquefort on top. Multi-storey it with sliced gherkin, some crispy bacon if you like, and more salad. Makes four big burgers – makes supper.

500g lamb or beef mince
6 spring onions, finely chopped
2 cloves garlic, crushed
2 tsp dried oregano or fresh thyme leaves
2 tsp Worcestershire sauce
½ tbsp Dijon mustard
100g mild Cheddar, grated
olive oil

To serve:
4 soft rolls or burger baps
4 tbsp mayonnaise
1 beef tomato, sliced
handful of salad leaves
4 tbsp Roquefort or other blue cheese, crumbled
4 fine slices red onion

Mix together the first seven ingredients, season to taste, then shape the mixture into four large flat burger shapes. Brush with oil, and cook in a preheated chargrill pan for about 2 minutes on each side.

To assemble, spread each half of the split rolls with the mayonnaise, then on to each bottom half add a couple of tomato slices and some lettuce, and plonk the hot burgers on top. Top this with the Roquefort cheese and the onion, then glue the lot together with the other dressed half of roll, and savour. (See image on page 11.)

Pitta burgers with humous and mint

Lamb, humous and mint, you can't put a foot wrong.

1 tbsp each of cumin and sesame seeds
1 onion, finely chopped
2 cloves garlic, crushed
olive oil
500g lamb mince
1 bunch mint leaves
4 pitta breads
150g humous
1 lemon, quartered

First toast the cumin seeds and the sesame seeds in a hot, dry frying pan until the sesame seeds are a light golden brown. Watch them, and turn them regularly, as they'll burn if left alone. Then mix with 1 tbsp sea salt. Next, fry the onion, garlic, and 2 tsp of the seed salt in a dash of olive oil until the onion is soft and transparent. Tip out of the pan then mix this with the lamb. Chop up about a third of the mint and mix this in too along with some black pepper. Shape the lamb mixture into burgers (they'll hold in the fridge for 24 hours at this stage), brush with oil, and grill in the frying pan – or on a barbie – for about 2 minutes on each side.

Meanwhile, pop the pittas in the toaster – or over the grill rack – to warm through, then split them open and slather the insides with humous and stuff in some mint – be generous. Shove in the burgers, sprinkle with a little of the seed salt, squeeze with lemon, and eat.

Home cheese and onion toasted sandwich

Trendy sandwich bars would use part-baked baguette – you know, the anaemic ones balloon-bagged in threes in the supermarket – then grill them on a ridged pan, and call them panini, *the Italian name for toasted sarnies. The garlic butter here can also be used to make 70s style garlic bread.*

60g butter
2 cloves garlic, crushed
2 sprigs thyme, leaves roughly chopped
8 slices bread or 4 small part-baked baguettes, split
2 good handfuls each of grated Gruyère and Cheddar cheeses, or other melty cheeses
½ Spanish onion or red onion, finely chopped
6 baby leeks, or 1 leek, cleaned and finely chopped
olive oil if necessary

Mash the butter with the garlic, thyme and a sprinkling of salt, then spread over one side of each piece of bread or baguette half. Toss together the remaining ingredients (apart from the oil) and season, then stack them on top of four slices of bread and sandwich with the remaining slices.

Preheat a heavy pan until smoking hot (preferably one that's ribbed). If it's not well oiled, brush the bread with a little oil. Then grill each sandwich, weighting it down with the base of a cooking pan on top, then carefully turn over, and do the same again. About a minute or so on each side.

Bowls of salad and mayonnaise

Come summer, when meat (that once was four legs) is too meaty; fish is just too fishy; veg means steam (and I'm not prepared to sweat it out); then it's leaves, ripe toms, oils and vinegars, and cold chicken time. Salad. Anything cool and crunchy, to be exact. There again, come winter, and a good salad saves me from over-dosing on mash, pies and too much roasting.

It's the home salads of old that do the rounds in my house with regularity. One in particular – Mum's French picnic salad: dwarf beans boiled with a rasher of bacon to flavour them, then tossed in a garlicky French dressing. And her various potato salads. A favourite is freshly boiled and skinned Jersey Royal potatoes, turned with lemon, olive oil and garlic while still warm, then showered with chopped spring onion, and blobbed with a few wobbles of thick mayonnaise; everything is then turned together until the little spuds are slicked with a slippery white creamy coat, dimpled green, and wafting tempered lemon and warm potato. Fantastic. With the addition of a few fried bacon lardons buried in the dressing, it's a meal in itself. Warm waxy potatoes will take on all the flavours you chuck their way, especially vinaigrettes and herbs.

Time and place and fresh things are all important to a good salad – and so is its dressing. I love mayonnaise. Everyone loves mayonnaise. My favourite lunch is a lovely fat crab, with a freshly baked baguette, a lemon and a little pot of thick mayonnaise, for dipping and dunking into. Everything gets more fabulous for mayonnaise. Go to a crab boil in Louisiana and they'll peg the table top with a piece of Fablon and tip a mound of steaming cooked crabs, corn cobs and potatoes across the top. The table is one heaving communal plate. There are no knives or forks, just implements for cracking open shells and wheedling out juicy flakes of meat. And there are no fancy sauces, just industrial-sized bottles of Tabasco and vast uncapped jars of mayonnaise. It's a hands-on job. A time to get really stuck into things and get your hands and face slathered in all that's sweet, salty – and mayonnaised.

Now, a good salad only gets as good as its dressing. Dressings are their make or break. It should enhance, rather than bully or swamp and slaughter. So sometimes the mayo won't do. For instance, with a bowl of nubile little spring leaves is when to use that pricy single estate olive oil you may have let lurk in the cupboard too long – and leave it at that. Or go one stage further and spill with a few drops of best balsamic vinegar. Lovely though an elegant film of the best virgin may be, there are those dead-end days when I lust for something more. When salad is something you munch through daily and has turned into a bit of a wade, it's time to unleash a bit of oomph and inject some event. Enter Asian-style dressings. Their explosive hot, sweet, salt and sour combinations work wonders – and shake the ass off the mundane.

Green salad should be just that. Green. A combination of the crunchy, the delicate and the smooth, and the sweet with the peppery. Now, those supermarket salad bags hold miserable stuff. Convenient, yes, but always full of bruised leaves that give-up-the-ghost once out. So buy them undeconstructed – that's as a good old lettuce, or loose from a farmers' market box. There's an encyclopaedia botanica of different named leaves creeping in now – all very dainty and embryonic, yet tasty. But the lettuce leaves of old are still the classics. Iceberg for one. Yes, iceberg, Mum's good old stand-by. Then the soft bright green round lettuce, so English – yet so favoured by the French in their *salade niçoise*. And the full-flavoured cos or romaine. I think it the most handsome flavoured leafy thing, of all edible leafy things.

Now, when tossing a salad together – which is the beauty of the thing – I rarely go to the elaborate lengths of actually cooking things to go in it. If I do, it has to be easy quick-kiss-of-the-pan type stuff. More usually, I just grab at what's already sitting in the fridge, shred, flake or chop it, and in it goes. Then I drop something effulgent into the dressing, to boot the whole caboodle into action. That said, there are occasions when leafage is *le plat du jour*, then the wayward smash-and-grab tactics are put in check and stuff is thought out and cooked from scratch.

Remember, crisper leaves – akin to cos – hold their ground with heavier dairy-type saucings, and won't go to mulch. And do make sure everything is rip-roaring fresh and not eaten over-chilled: well-sprung turgid leaves equal big flavour, and all the crunch and green will be in there, too. Green stuff that's at death's door, you won't have a party with.

Here are the favourites, with lots of mayo, and lots of chickeny ones – and all damn good, but of course. And a salad can be just for Christmas, too, so there's the best in coleslaws, and other ideas – but not as mum would have dared it.

And PS Do not go near lollo rosso: the most misguided, pappy, frothy, tasteless, big-girl's-blouse of whoring low-life, the most wishy-washy pile of leaves ever created.

The perfect mayonnaise

Mayonnaise is the combination of an egg yolk with a load of oil. It's as simple as that, but can be tricky to pull off. So, if you're not into making mayo...use a jar. They're perfectly good – and skip over the next few pages. But, if you are, it's good to get some kind of grip on what you're doing here. The egg has to be emulsified with the oil, which means that the two – with your measured assistance – must thoroughly bond with one another as they meet. If not handled correctly the party

won't take off, and the oil and yolks part. A good mayo for me is not made with olive oil, for it should taste bland and faintly eggy, not peppery, fruity and green.

What's the fail-safe way to make it? I'd say in the food processor. However, if your processor is one of the larger models, you may find you have to make a double quantity as the blades may only skim the surface of the yolks, beating them insufficiently when the first drops of oil are added. Alternatively use a hand whisk and a bowl, and anchor it by sitting it on a folded damp tea-towel – to prevent spin as you beat. Beating maniacally with the one hand and gingerly pouring the thinnest stream of oil from a jug in the other, can be tricky. Always make sure your eggs are at room temperature: cold eggs are less willing, and sometimes downright refuse to behave.

How do I start? Process the yolks with the specified mustard powder and salt, then allow a few intermittent drips – that's delicate drips, not splashes – of oil to drop through the feed tube into the spinning blades. It doesn't matter which oil goes in first. Keep going, allowing each batch of drops to be thoroughly incorporated into the eggs before adding the next – for about a minute. Then slowly – and I mean so slowly that you're really concentrating on how slow you're going – increase the drops to intermittent needle-thin drizzles. They should be short sharp injections, not free-flowing streams.

Do this over the next 45 seconds. This is the most vital make-or-break stage in the process. So don't get cocky with it and think you can hurry things up.

You'll now notice the mixture has paled, looks silky and is beginning to resemble mayonnaise. Start to increase the drizzle to a very thin stream but break the stream every couple of seconds until you're convinced that the emulsion is happening. It's easy to be kidded as separation is not always apparent at first. So turn off (or stop whisking) and take a close look at the mixture: tiny white flecks are curdles, which mean it's going nowhere. If all is okay, carry on. Increase the flow of the oil to a steady, but still thin, stream. As you progress, the likelihood of curdling decreases – thank God. Add the lemon juice toward the end and, after tasting, more salt if it needs it.

And if the mixture separates? This is not a catastrophe. For you can start again with fresh egg yolks – minus mustard and salt – and still use the aborted mix. Once you've established an emulsion, start slowly adding the curdled mixture which will, amazingly, take to it. So no waste.

Too thick? Then 'let it down' with a drop of warm water. So, with the motor running, add about a tbsp of warm water and then test its fluidity. For me it should still hold a swirl but shouldn't allow a tsp to stand upright in it. For once left, it will firm further, and if chilled, will firm up more – with a nice wobble.

Mayonnaise

Now you've read the information opposite, follow this for a quick guide. These quantities make about 300ml.

2 large egg yolks, at room temperature
1 tsp English mustard powder
250ml groundnut, sunflower or vegetable oil
50ml olive oil (not virgin, optional)
squeeze of lemon juice

In a processor or using a whisk and bowl, beat the yolks with the mustard powder and ½ tsp salt, then at the same time add a few tiny drops of oil. Then slowly increase the drops to an intermittent ultra-thin drizzle, all the time processing or beating. Start to increase the drizzle to a very thin stream but break the stream every couple of seconds until you're convinced that the emulsion is happening. Then increase the stream, until you have a nice thick mayonnaise. Now beat in a squeeze of lemon juice and stick in your finger for a taste – then add more lemon or salt, if needed. And if it's too thick, beat in a dash of warm water.

Take it a step further Mayonnaise is the master behind the **marie rose sauce** for prawn cocktails (see page 38); it makes the French Provençal garlic mayo, **aïoli** (just beat in 2 crushed garlic cloves); and this with the addition of a little more mustard powder and smoked paprika or pounded roasted red peppers, makes **rouille** – to dollop on to croûtons for bouillabaisse and fish soups. It's the base for **tartare sauce** for battered or breadcrumbed fish; and with soured cream and blue cheese, it makes an **American blue cheese dressing**. For something hot, add a tsp of wasabi (Japanese horseradish); or for **Thai mayo** add fish sauce, lime juice and basil – and so on. For a **rosemary aïoli**, pound 2 fat garlic cloves with a smidgen of sea salt until paste, then pound in around 3 tsp chopped rosemary needles. Once it looks like a green sludge, beat in 200ml mayo and sharpen up with enough lemon juice to suit your mood. This is fab with pan-roast cod, and if mixed with 200ml thick yoghurt makes a brilliant dip for crisps. Be creative, but only add one or two ingredients, otherwise you'll end up – as one Aussie said to me, 'with a right sha-mozzle – a bloody mess, mate.'

Classic French dressing

How you make up this classic is your shout. Essentially, its foundations are one part vinegar to three parts oil and usually – but not always – a little mustard, to which one or two other bits and pieces can be added, such as crushed or chopped garlic. If crushed is used, the dressing shouldn't be left lying around for more then two days, as it will turn rancid. Chopped garlic can be fished out. The process, no matter how simple, is still a creative one, as it involves a layering in and building of flavours – relying totally on your oils, vinegars and desires. Chopped soft herbs can be thrown in too.

2 tbsp white wine vinegar
2 tsp Dijon mustard
6 tbsp extra virgin olive oil or olive oil

Put the vinegar in a bowl with some salt and pepper and the mustard. (You may like to add about a ½ tsp sugar here too.) Next, using a whisk, beat the mustard into the vinegar until smooth. Then slowly add the oil, beating all the time, and carry on until it's formed a gloopy, homogenised liquid. Add more salt and pepper and beat in. Stick in your finger and give it a suck – it should pucker lips and tongue a little – then, remembering its force will dilute once on the leaves, add more seasoning if needed. If it's left to stand, and separates, just beat it together again. Then there's the cheat's way: put everything in a screw-top jar and give the lot a jolly good shake. Should have told you that in the beginning.

Asian dressing

This is the dressing in my kitchen. It turns the bland into fantastic. It's dairy free, oil free and – not that this ever dictates what I eat – it's healthy, so a great one if you're clocking the calories. It has to be a classic now. It's simply what the Vietnamese use as a dipping sauce. Add a handful of crushed and toasted peanuts on top of any pile of bits and pieces tossed with this and you're off. A little goes a long way, so use more sparingly than, say, a French dressing. And add a drop of oil, if you prefer. And if you want to use it as a dipping sauce, dilute with 1 tbsp of water.

2 small red bird's eye chillies, finely sliced
2 cloves garlic, crushed in a press
3 tbsp caster sugar
4 tbsp each of fish sauce, lime juice and rice
   vinegar

Whisk together all the ingredients (or shake up in a screw-top jar) until the sugar has dissolved, then leave to stand for about 20 minutes to allow the chilli and garlic to do their thing. Easy.

Chunky guacamole

If your coriander has roots, don't dump them: scrub them, then pound them with the garlic and a sprinkling of salt and work them into some of the lemon juice and add to the mix. Eat with anything or chuck over some crispy bacon – or have just as it is, on toast or stuffed into grilled pitta. It's also good with wok-fried chicken and rolled into a warm tortilla with a blob of soured cream – and more Tabasco for those that like it hot.

3 ripe avocados, halved and de-stoned
2 limes
2 cloves garlic, crushed
4 spring onions or ¼ red onion, chopped
4 good tomatoes, chunked, or handful of cherry
   tomatoes, halved
Tabasco sauce
extra virgin olive oil
big bunch of coriander, well washed
1 long mild red chilli (optional), finely shredded

Using a tsp, scoop out the avocado flesh in chunks into a bowl, then squeeze over the lime juice and toss through. Chuck in the garlic with the onion and tomatoes. Then splash to taste with Tabasco, sprinkle over salt and pepper, and add a good slosh of the oil, and turn through. Pull the coriander leaves from their stems over the lot. Turn through and give it a taste: make it hotter or perhaps add more lime juice to taste. To serve, chuck the chilli on top (if using) with more coriander.

Variation To make a more dip-like guacamole, mash the avocado to a paste before stirring in the other ingredients (good with Chilli con carne on Page 132).

Delicious grilled chicken, bacon and avocado salad with blue cheese dressing

This is comfort salad. And although you're stuffing yourself with calories, you can at least kid yourself they're the healthiest – after all, it's a salad.

2 large boned chicken breasts
oil (olive, vegetable or sunflower)
6 rashers back bacon
2 ripe avocados, de-stoned and peeled
juice of ½ lemon
30g blue cheese (any sort)
2 tbsp each of mayonnaise (see page 17) and
 soured cream
4 big handfuls young salad leaves (spinach,
 lamb's lettuce, rocket)

Remove the feather fillets, the pieces of meat found on the inner sides of the breasts. Next, using a rolling pin, lightly beat the thicker fillets to flatten them just a little. Then salt and pepper the meat and rub with oil. Next, either grill in a hot heavy pan, for about 2 minutes on each side or until cooked all the way through – testing with a knife for doneness (the juices should run clear) – or cut into chunks and fry until golden. Leave the chicken to rest while you grill or fry the bacon until cooked. Meanwhile, slice the avocado flesh into chunks or slices and toss with the lemon juice. Mash the cheese with the mayonnaise and soured cream, then beat together until smooth.

To serve, slice the chicken (if grilled), and chop the bacon into strips. Toss the leaves with the dressing until well coated, then tumble everything together Yum.

The best Caesar salad

Many ideas fly around on this one's dressing. Some put mayonnaise in, I don't. I prefer to use the richness of real yolks and then add my own olive oil – but use a bought mayonnaise if you can't eat raw egg. Others put lemon juice in, I prefer vinegar, and some over-anchovy it. Mine is what you're getting – and I know you'll like it. Don't be the snoot over which anchovies you use here. The ones packed in salt that you have to then soak for ages, de-bone and fiddle about with are a waste of time in this – and I think them too salty. Use regular bog-standard canned anchovies in oil – those little silver and white pickled ones can be nice, too. Add chicken and bacon too if you like. One thing we all agree on – the leaves gotta be cos.

2 large egg yolks
2 cloves garlic, crushed
2 tbsp sherry vinegar or white wine vinegar
250ml olive oil
1 x 50g can anchovies, drained
2 tbsp single cream
block of Parmesan
4 thick slices white bread (or baguette)
1 large feisty-looking cos lettuce, roughly torn

There's nothing tricksy to this – it's plain sailing all the way. So start by hand whisking the egg yolks with half the crushed garlic, adding the vinegar and a small dash of sea salt and black pepper. Go easy on the salt as you'll be adding anchovies next. Once well amalgamated, whisk in 200ml of the olive oil thoroughly, then add 4 chopped anchovies. You're not making anything like a mayonnaise, but try and add the oil in a thin steady stream. This could all be done in the processor if you prefer but is actually just as easy by hand. Then beat in the cream and then grate in around 30g of Parmesan. Beat together to make a flecked but smooth, creamy dressing.

Next, swirl the remaining garlic in the remaining olive oil. Tear up the bread into crude-shaped croûtons or cut into neat cubes, and toss in the garlicky olive oil. Then spread them over a baking sheet and bake in a 200°C/ 400°F/Gas 6 oven until crisp and crunchy.

In bowls or plates, layer the croûtons with the roughly torn cos leaves and a few whole anchovy fillets. Slick with the dressing and snow with grated or shaved Parmesan, as you pile. It's best dished up already portioned, otherwise things can get messy at table.

Poached egg and bacon brasserie salad

Curly endive (winter frisée), the lettuce that looks like a janitor's mop head, is the only leaf that will do here. Bitter tasting, strong and feisty, it's made for the powerful mustard and vinegary dressing and the pan-hot fat and bacon that's lavished upon it. Our supermarket summer frisée will sort of do, but sulks miserably when drenched – for it's a mere pauper to the true curly kind. Escarole lettuce is better, and is a relation of the feisty one. And spinach, although not authentic, is nice, too. When in Paris, I head for Les Halles, and frisée aux lardons, *all jumbled with garlicky croûtons, is the first thing I set to. The dog's bollocks – if you'll* pardonnez-moi.

12 slices baguette
olive oil
3 shallots, finely chopped
1 fat clove garlic, crushed
1 quantity Classic French dressing (see page 18) made with 1 tbsp Dijon mustard and an extra 2 tbsp vinegar
1 large curly endive lettuce, well washed and drained
big handful of flat-leaf parsley leaves, roughly chopped
4 tbsp white wine vinegar (for poaching)
4 very fresh large eggs
250g smoked fatty bacon lardons

Lay the slices of baguette across a roasting tin, slosh with oil, then bake in a 190°C/375°F/Gas 5 oven until crispy brown. Meanwhile, mix the shallots and garlic with the dressing. Discard the central core of the lettuce and toss the leaves into a big bowl with the dressing and parsley. Next, put the vinegar in a wide pan of water and bring to a simmer. Crack in the eggs, very carefully slipping them into the gently murmuring water, and poach for 2 minutes. The whites must be firm and the yolks soft. Scoop them out using a perforated or a wire basket spoon (a spider).

Meanwhile, fry the bacon until crispy – you may need to add a tbsp of oil to the pan to get the fat on the run – then chuck the lardons with all their hot fat over the bowl of dressed leaves, and turn through. Spoon on to deep plates, over the crunchy bread slices, pop an egg on top of each, smatter with pepper and a touch of salt on the egg, and you're away.

Salmon, new potato and egg mayonnaise salad

Simple and effective.

1 tbsp white wine vinegar
extra virgin olive oil
1 clove garlic, crushed
small bunch of chives or spring onions, snipped in half
500g new potatoes, boiled and peeled
2 x 300g pieces salmon fillet
2 tbsp each of crème fraîche and mayonnaise (see page 17)
1 head cos lettuce
6 large eggs, hard-boiled and halved
200g dwarf beans, blanched
3 beef tomatoes, quartered
1 tbsp capers or caper berries

Whisk the wine vinegar with 4 tbsp of the olive oil, the garlic and some salt and pepper, then stir in the chives. Toss with the freshly cooked potatoes, while they're still warm. Next, salt and pepper the salmon, rub with olive oil, then sear in a very hot heavy frying pan, without moving it about, for about 2 minutes on each side – it should be rare in the middle. Allow to cool a little then flake into big chunks and discard the skin. Beat the crème fraîche with the mayonnaise, and chill.

To serve, tear up the cos leaves and arrange them with the eggs, potatoes, beans, tomatoes and salmon on plates or in bowls, spoon over any remaining dressing, and chuck over the capers. Serve with a big dollop of creamy mayonnaise.

Mum's big teak bowl cucumber salad

This is one of life's basics in our house. It's the no-frills of green salads and it contains that most scorned of lettuces, the iceberg. It tastes wonderful. Iceberg has a good bland flavour and is best when chilled and crisp. No other lettuce will do here. This great salad, Mum makes in vast quantity with loads of highly peppered cucumber, tossing it all up in her big 60s teak salad bowl – and no patio barbecue is complete without it. I think she picked up the peppered cucumber bit when we lived in Germany. It's a real home salad, I can't enthuse enough…so let's get on with it.

1 large tsp Dijon mustard
1½ tbsp white wine vinegar
½-1 tsp caster sugar
4 tbsp olive oil (*not* extra virgin)
1 iceberg lettuce, not too big
1 medium cucumber

Put the mustard, vinegar, sugar and a pinch of salt into the base of a big salad bowl and beat them together, then beat in the oil. Next, quarter the lettuce, then pull it apart, letting it tumble into the bowl. Then peel and slice the cucumber into rounds very finely, and scatter it all over the iceberg in the bowl and twist it with lots and lots and lots of black pepper. finally, using salad servers, dig down deep and toss the salad together well, so that everything is awash with dressing.

Holiday seafood salad

Holidays around the Med. This is the one that does it for me.

4 cloves garlic, finely chopped
good olive oil
500g mussels or clams, scrubbed and soaked
2 medium squid tubes, cleaned and sliced into rings
12 uncooked prawns in the shell
300ml white wine
½ medium red onion, chopped
3 tbsp white wine vinegar
juice of 1 lemon
1 small bunch flat-leaf parsley, roughly chopped
2 large mild red chillies, deseeded and finely chopped

Gently fry half the garlic in 3 tbsp oil for 30 seconds, without colouring, then add the seafood. Pour in the wine, season, cover, whack up the heat and bring it to a lid-puffing bubble. Cook for around 2 minutes, then turn off the heat and leave to cool a little. Scoop out the seafood into a large bowl and de-shell most of the mussels, adding the meat back to the bowl (discard any shells still closed). Spoon in 5 tbsp shellfish juices from the pan, then add all the remaining ingredients and jumble through. Leave to bathe for 4 hours or overnight, chilled. Dress with 5 tbsp olive oil, taste for seasoning again, and serve with good bread.

Wonderful cherry tomato panzanella

Panzanella *is a Tuscan salad classic. Tomatoes in panzanella is not Italian – but then I'm not Italian. Without the toms it wouldn't be in this book, but with them it's fantastic. (Our everyday tomatoes are low on flavour, so I use the cherry ones – and sometimes chuck in some wedges of semi-dried tomatoes.) Traditionally the salad is tossed with day-old bread but ours is not strong enough even when stale, so to avoid a nasty slop, I tear fresh bread into chunky shapes and briefly bake them, like croûtons. Anchovies can be added, and peppers, which can be roasted and peeled (if you prefer them that way). To make this salad work, make sure you mix everything together – minus the croûtons – a good hour or so before you need it, time to allow the tomatoes to give up their juices to the dressing. For this salad completes its own dressing as it sits – and there's lots of it.*

¼ **white country loaf**
extra virgin olive oil
2 **fat cloves garlic**
1 **large mild red chilli, deseeded**
3 **tbsp red wine vinegar**
pinch of caster sugar
600g **cherry or baby plum tomatoes, halved**
1 **red pepper, deseeded and cut into smallish chunks**
½ **large cucumber, chopped into chunks**
2 **big sticks celery, finely sliced**
1½ **tbsp capers, rinsed**
4 **spring onions, chopped**
¼ **red onion, slivered**
small bunch of flat-leaf parsley or basil

Tear the bread into large croûtons – about six small chunks per person – then scatter the chunks across a baking sheet. Slosh here and there with a little oil – you could season the oil with some crushed garlic first – and sprinkle with salt, then bake in a 200°C/400°F/Gas 6 oven for about 10-15 minutes or until golden and crunchy. Once cooled, they'll keep fine for a day or two in a sealed container.

Meanwhile, crush the garlic with a small sprinkling of salt in a mortar, then chop up the chilli and crush this too, to make a coarse paste. (If you don't have a mortar and pestle, use the back of a spoon on a plate.) Add the vinegar and a spot of sugar, mix together, then tip into a large bowl. Add about 200ml extra virgin olive oil – yes, that's 200 – and beat together.

Pile all the remaining ingredients into the bowl, add a touch of salt and lots of black pepper, then toss together and leave at room temperature to stand for a good hour, turning through every 20 minutes or so.

To serve, arrange the croûtons in big bowls, pile salad on top of each and tip over the collected juices, then scatter more herb leaves over the heaps and serve.

Mum's potato salad

I don't know if Mum gets it slightly wrong but she always undercooks the spuds a little, and this is how I love it. A slight bite to the potatoes, along with her magic ingredient – a drop of Maggi sauce. Strange, I know, but it gives it a savoury edge, and perfects it. Always a winner at barbecues. Mix while hot, and eat when cold.

600g **new potatoes**
½ **fat lemon**
4 **spring onions or 1 small bunch chives, finely chopped**
1 **tsp Maggi sauce, or soy sauce (optional)**
4-5 **tbsp mayonnaise (see page 17)**

Boil the potatoes, peeled or in their skins (and peel afterwards) in salted water until just tender, but with a little bite. Pierce with a knife to test – there should be some resistance to their middles. Slice the potatoes into thick rounds or chunks, and while still warm, squeeze over the lemon juice and toss well with the rest of the ingredients, then leave to go cold.

Boxing Day coleslaw

All the food processor attachments come out for this one every year. We never remember which one does the job best. Once found, it shreds everything in seconds – and then we get trigger-happy, and always end up with way too much. But it all goes, and quickly. For bland and plain – without knobs on – it's the job.

1 eating apple
½ lemon
1 small white cabbage, cored and finely shredded
2 big carrots, coarsely grated
½ medium Spanish onion, coarsely grated
3 tbsp sultanas (optional)
6 tbsp mayonnaise

Coarsely grate the apple into a big mixing bowl, then squeeze it with lemon juice and toss. Mix in everything else until all is coated snow white. As per usual, taste, and add more salt, pepper or a squirt more lemon juice if you deem it needs it. All done.

Variation When enough is enough on the regular slaw front, I make this **delicious Asian slaw**. Sort of Mum's slaw goes to Thailand. If we'd done Thai in the 70s, this one we'd have concocted then. It's friendly and gorgeous, and a good one with any steak, chop or cutlet. Great too with rare roasted blackened beef – leftovers or deli bought. Simply mix the mayonnaise with 5 tbsp Asian dressing (see page 18) and the finely grated zest of ½ lime, and fold through all the ingredients, also adding 4 finely slivered mild red chillies and spring onions and some wedges of de-pulped tomato. Then rip basil, coriander and mint from their stems (a small bunch each) into the bowl (discarding the stems), and toss everything through again. If you have a Thai shop nearby, then use Thai sweet basil and kaffir limes – they'll put more rip into its freshness. A few very finely shredded kaffir lime leaves make it more zest-brilliant, too. Chuck lots and lots of herb into this. Bliss.

Sticky Asian pork and herb salad

I'll scoff this any day. It's got all the wham, whack and soothe that any salad could muster. It's Vietnam in a bowl. Fantastic.

3 tbsp unsalted skinned peanuts
500g free-range pork fillet (or chicken breast)
3 tsp five-spice powder
2 tbsp soft brown sugar
1 tbsp fish sauce
3 tbsp soy sauce
2 sticks lemongrass, trimmed and finely shredded
3 large mild red chillies, deseeded and roughly chopped
3 cloves garlic, crushed
3 shallots, finely chopped
3 tbsp Asian dressing (see page 18)
½ large cos lettuce or other crisp leaves, torn up
handful each of basil, mint and coriander leaves
1 cucumber, peeled, deseeded and shredded
4 spring onions, finely shredded lengthways
2 tbsp vegetable or sunflower oil

Scatter the peanuts over a roasting tray, then toast in a 200°C/400°F/Gas 6 oven for about 15 minutes, shaking once or twice, or until evenly brown all over. Then crush them to chunky crumbs. They'll keep like this, sealed in a tub, for a good month or more – so do extra if you make lots of South-East Asian things.

Slice the meat into 1cm thick sections and toss with the five-spice powder. Then mix the sugar with the fish sauce, soy sauce, lemongrass, chilli, garlic and shallot, tip this over the seasoned sliced pork, and stir through. Leave to marinate for about an hour if you can – although the results are still damn good if you're time-poor and have to sling it straight in the pan. Next, toss the Asian dressing with the torn-up cos leaves, herbs, cucumber, spring onion and toasted crumbled nuts.

Heat the oil in a heavy frying pan and fry the marinated pork without moving for about 1 minute, then turn and fry for another minute, then sling over any remaining marinade and cook until varnished brown and sticky. To serve, fold the pork with all its caramelised bits and bobs through the dressed salad leaves and other ingredients. And dig in.

Asparagus and easy firsts

A while back, I went to this place called Mario's, a little restaurant on the east coast of Northern Ireland, in Newcastle. It was a gem. The menu was in one of those burgundy, spongy-backed plastic folders and read like a list of edible ladies: prawns marie rose, garlic prawns à la duchesse, consommé princesse, chicken louisette, steak diana, pear hélène and so on. Not an Asian this, diver-caught that, pan-fried something-or-other, or chargrilled thingy in sight.

Food was upstairs, where curtains matched menu; glasses sprouted pleated napkins; copper cauldrons dangled vines; and the piped sounds of 'Evergreen' by Streisand and Kristofferson made it bedroomy. Feeling really comfy, I tucked in. Everything was exactly what I wanted to eat. I was cast back to the 70s in a place that hadn't changed in 30 years – and loving it. The decade when Graham Kerr was Mum's pin-up, Robert Carrier was one of Mum's kitchen deities, and lobster thermidor was the *pièce de résistance* of every hostess worth her weight in copper flambé pans.

First up, came creamy garlic prawns in a white ceramic scallop shell – of the Joan Collins soap dish variety – with grilled swirls of piped mash, followed by steak in a thick cream peppercorn sauce. I couldn't stretch to pud but settled for an Irish coffee in a wine glass with its two complimentary After Eights. It wasn't poncy, it wasn't hip, it was just what it was – honest good stuff. I wanted all the starters. And they were the simplest things out. Most of us don't know how to make them now. After all, when they were in vogue we were too busy listening to albums, sticking smilies on our flares or a mere twinkling somewhere. So, it's some of these firsts I've revisited, with a gentle re-shape here and there. Flavours just as we remember, and some so simple they barely need a recipe.

One of the easiest and most English of starters must be asparagus: a few flash-boiled spears to be dipped in butter or mayonnaise, or dressed with vinaigrette. However, it's not always been like that. My first asparagus came from a tin. Small spears of white stuff – brined and limpid. My mother used them in something called 'asparagus mould': a Cordon Bleu style ring mould of wobbly mousse-like cream, ham and pale asparagus. The recipe I'm sure stipulated canned. And I adored it. It was made for birthdays, dinner parties and Christmases alike. Seasonality never entered the equation. Asparagus I was told was a *luxury* and I knew it as such – from a can. We all now know it as green, and inexpensive. A luxury now only because of its short season. It's the one veg that's worth the wait and then overdosing on when it's about.

One more thing on starters. Three-course dining went out with the Ark. It's okay now to whip up one course with perhaps some cheese for afters, or do startery type things as mains or for suppers. Rules at table don't make good food. Thankfully we've abandoned the starch of formality. After all, enjoying food is not about order and how much we eat, it's more about *what* we eat. As long as what goes in tastes wonderful, then we're happy. Eating is about sharing, enjoying food with others, so why make it a formal course thing? Leave that to restaurants.

You could serve a selection of startery things as a mezze – for everyone to dive in on together. I'm all for promiscuity at the dinner table. Even with those I hardly know. I don't mean a furtive under-table toying with legs and feet but more a blatant above-board pillage and plate rape. My fork makes a bee-line to next-door's plate and it's usually only when the prongs have landed on target that I actually ask next-door if it's okay. By that time of course no one says no. We always want what we haven't got – and stolen stuff tastes better. I have it down to a fine art when eating out with my good friends, Alasdair and Rebecca: at the command of 'all change' everyone lifts their plate and places it in front of the person on their left. The command to change gets faster, as there's always someone with something they don't want or someone wishing to return to something good. It doesn't go down too well with the waiters and judging from the wistful looks around, makes those on adjacent tables feel left out. I eat out with them a lot.

Use starters how you wish – they often only need a wad of extra leafage and some bread, to bump them up into something more main. And do remember you don't have to 'cook' to produce something noble to eat. In fact, sometimes things are at their best – and are best enjoyed – when plonked on a plate as nature intended. Think: a plate of pink prawns in the shell or a pile of those salty little brown shrimps, with brown bread and butter; or an elegant antipasto plate of prosciutto, perhaps with a wedge of ripe melon in summer.

Perfect asparagus

Shun the miserable foreigners you see sitting on the shelves all year round. You want home-grown spears, ones with attitude, that come bundled and rubber-banded, towards the end of April. Fresh and sweetly astringent, these need little messing about with. Yet select carefully: don't opt for a bargain bagful at the market to discover it's a mass of over-woody stems and squidgy heads – after all the trimming you'll end up with a pitiful lot of butchered green stumps. And the fancy asparagus

pan? Forget about it. It's only good for fat stems: anything waspishly slim will slip through the mesh and slither all over the floor when the basket is pulled from the pan. Just boil it in a wide pan.

And the classic way to cook it? Most asparagus can be cooked straight as it is, after the woody ends to the stems have been trimmed off, and it cooks in less time than you imagine it might. Older stuff may need a bit of a peel – a swivel peeler does the job. Medium width stems need only a 3-minute spell in lots of rapidly boiling salted water and fat stems maybe a minute more, whereas the white sort needs a good 10 minutes or so and shouldn't be at all al dente but limp and suggestively floppy. Test it with the point of a knife for doneness. Slender tips only need a minute or so, or a mere toss in a wok, if you want to keep some crunch. If not eating immediately, plunge the cooked stems straight into cold water to keep them ultra green looking.

And some simple ways with? Asparagus pooled with melted butter

is classic but the butter can be flavoured. For **lemongrass butter**, finely shred 2 sticks lemongrass and gently warm through with about 120g melted butter and a sprinkle of sea salt for about 10 minutes. Strain into a clean pan, leaving behind all the milk solids that will have separated to the bottom of the pan. Then reheat this clarified butter and serve in a preheated dish piled with a salted bundle of blanched or roasted asparagus. A little chopped chilli or some herbage could be added to the dish on serving up. Alternatively flavour the butter with crushed **garlic** (or **wild garlic** if you pick it), plus some sea salt. (For me, a crunchy bit of salt makes everything.) Parmesan can be shaved over too. If you like wokking, **stir-fry slim stems of asparagus** with sugar snaps, mangetout and sliced shiitake mushrooms in a dash of oil and sesame oil and chuck in some chopped garlic, then stir through some beansprouts, shredded spring onion, salt and pepper and serve up thatches of the stir-fry on plates, topping each with a fried egg. Something more elegant can be concocted with **fried quails' eggs**, salad leaves and vinaigrette.

Asparagus and crab mayonnaise

I'm a big fan of crab. If you can't face handling a whole one, or don't know how to de-flesh one, prepared fresh crab meat, the brown and the white, can be bought from fishmongers. The hand-picked crab meat from Cornish or Norfolk crabs is the best. And the tinned? Don't bother. It's tasteless wadding. If you're not partial to Thai flavours, make up a simple asparagus and crab mayonnaise toast, flavoured simply with lemon and snippets of chives. The crab mayo is good piled into halved avocados too.

1 large cooked dressed crab, white and brown
   meat separated
1 bundle asparagus, trimmed
butter or olive oil
4 generous slices sourdough or other rustic
   bread
2 lemons, halved
handful of basil leaves

Thai mayonnaise:
1 clove garlic, crushed
½ large mild red chilli, deseeded and finely
   chopped
finely grated zest and juice of ½ lime
3 tsp fish sauce
4 tbsp mayonnaise (see page 17)
1 tbsp each of chopped chives and coriander

Make the mayonnaise, using a fork, by beating together all the ingredients. Fold in the white crab meat so that it's well incorporated but hasn't lost its flaky chunks. This can be knocked up the day before and refrigerated.

Cook the asparagus just before serving if you want it warm, and toss in butter. Alternatively pre-cook and cool it, then toss in a splash of olive oil, if you'd prefer it at room temperature. Cut thicker stems in half lengthways.

Toast the bread and spread with a little butter, then spread each slice with a wodge of pasty brown crab meat and season with pepper and a squeeze of lemon. Pile with asparagus, a spoonful of the Thai crab mayonnaise and a few basil leaves.

Dad's prawn cocktail

Dad made this for dinner parties, while Mum got on with the coq au vin. He always used the bright green round lettuce with the floppy soft leaves, and after sprinkling the finished cocktails with paprika, would stick a fancy disc of lemon on the rim of the glass. We were so impressed. Dads always know how to steal a mum's thunder with little work. Prawn cocktail survived the decade of the buffet spread, and deep-down we still hanker for it. Use those boiled pink seaside-type prawns in the shell – they're sweet and juicy. Tropical-sea prawns, such as tigers, have no place here. And avoid the frozen peeled bagged ones. Serve in halved avocadoes if you like, and, like all retro salad things with mayo, it's a winner as a sandwich filler.

generous 600ml cooked pink prawns in the shell
1 small English round lettuce

Marie rose sauce:
4 tbsp mayonnaise (see page 17)
1 tbsp each of tomato ketchup and double cream
good squeeze of lemon juice
few drops of Worcestershire sauce
dash of brandy (optional)
hint of Tabasco sauce

De-shell the prawns, leaving on the tails, if you like. Then beat all the sauce ingredients together well.

When ready to serve, put the lettuce, larger leaves sliced, with the prawns into four small bowls, tumblers or glasses, and spoon over the dressing.

Big bowl of mussels

The 'r' in the month rule to eating or not eating mussels doesn't strictly apply any more. It was there to stop us from poisoning ourselves on – wait for it – potentially toxic summer-spawning dinoflagellates (that's weeny plankton) ingested by wild mussels in the days before mussel farming became the norm. It still has some relevence, though, as bivalves – that's all hinged shells – are sexually active in summer. One mussel can spew out between 5-12 million eggs in one go, and no one would be in any shape to be devoured after that. So, if going for the sea-harvested big boys, perhaps wait for summer to pass and meantime use the loch rope-grown ones.

One of the delights about mussels is their juice. It holds the guts of the sea. And it's this neptunous eau de vie that makes cooking with them so very good. The mussels almost make their own sauce, and there's lots of it, so arm yourself with plenty of bread. And when eating, do as the French do, use an empty shell as a pair of tweezers to pull out each lobe of flesh.

1kg mussels
4 shallots, finely chopped
3 fat cloves garlic, finely chopped
30g butter
400ml white wine
250ml double cream (optional)
1 medium-sized bunch parsley, curly or flat-leaf, coarsely chopped

Before cooking, allow the mussels to soak in cold water for a good 2 hours or so, so that they have a chance to expel any grit. Loch-grown ones won't require this. If they have barnacles attached, scrape them off with a stubby knife, as I think they can turn the cooking juices a bit smelly. Give them all a scrub – I use a plastic scourer – and discard any that remain open.

In a large saucepan, gently fry the shallot and garlic in the butter without colouring and until softened. Pour in the wine, season and bring up to a bubble, then tip in the mussels, cover and turn up the heat to very high. Once bubbling again, cook for 2-3 minutes only, and halfway through their time, using a big spoon, turn the top mussels to the bottom of the pan. Next pour in the cream (if using) and bubble up, then chuck in the chopped parsley and jumble through again. Now ladle mussels and juices into big bowls and supply with lots of baguette for dunking (a pat of butter on the table for the bread will not be left alone either). Put a big empty bowl in the middle of the table for spent shells.

Variation For **grilled pesto mussels**, use the big ones – deep black-blue and contoured. The teenage-sized supermarket ones, that haven't had time to flex their muscles, don't appear to have those deep-orange lobes of flesh I so like. Soak 500g mussels as above and cook as above, but in a splash of water only. Once open they're cooked and juicy – don't leave them any longer or you'll be eating rubber. Remove the top shell on each and discard any that are still shut. Mix 60g breadcrumbs with 4 tbsp fresh pesto and smother each mussel in its shell with this mixture. Dab each with a spot of butter and place under a very hot grill for a couple of minutes. Eat them with lots of sliced baguette.

Garlic and parsley buttered jumbo prawns

This for me is one of those fantastic excuses for a paddle through loads of garlic butter. The prawns are the thing too – but you know what I mean. Half the joy here is the constant lick of fingers and sucking on the shells. Suck on the heads to get at the hot liquor inside – this is not gruesome but a joy. Remember the bread, baguette or whatever, for mopping up.

12 uncooked jumbo prawns or 4 massive ones, in the shell
120g butter
4 cloves garlic, chopped
handful of flat-leaf parsley leaves or garlic chives, chopped

If the prawns are those massive creatures, the size of small lobsters, then cut them in half lengthways (as you might a lobster). Heat about a third of the butter in a large heavy roasting tray, then lay in the prawns and sprinkle with sea salt. Place over a medium heat until they start to fry and blister on their shells. Next, sprinkle in the garlic with the remaining butter, then turn everything over and let it all cook for another 2 minutes or so. Chuck over the parsley, jumble the prawns around a bit, so that they're coated with everything and looking gorgeous, then serve – 2 or 3 to a plate, with garlic butter poured over. It's a good idea to preheat the plates here.

Variation For **chilli-salt prawns**, add 2 chopped mild red chillies, 3 tsp chopped fresh root ginger and 2 tsp sugar to the pan too, then squeeeze over the juice of $^{1}/_{2}$ lemon once things have frazzled, finally tossing through a handful of chopped garlic chives, chives or the green tops of spring onions. Devour the prawns with the scraped-up caramelised pan bits. Yum yum.

Grilled goat's cheese salad

This screams 80s. Goat's ruled salad then. I like it with French green beans and some walnuts myself. If you don't want to use goat's cheese, use chunks of ungrilled Gorgonzola or oozing Brie instead. Good with a few ripped ripe figs thrown in too.

250g dwarf beans, trimmed
handful of walnut kernels, crumbled
4 small handfuls rocket or young salad leaves
4 spring onions, shredded
2 tbsp fruity extra virgin olive oil
2 tbsp walnut oil
1 tbsp balsamic vinegar
4 slices baguette
4 thick slices goat's cheese

Cook the beans in salted boiling water for about 2 minutes – they should be still be slightly crunchy – then plunge into cold water to cool. Drain, then toss with the walnuts, leaves, spring onions, oils and vinegar, with a little salt and a good twist of pepper. Next, lightly toast the baguette slices, then top each with a slice of cheese and whizz these under a hot grill until golden and bubbling. Meanwhile, divide the bean salad between four plates or bowls, then plant a grilled goat's cheese toast on each.

Bacon roast asparagus

If you want to pull out all the stops, serve each of these parcels with a poached or fried egg on top – for a bacon 'n' egg asparagus. Alternatively shave or crumble over some salty nuggets of Parmesan.

20 medium to thick asparagus stems
extra virgin olive oil
8 large slices prosciutto crudo, Parma ham,
    Black Forest ham or thin-cut bacon
4 tsp balsamic vinegar

Briefly boil the asparagus stems in salted water for about 1-2 minutes, then drain and slosh with a dash of oil. Next, bundle up five stems in an overlapping, spiralling wrap of two slices of the ham. Do the same with the rest of the asparagus and ham, to make four parcels, then lay them all on a baking sheet. Sea salt and pepper them, then douse with a bit of oil, and roast in a 200°C/400°F/Gas 6 oven until the ham has crisped a little. If you're convection, you may need to protect the tips of the asparagus with a loose cover of foil over each.

Place each parcel on a warmed plate, and dress with a splash more of olive oil and a few drops of balsamic vinegar.

Rare beef, asparagus and Parmesan

This can be as dainty or as robust as you care. Turn it more main-course-like by bumping up the leafage and beef. Use either carpaccio-thin slices of uncooked beef fillet, or rare beef that's been briefly seared or roasted. Pinky-red carnivore-looking material is the taste and look you want. Those up for cooking their own rare beef, see page 89. Beef, asparagus and salty Parmesan, je t'adore.

8-16 thin slices rare beef (depending on your
  joint's width)
1 ripe avocado
juice of ½ lemon
4 handfuls young lettuce leaves (rocket or lamb's
  lettuce are good)
1 bunch watercress
1 small bundle slender asparagus, trimmed and
  blanched (see page 32)
4 spring onions, shredded or chopped
handful of mixed herb leaves (chives, flat-leaf
  parsley or basil)
1 punnet cress, snipped from its box
extra virgin olive oil
balsamic vinegar
big handful of Parmesan shavings

In brief, once you've sliced, shredded and chopped everything up, you're ready to serve. Peel and de-stone the avocado, slice it up into segments lengthways, then toss it in a little lemon juice to keep it from discolouring. Next, gently toss all the green things together in a big bowl with one of your finest oils, plus the teensiest amount of salt, yet a good twist from the peppermill. Pile into bowls or on to plates, layering in – as artfully, yet as naturally as possible – all the beef and Parmesan as you go. Splash with some vinegar here and there and dribble around a dash more oil, *et voilà* – something bountiful and beauteous to eat.

Grilled vegetables with Parmesan

Grilled vegetables, you'd think they were now ours, we love them so much. Remember?...they're Italian. Make this with just one or two vegetables or several, as below. Good with crumbled feta or grilled goat's cheese too.

2 courgettes
1 slim aubergine
1 red pepper
1 red onion
1 vine of baby tomatoes
extra virgin olive oil
bunch of basil or rocket
splash of balsamic vinegar
block of Parmesan (or buffalo mozzarella)

Slice the courgettes and aubergine into thick slices; halve, deseed and de-rib the pepper and slice this into chunks; and peel and cut the onion into fat rings. De-vine the tomatoes. Tip everything into a big bowl as you go. Next, twist over a good amount of black pepper and sprinkle with salt, then slosh over about 4 tbsp of the oil, and then jumble everything together.

Heat a heavy frying pan until hot, then sear the vegetables on either side in batches, until just cooked, and not squishy.

Toss with basil leaves, pile on to plates, then dress with more oil and a splash of balsamic vinegar, plus some shavings from your block of Parmesan. (Alternatively, tumble through with some torn chunks of mozzarella.) Bread is required.

Variation Quartered treviso (a long radicchio) is good sprinkled with sea salt and drenched with olive oil, then lightly charred along its cut seams on a hellishly hot cast-iron grilling plate, and dished up with a roof of Parmesan shavings. The salt and oil kick in, the bitterness of the leaves cleanses – and you go back for more, and more. Compelling really.

Home soup and big bowls of noodles

Now, hand on heart, I don't think I have ever thrown away the remains of a chicken without sticking the lot in a pot first and making a stock. It would be sheer sacrilege. Holier than thou in the kitchen I am not, yet time and time again, I see it happen elsewhere: gorgeousness slung in the bin. Good soup comes from good stock, and chicken broth is the good all-rounder. It brings out everything you add to it. It takes no time to make a stock, as it's simply a case of bunging a handful of things in a pot, sticking it on the hob and walking away for an hour or so. Easy. And the result is the base for countless good soups afterwards, including seafood soups, especially Asian-style ones, and lots of noodley things too. And you can freeze it. If you don't have a carcass, a whole bird can be used and the poached flesh can be used in a pie or in salad, or thrown back in the soup again for serving. Chicken bones of some sort are essential – it's these and the cartilage that give it depth, body and soul.

There are many good soups not included here; however, once you've made your stock, anything blended or coarsely chopped and thrown into it will be good. Such as stock-poached parsnip whizzed up with a little curry powder and cumin, then ladled out, smooth and fragrant, each serving with a blob of mango chutney at its heart; or a stock simmered with sweet carrots and warm root ginger and then whizzed up with a feisty bunch of coriander. That sort of thing.

I'm not thrilled by chilled soups. To me they taste of fridge. You know, the refrigerated leftovers you might unfortunately take a snick on when driven – and then wish you hadn't. Gazpacho has never been on my must-have list either. Sorry. I'm a hot soup guy. And I do love some of those old-style soups like oxtail and lobster bisque that we haven't seen for yonks. A bisque may smack of grand hotel dining, silver service and gourmet night on *Fawlty Towers*, but it's an excellent way with a lobster, and every time I stumble on it I love it, to death.

Now, just a quick word on noodles. Don't be daunted by them. My mum hasn't got a clue about them – I suppose it's a generation thing, although my sister's not much better – and would run a mile from any recipe with noodles in the title. They're just like spaghetti – but actually quicker. I know there are loads of noodles to choose from, but essentially they're all pretty similar. To simplify things, you have two types – those made from rice flour and those made from wheat. The wheat ones go mainly in Chinese things, and the rice noodles belong to all things South-East Asian. And they come in different widths, like with pasta's tagliatelle, linguine, spaghetti and vermicelli: broad to thin, to round to fine. Yet they're easier than pasta to cook – for most noodles need only a few minutes' soak or a 3-4 minute spell in boiling water, and they're done. They are fast food personified.

The perfect chicken stock

If using a carcass (the remains of a cooked bird) to make your stock, remove any large chunks of chicken first, and keep to add back to the soup later – if, say, you're making a chicken soup. Then break up the carcass and tumble the bits into a big pan and pour in 2 litres water. If you haven't a carcass, buy a leg, thighs or some wings and use these, chopped. This is still much, much cheaper than buying those minuscule ready-made tubs when you need stock in quantity. Next, bring the pan to a rumbling boil and skim off any flotsam, then add a small bunch of herbs (say, parsley, bay and thyme), a couple of peeled onions, some sea salt and 1 piled tsp black peppercorns, some chunks of peeled carrot to add sweetness and, if you have it, a celery stick (though it's not vital). Cover and leave everything to gently bubble for a good hour or so, then strain it through a sieve and discard all the spent bits – including any meat – as it will have poured all its life treasures into the broth and will now taste of nothing.

To poach a whole chicken With this you get lovely stock as well as some delicious poached meat. Place a whole bird in a pot, pour in enough water so that the chick is covered, then bring to a rumbling boil. Skim off any flotsam, then add everything else (as above). Turn down the heat, cover, and very gently bubble for about 45 minutes (for an average 1.5kg bird). It's the low murmuring that keeps the stock clear – boiling it now will turn it cloudy. Turn off the heat, and allow everything to cool for a while. Then hoik the bird out the pot. To avoid the bird belly-flopping back in and bombing you with liquid, stick a long-handled wooden spoon up its cavity, and lift out this way. This'll give you perfect control. Then strip off and discard the skin, and flake off the meat – not forgetting the two delicious oysters of meat found either side of the backbone. Next, strain the broth of all its spent bits and bobs.

You want extra thick stock? If you want a stompingly good stock, of the sort that when refrigerated will set to a dense jelly, then return the carcass, broken up, to the pot of stock. Allow it to bubble away very gently again for the same amount of time, then strain. And if you refrigerate it, you can scrape off the fat once it's set. If you've got your stock right, you'll get your soup right.

Asian stock Just add 4 halved spring onions and about 5cm thickly sliced fresh root ginger to the pan with salt and the carcass – nothing more – then strain and discard all the bits after the hour is up. If you're poaching a whole bird with these flavours, the meat is wonderful served on steam-boiled rice with lots of fresh coriander shoved on top, accompanied by a little bowl of the fragrant poaching broth (for sipping on or splashing over the rice) and a dipping sauce (made simply from soy sauce or fish sauce and grated ginger). Mmmm, my kinda food.

And PS I know it's just stock, but please use a bird that's had a life.

Mum's chicken soup

This for me is classic chicken soup. Perfect if you're feeling a bit under the weather. It's a flexible soup, so add any roots you like and leave out the ones you don't. It almost doesn't need a recipe, it's so easy. When like homing pigeons, my sister and I descend unexpectedly on the nest, Mum makes a quick version of this – by bunging everything in her pressure cooker. Pressure cookers make excellent chicken broth.

1 medium onion, chopped
2 sticks celery, chopped
2 tbsp olive oil
800g mixed roots (such as carrots, turnips, swede, parsnips or celeriac), roughly chopped
about 1.5 litres fresh chicken stock, made with 1 small whole chicken (see above)
small handful of flat-leaf parsley leaves, roughly chopped
½ lemon

In a large saucepan, gently fry the onion and celery in the olive oil until soft, then chuck in the roots. Add the stock, then simmer for about 15 minutes or until everything is tender. Stir in some of the flaked chicken (the remainder will make great sandwiches) and the parsley, sharpen with lemon juice, then taste and add more seasoning if it needs it. Eat with lots of buttered bread.

Spring chicken and vegetable soup with pesto

This is pistou, a Provençal green bean soup blobbed with a pounded mixture of basil, pine nuts and garlic. Eat with good bread, or cook in some chopped-up spaghetti or other small pasta. Frozen peas and broad beans are fine.

4 shallots, chopped
2 sticks celery, chopped
2 cloves garlic, crushed
extra virgin olive oil
2 litres chicken stock and some poached chicken
350g fine green beans, trimmed
200g each of podded peas and broad beans
2 courgettes, sliced
bunch of mixed herbs (to include basil, tarragon, chives or chervil), chopped
4 tbsp fresh pesto
pile of Parmesan shavings

Fry the shallot, celery and garlic in 3 tbsp oil until softened but not coloured, then pour in the stock, and gently bubble for 10 minutes. Add the fine beans, peas, broad beans, courgette, a tbsp more of olive oil, and some of the flaked chicken, and continue to cook for a further 5 minutes, or until the vegetables are just tender. I like a little bite to them – although the courgette soft is fine. Remove from the heat and stir in three-quarters of the chopped herbs. Serve in bowls with a fat dollop of pesto in each, a scattering of the remaining herbs and lots of Parmesan shavings.

Rocket and pea soup

Let the weather be your guide as to what you add on serving. I add shavings of Parmesan and a good slug of virgin olive when it's warm, crisp bacon lardons when it's cold, or chopped chives when I need that inner spring clean-up. This one's fine if prepared the day before and stored in the fridge. If you're vegetarian, leave out the bacon flavouring – it's there to ham the stock up a bit.

650g podded peas
1 litre fresh chicken (see page 47) or vegetable
  stock
2 rashers smoked bacon
1 Spanish onion
extra virgin olive oil
180g rocket leaves
Parmesan flakes, crisp bacon lardons or chopped
  chives

Cook the peas in the stock with the bacon for about 5 minutes. Meanwhile, chop up the onion and then fry in 4 tbsp of the oil in a large saucepan, until soft but not coloured. Stir in the rocket leaves, then add the stock with the peas. Simmer for a couple of minutes – just long enough to wilt the rocket without robbing it of its oomph - then discard the bacon, and whizz the soup in batches in a processor until smooth. Add more stock if the soup is too thick, and give it a taste. Then ladle out, slop each portion with some virgin olive oil, and add some Parmesan – or the other bits and bobs suggested above.

New England lobster bisque

Now, don't be concerning your goodselves with the ins and outs of home slaughter – there's no killing to be done here. Another put-off can be that lobsters look all big and plentiful on the outside, then once you're in there's little of them for their money. The little that there is, however, is very good and can be made to go a long way.

1 large cooked lobster or 2 small ones
2 tbsp olive oil
2 tbsp brandy or sherry
2 each of carrots, tomatoes, sticks celery,
  shallots and leeks, all finely chopped
60g butter
2 cloves garlic, chopped
2 sprigs thyme
3 tbsp tomato purée
2 tbsp plain flour
150ml single cream

Turn monsieur lobster upside down, then using a serrated bread knife, cut him in half lengthways. Remove the white meat and the soft meat – that's the creamy stuff and any coral (roe) – and keep to one side. Then crack the claws and extricate this meat as intact as possible, and keep this separate, too. Smash up all the de-fleshed lobster shells and the whole legs with a rolling pin until well broken, discarding the feathery gills.

Fry the jumble of shell and bits in a saucepan in hot olive oil with a little salt until well singed and brittle (about 5 minutes), then pour over the brandy and let it sizzle up. Chuck the veg into the pan, along with half of the butter, the garlic and thyme, and continue to fry until the vegetables have softened. Stir in the tomato purée and fry for a minute or so further, then add 2 litres water, season well and gently bubble for about an hour, reducing to around 1.5 litres. Pass everything through a sieve into a clean pan, pushing through anything soft – and discarding all the spent veg and carapace.

Next – and remembering to keep the claw meat separate for serving – crush the body meat by pulsing in a processor, along with the saved creamy flesh, the remaining butter and the flour. Then, using a hand whisk, beat this mixture into the soup, until well blended and satiny looking, and allow to gently bubble for about 10 minutes. Stir in the single cream and bubble for 10 minutes. Taste again for seasoning, then ladle into bowls with a little claw meat in each. Posh.

Creamy mushroom soup

If you want to turn this fancy, then make it a touch smoky by adding a few pre-soaked dried morels plus their soaking water. Eat with warm buttered toast.

750g chestnut mushrooms, quartered, or
   regular buttons, halved
2 tbsp olive oil
30g butter
6 shallots, chopped
1 clove garlic, chopped
2 sprigs thyme, leaves only
1 litre chicken stock (see page 47) or vegetable
   stock
2 tbsp crème fraîche

Fry the mushrooms in the oil and butter in a saucepan until browned. Add the shallots and garlic, the thyme leaves and some salt and pepper, and fry, without browning the shallot, until soft. Next, pour in the stock, then gently bubble for 10 minutes. Ladle the chunky mixture into a processor and then whizz up until smooth. Stir in the crème fraîche and reheat before serving.

Pumpkin soup with goat's cheese

This one's velvety and smooth.

1.5kg dense-fleshed pumpkin or butternut
   squash, halved, deseeded and skinned
1 large onion, finely chopped
2 cloves garlic, finely chopped
1 tbsp olive oil
1 tsp cumin seeds, toasted
2 sprigs thyme and 2 bay leaves
½ tsp each of grated nutmeg and ground allspice
1.5 litres chicken stock (see page 47)
1 small soft goat's cheese log, sliced into 4

Cut the pumpkin flesh into chunks. In a deep pan, fry the onion and garlic in the olive oil until soft, without colouring, then season and chuck in the cumin seeds, herbs, nutmeg and allspice. Fry for a further minute, then tip in the chopped squash and stock, then gently simmer for half an hour or until the pumpkin flesh is soft. fish out and throw away the bay and any twiggy bits of thyme, then whizz everything in a processor until smooth. You'll need to do that in a few separate batches, to avoid overflow. Reheat the soup when you're ready to serve. If it's too thick, then let it down with a drop more stock or a dash of water. Plop a slice of goat's cheese in each bowl, once ladled out.

Delicious shrimp pad Thai noodles

This is a Thai's classic stir-fried noodles – and one of ours now. I don't want to give you a watered-down version, but something authentic, as we now have the ingredients in our supermarkets. Ideally you want peeled tiger prawns, with tails left on. The method looks intricate, but once all is prepared the cooking time is literally around 4 minutes flat.

300g dried rice stick noodles, or other rice
   noodles
5cm white radish or 4 regular radishes, finely
   shredded
3 tbsp rice vinegar
2 tbsp caster sugar
fish sauce
2 hot red chillies, sliced into rings
500g uncooked tiger prawns
2 big handfuls beansprouts
3-4 tbsp vegetable oil
3 large eggs
6 cloves garlic, finely chopped
2 shallots, finely sliced
6 spring onions, cut into short lengths
4 tbsp roasted peanuts, crushed
1 tsp ground dried chilli or chilli flakes
handfuls of coriander leaves

The secret here, as with all stir-frying, is to have all your stuff ready for the pan, then it's a simple process of slinging things in when you come to cook. First, soak the noodles. Toss the radish with the rice vinegar in a small bowl, and leave for about 30 minutes, then lift from its vinegar bath and put on one side. Stir the sugar, 2 tbsp of fish sauce and 1 tbsp water into the vinegar. Pop the chilli rings into small dipping bowls filled with fish sauce ready for serving. Now, display everything – including the prawns and beansprouts – in little piles or in bowls by the hob, ready for the off.

To cook, heat about 1 tbsp oil in your wok and swirl around, then crack in the eggs and scramble them: once they begin to set, keep scraping up and jumbling over until they start to gain a little golden colour, then scrape out into a small bowl. Next, heat 2 tbsp of oil in the wok and chuck in the garlic. After about 20 seconds, chuck in the prawns and stir-fry until they turn pink. Throw in the shallots, then stir in the vinegar mixture and let it bubble up, then tip in the noodles, vinegared radish, spring onions and peanuts and stir-fry for about 2 minutes or until the noodles have absorbed the liquid. Chuck in the beansprouts, sprinkle over the dried chilli, and once more stir through. Pile on to plates and scatter with coriander. Zing it up by adding rings of chilli and dribbles of hot fish sauce as you eat.

Hanoi pork noodles

Those in the East are the masters of one-bowl food. It's that combination of ingredients they get so right: noodles, sticky caramelised bits and bobs, and leaves, all dressed with aromatic sprinklings and sloshes of this and that. When layered into one bowl, these hots, salts, sweets and sours play beautifully together. You could use this marinade on any pork and on chicken or beef, and barbecue it if you like – then slice it up and toss it with everything else.

3 sticks lemongrass, trimmed and finely chopped
2 small red chillies, deseeded and finely chopped
2 cloves garlic, crushed
3 tbsp caster sugar
4 tbsp each of fish sauce, lime juice and rice vinegar
500g pork tenderloin, cut into 1cm thick slices
1 bunch spring onions, finely shredded
1 tbsp dark soy sauce
1 large carrot, finely shredded
200g rice vermicelli noodles
vegetable oil
handfuls of coriander leaves and tender salad leaves
1 cucumber, finely shredded
4 tbsp roasted peanuts, crushed

Mix together the first five listed ingredients (up to the rice vinegar) and stir until the sugar has dissolved, then divide this dressing equally between two bowls. Put the pork, spring onions and soy sauce with one batch of the dressing, and add the carrot to the other and toss through. Leave both to bathe for about an hour. Submerge the noodles in a big bowl of cold water for 20 minutes. Then drain them and boil in plenty of boiling water for about 2 minutes, stirring to prevent clumping. (If using different noodles, cook according to packet instructions.) Rinse under running cold water and leave to thoroughly drain.

Remove the pork from its marinade, rub with some oil and sear in a smoking hot, heavy frying pan for about 1 minute on each side, then tip in the marinade and reduce until sticky and glossy, and clinging to the pork. Pile some salad leaves and noodles into four bowls, and top with the cucumber and the carrot and its dressing. Stick on the caramelised pork, shower with crushed roasted peanuts and coriander leaves, and tuck in.

Wagamama noodles

This is a great get-together of storecupboard stuff that, with the addition of some fresh salmon and a few crunchy leaves, is unctuous yet invigoratingly fresh – and my perfect one-bowl supper. Similar soups are served in Wagamama, the Japanese noodle restaurant chain.

4 x 150g slices skinned salmon fillet
5 tbsp bottled teriyaki marinade
400g soba (buckwheat) noodles or other wheat noodles
1 tbsp dried wakame seaweed (optional)
vegetable oil
1.5 litres Asian chicken stock (see page 48) or use instant dashi stock (if you know it)
1 tbsp sesame seeds, toasted
4 spring onions, finely shredded
good handful of young crunchy leaves, such as watercress or anything oriental

Rub the salmon fillets with a little salt and pepper, place in a sandwich bag and pour in the teriyaki marinade. Lightly massage it around the fish, then leave for about an hour or however long you've got, turning occasionally. Meanwhile, cook the noodles in plenty of boiling water until al dente. Depending on the thickness of the noodles this should take anything from 3-5 minutes, but check the packet instructions. For perfectionists only: to perfect your noodles, add half a cupful of cold water to the pot twice during cooking, allowing the water to come back to the boil after each cupful – this arrested cooking technique firms them up. Then drain, and rinse them under cold water.

If using the dried seaweed, stick it in a bowl and cover with cold water: it will swell incredibly, so lots of water. Leave it to soak for about 20 minutes or until rehydrated, then drain it. Remove the salmon from its bath, rub with a little oil and place in a preheated (preferably non-stick) frying pan. Sear for about 2 minutes on each side, splashing in a drop of the marinade towards the end – this will bung in the teriyaki flavour and caramelise it beautifully. It will be deep pink in the middle. And no shifting it about while it's searing.

Bring the Asian stock to a bubble and chuck in the noodles, just long enough to reheat them, then stir in the softened seaweed and divide between four generous bowls. Sprinkle each with sesame seeds, add some shredded spring onion, top with the salmon and some leaves. Eat with chopsticks and spoons.

spaghetti bolognese

and more pasta

Roast cherry tomato spaghetti with basil

Simple and delicious.

2 cloves garlic, finely chopped
1 long mild red chilli (optional), deseeded and
   chopped
olive oil
2 tbsp tomato purée
1 big punnet cherry tomatoes, 10 of them finely
   chopped
1 bunch basil
400g spaghetti
block of Parmesan

Gently fry the garlic and chilli in 3 tbsp oil in a medium pan until the garlic begins to colour, then stir in the tomato purée and chopped tomato, and cook for a minute or two. Add a good splash of water – about 100ml – and some seasoning. Remove the basil leaves from their stems, then tie the stems together and throw the latter into the pan too. Bring to a rapid spluttering bubble, then lower the heat and let it gently reduce to a thickish sauce, then fish out the stems and discard them.

Cook the spaghetti according to the packet instructions, and then put the drained pasta back in its cooking pan to keep warm. Meanwhile, scatter the remaining tomatoes across a baking sheet, sprinkle with salt, pepper and a little oil, then roast in a 220°C/425°F/Gas 7 oven for about 6-8 minutes or until they begin to split. To serve, tip the chilli tomato sauce over the pasta, adding a good twist of black pepper, then tear over some basil leaves and thoroughly mix. Fold through the roasted cherry tomatoes plus the remaining basil leaves, and serve with grated Parmesan. (See image page 65.)

True comfort spaghetti

This is an Italian comfort spaghetti – made with butter, not olive oil. Antonio Carluccio made it for me once, when we both agreed we'd had it up to here with all things fancy and longed for something completely undemanding yet full of appetite. Makes supper in 10 minutes.

400g spaghetti
1 onion, finely chopped
2 big knobs butter (about 30g)
1 tbsp tomato purée
1 x 400ml can chopped tomatoes or bottled
   passata
grated Parmesan

Cook the spaghetti in plenty of boiling water according to the packet instructions until al dente. While you are waiting for the pasta water to boil, fry the onion in a big knob of butter until soft. Season and stir in the tomato purée and the chopped tomatoes. Allow to splutter away and reduce while the spaghetti cooks. Toss the pasta with the tomato sauce and shower with grated Parmesan and black pepper.

Variation For an **uncooked marinated tomato sauce** – *pomodoro crudo* – roughly chop about 750g cherry tomatoes and mix with 1 tsp each salt, ground black pepper and sugar, 2 cloves crushed garlic and 6 chopped anchovy fillets, and leave to sit for a good hour. Then stir through some shredded basil and about 100ml extra virgin olive oil. Toss with the just-cooked spaghetti.

Buttery asparagus pappardelle with lemon and herbs

Need I say more? Sublime. Till-the-cows-come-home food.

1 bundle asparagus, trimmed
300g dried egg pappardelle or other ribbon pasta
50g butter, softened
a dash of extra virgin olive oil
grated zest of ½ lemon
1 mixed bunch basil, mint, chives, dill, chervil,
  tarragon or parsley, roughly chopped
Parmesan, shaved from a block

Blanch the asparagus in boiling salted water for about 3 minutes or until just tender but still retaining some bite and drain, then slice each stem into three sections. Meanwhile, cook the pasta according to the packet instructions, until al dente. Then toss it in a dash of its cooking water, salt, pepper, butter, olive oil, lemon zest and herbs, then mix through the cooked asparagus. Pile on to plates, topping with shaves of Parmesan, and some more twists from the peppermill.

Mushroom and chestnut penne with sage

It's as good without mushrooms, so if you're not hot on them, leave them out. However, when you're up for a treat, fresh porcini (ceps) are fabulous in this.

400g penne pasta
olive oil
16 vac-packed cooked chestnuts, halved
300g mushrooms, cleaned and thickly sliced
1 bunch sage
5 tbsp fresh pesto
grated Parmesan, to serve

Cook the pasta according to packet instructions, reserving a half cup of the pasta water once cooked. Meanwhile, heat 3 tbsp oil and flash-fry the nuts and sliced mushrooms until they begin to colour a little, adding more oil if need be. Next, throw in the sage leaves and allow to go crisp, then remove from the pan. Toss the cooked and drained pasta with the pesto, crispy sage, chestnuts and mushrooms – lubricating it further with the pasta water, if it needs it. Season and shower with grated Parmesan.

Butternut squash and sage spaghetti

Pumpkin and sage is another of those twosomes I can't live without.

1 small butternut squash, halved, deseeded and
   skinned
400g spaghetti
60g butter
2 tbsp olive oil
2 fat cloves garlic, finely chopped
bunch of sage leaves
good grating of Parmesan

Cut the squash flesh into small chunks. Poach in enough salted water to barely cover for about 5 minutes or until just tender, then drain – but keep a small cupful of the water. Meanwhile, cook the spaghetti in plenty of boiling salted water, according to the time on the packet. Fry the butternut chunks in the butter and oil with salt and pepper until they take on a warm glow, then add the garlic and sage leaves and fry until the sage has wilted and turned a little crisp. Add the cooked spaghetti to the pan and toss through with a dash of the reserved butternut juices and some Parmesan. Tong into bowls or on to plates, shower with lots of Parmesan and twist over that pepper again.

Egg 'n' bacon spaghetti

Spaghetti alla carbonara is a classic. I'm with the Italians on this one – I don't add cream to mine. Apart from the frying of the bacon, the sauce makes itself around the spaghetti – and it all only takes as long to make as it does for the pasta to cook.

400g spaghetti
400g bacon lardons or bacon, chopped
splash of olive oil
4 large hen or duck eggs
lots of freshly grated Parmesan

Cook the spaghetti in plenty of salted boiling water, according to the packet instructions, until al dente. While you're waiting for the pasta, fry the bacon with a small splash of oil – to get the fat running – until beginning to crisp, but not frazzled. Then crack the eggs into a bowl and lightly beat together with some pepper and salt.

Drain the pasta, reserving a little cooking water, then tip back into its still-hot cooking pan. Next, toss the eggs through the spaghetti, so that all strands are well slicked – the heat from the pasta will cook the egg – then add a touch of the kept water, if it needs it. Then tip in the bacon and a very hearty grating of Parmesan, and toss through again. Eat snowed with more Parmesan – and that peppermill should be at hand, too.

Bowls of rice and good curries

Sometimes I come unstuck. Completely at a loss over what I want to eat. I reach stalemate. Nothing entices. Nothing stirs. Nothing clicks. Should be the cue for starting the diet. But no. It's only momentary, this loss of appetite – a day or two. It's when what's in and what's out is unclear. And I'm not talking handbags either, but seasonal ingredients. Spring hasn't quite made up its mind and wintery things still nag; flavours feel samey and a lift is urgently required. Something gentle and fragrant and layered with spice, with a hint of root and a flash young leaf, is what I'll be after. Exotic, but without the ram-rod smash of too much chilli. And that's Indian food, believe it or not. A gentle curry is just the job. For Indian curries can be far removed from chillies.

Indian curries were my first exploration into spice territory. When I first started to cook curry, our high priestess of curry writers, Madhur Jaffrey, had just brought out a book, *Indian Cookery*. All very do-able, yet authentic and above all, exciting – for I learnt that a curry's character has little to do with heat and more to do with the careful blend of aromatic spice. Thanks to Ms Jaffrey's enthusing, India became my first far-flung travel destination, and it now holds a very special place in my heart – of colour, thrill, magic and elation. Since then I've travelled all over. It's a sensual haven and a world I can still find without having to step on a plane, when I throw spices into hot oil in a pan at home on my hob.

A cloud of spice, as if blown in from Kerala's Cardamom Hills, steeps me and my kitchen for days afterward. Cardamom. That's the spice that does it for me. My favourite. And it inhabits our best-loved curries.

Ever bitten into a green cardamom pod by accident? It bites back. It's an anaesthetic, gum-numbing experience, like chewing on a capsule of eucalyptic explosive. The shock sends your tongue into autonomic spasm and you spit the little spice bomb out on to your plate, but then cardamom isn't meant to be eaten. However, I enjoy the sabotage, and will chomp on the pod with pleasure. What makes it such an amazing spice is its ability to add nuances of fragrance and flavour. Isolate a single pod and the aromas – far from the medicinal chest-rub whiff you'd expect – are of liquorice and molasses, allspice leaves and betel nuts. Sprinkle some into a curry and it will steep the food with the same elusive blend of exotic perfumes and tastes. Now, if your jar of cardamom has been sitting on the shelf for more years than you care to remember and the desiccated pods now look like straw-coloured gerbil food, it won't have the desired effect – so chuck 'em out, and invest in some more. This is the same for all spices: they won't keep for ever, so buy in small packets only.

All spices are best bought whole – in seed or stick form – then lightly toasted in a dry frying pan, and ground by your own fair hands, just

before you sling them into your pot of curried gloriousness. Yes, very nice. Truth is, we often don't have the time for such labours of love and the pre-ground packets happily fit the bill. If you have time, do it – I don't always, and still make great curry. Same goes with bought curry pastes and spice mixes – they're good, and save time intelligently. They're the one breed of cook-in sauces that work. Try and make your curry in advance, for the wait – and preferably an overnight one – will do it extra good. South-East Asian curries are different, they're more last-minute cooking and more soupy, yet can be whacked together much faster. Excellent for those that like things light and their veg with crunch.

And when you dish up an Indian curry, try and serve a few little dishes of chopped-up bits and bobs. This could be just be some sliced white onion jumbled with lemon juice and dried mint (yes, the dried here is good) or a dish of chopped cucumber with fresh coriander, or simply some toasted flaked almonds. Mum's comfort Raj-style curry is naked without them. And don't forget the bought pots of chutneys and pickles. Contrasts are everything.

Cooking rice to accompany those curries – or other rice dishes – can be like asking some of us to go and bunjy-jump. Completely no-do. So many packets of rice and different people's recipes say conflicting things – often too much water and too long cooking times are stipulated. It used to instil terror in my sister Catherine. My father rubbished her rice for being too sloppy and overcooked. And showed her his way – boiling it, then rinsing it and drying it in the oven. Interesting, but not correct either. Sorry, Dad. She now does it my way, and gets pin-point perfect rice every time.

Perfect boiled rice

You may think this obvious, but I'm going to tell you anyway – even if just as a comparison to the rest. When boiling rice in lots of water use American long-grain rice; my Mum uses Patna rice. Wash the rice first in cold water to rinse it of excess starch: either stick it in a sieve and hold it under the tap, or tip it in a pan sat in the sink, letting the cold water tap run into it for 3 minutes with a gentle overflow, swishing it around with your hand every now and then. Then drain and put the rice straight into plenty of salted boiling water, turn down the heat to a fast but gentle bubble and simmer for 11 minutes – that's 11 minutes on the dot. Next, tip it into a wide colander to drain (do not rinse) and then spoon it around for a few seconds so that it billows up its steam and dries a bit. It should be slightly moist but not wet, nor bone-dry, when served. A knob of butter stirred through boiled rice just before serving makes it rather good.

Perfect steam-boiled rice

It's easy to get befuddled on this one. What is normally meant by steamed rice is actually steam-boiled rice. The only true steamed rice – where the grain is set over a steamer – is sticky (glutinous) rice and this requires an overnight soak before setting in a muslin-lined tray and steaming for 20-25 minutes. All other rices are steam-boiled. This means that a set amount of water is put with a set volume of rice and the grains boil first, then once all the liquid has evaporated, they cook further in their own steam. It will give you rice that sticks with a lovely wobble – the sort you'd get at your local Thai or Chinese – and the same treatment is applied to basmati rice to make perfect pilau rice. This is how you should cook Thai jasmine, Chinese, Japanese (for sushi), basmati and, if you like, long-grain rice.

I like to use the cup method for measuring rice because you can then measure out the water with the same cup and it doesn't get complicated. For me millilitres and grams have no place here. It doesn't matter what a cup is, as long as you stick to the one volume for everything but for those that are desperate to know, it's a tea cup… okay, a sort of 200ml cup. So, measure out the amount in cups (you'll need about 1 cup per person where rice is the hero of the meal), then wash it or rinse it in cold water. Next, drain it and tip it into a heavy-bottomed saucepan, so that it's about 4-5cm deep. The more rice, the wider the pan. Then for every cupful of rice add just under $1\frac{1}{4}$ cups of water – using, of course, the same cup. Alternatively, add enough water so that when you lower your index finger to touch the rice, the water comes no higher than the first joint on your finger. Get the volume ratios correct, and you're halfway there. Now get the bubbling and steaming bit down to a tee, and you're home and dry.

Next, salt the water and bring to a boil. Bubble for 2 minutes, then cover with a well-fitting lid, turn down the heat to very, very low and cook for a further 7-8 minutes. Then turn off the heat and leave to steam-cook for a further 10 minutes. Some would say you should put a tea-towel at this stage between lid and pan to catch any drips, but I found it made not a jot of difference. Then fluff through with a fork and serve.

Take it one step further You can flavour the rice all sorts of ways and with all sorts of stuff when cooking: use a thinned chicken stock instead of water or use half canned coconut milk to water and enrich further with more thick coconut cream stirred through at the end. When putting the rice in the pan, add a couple of smashed stems of lemongrass to jasmine rice or slices of root ginger to Japanese rice. A dash of rice vinegar is good paddled through Japanese rice once cooked.

Perfect pilau rice for curries

This is what I call my Keralan hill rice – my all-purpose stand-by for all Indian curries that need a pilau rice attachment. Once you know it, you'll whack it together without thought or reference. Tip 500g basmati rice into a sieve and stick it under the cold tap, jigging it around a bit to wash it, then leave to drain. Heat 1 tbsp vegetable oil in a large heavy-based saucepan, then add some spices – 12 cardamom pods, 6 cloves, 2 large cinnamon sticks, 2 dried bay leaves – and heat for a few seconds or until they smell fragrant and begin to make popping noises. Stir in the rice, then add about 700ml water, or enough to cover the rice by about 2cm, and a good shake of salt. Bring to a boil and bubble for 2 minutes, then cover with a well-fitting lid, turn down the heat to very, very low and cook for a further 7-8 minutes. Turn off the heat and leave for at least 10 minutes, before fluffing through with a fork. It will sit happily like this, lid on, for a good half-hour, or can be reheated in the

microwave. Fluff through again when ready to serve. And remember not to eat the whole spices – although I like the cardamom pod surprise, it's a mouth freshener.

Perfect risotto

A risotto, in my Mum's book, is still a mound of fluffed-up long-grain rice with lots of leftover bits and bobs tossed through it. Very 1970s, made more like a paella or pilaff. Once cold and then stirred and coated with mayo, it became one of those rather dubious rice salad concoctions. In fact, Mother is not too struck by a true Italian risotto – the wet ones we make now with the correct rice and cooking technique. She remains unconverted.

What's the secret behind a good risotto? It's all in the timing and having an understanding of what you're doing and achieving. A risotto can't be rushed. It has to be nurtured, tended and gently fed so that you end up with a delicious starchy mulch of rice dotted with the things that have flavoured it. The grains should be tender and fat – but not split – and should have just an edge of bite to them. More skivvy and less skive make for a good risotto. Once you've got the basics, there's a never-ending list of wonderful risottos you'll create. Keep it seasonal – buying tip-top vegetables that taste – and you'll always end up with something good. And PS, I think I have to say this: never ever wash rice for a risotto.

So which risotto rice do I use? Don't fret over this too much, all sorts will do. But for those who want the knowledge, here's the low-down. Some risotto rice is simply labelled risotto rice and is usually the arborio sort. This is a good all-rounder but can be a little sticky as it doesn't absorb water as well as the next two, vialone nano and carnaroli rice. Vialano nano (meaning dwarf vialone) has short fat grains that are high in amylose (starch) and accept liquid readily. Carnaroli is similar but slightly superior to (and a tad more expensive than) vialone nano as it's even starchier and has the ability to stay firm during cooking. It's a pretty failsafe one, which makes it *the* Rolls-Royce of rice for risotto purists.

How do I know when my risotto is ready? Totally subjective. I can't give you an exact time or absolute rice texture as it's down to the rice and you. It's ready when you feel it almost tastes right. I say almost, because the rice will continue to cook once off the heat – so bear that in mind. Essentially it will take 18-20 minutes to cook (some would say 2 minutes more). Again, like pasta, Italians like the heart of the grains to be chalky, whereas I prefer mine with only a hint of the al dente about their gills. Take it too far and they'll become too pudding like. So keep focused toward the end, constantly tasting to catch it right. Add more seasoning, too, if it needs it.

Thai green jungle curry

This is your classic Brit-Thai curry, and very friendly, for it will happily bend to suit what's on offer from your fridge. I like mine bristling with seasonal green things. And if you eat meat you could add some sliced raw chicken breast (cut 1cm thick) at the coconut-milk-adding stage (or leftovers from a roast). A big bowl of steam-boiled rice (see page 72) is a must here.

2 fat cloves garlic, finely sliced
1 stick lemongrass, trimmed and finely sliced
vegetable oil
2 tbsp Thai green curry paste
2 x 400ml cans coconut milk
400ml chicken stock (see page 47, but a cube is
    okay)
1-2 tbsp fish sauce
3 tsp caster sugar
juice of ½ lime
4 handfuls green things, such as dwarf beans,
    stringless runner beans, broccoli (cut into
    small florets) and mangetout
2 handfuls beansprouts
handful of basil leaves or watercress

Fry the garlic and lemongrass in 2 tbsp oil in a wok or shallow pan until the garlic begins to turn golden, then stir in the curry paste and a touch of salt and gently fry for about 30 seconds, giving it a stir. Next, slowly stir in the coconut milk, then the stock, fish sauce and sugar. Bubble for about 8 minutes or until slightly thickened, then squeeze in some lime juice to sharpen it. It will be, and should be, very soupy.

Near to serving, cut the beans into short lengths, then plonk them with the broccoli florets (if using) into a pan of boiling water and bubble for a couple of minutes. Chuck the mangetout and beansprouts in, then shift off the heat and drain. Pile the vegetables into bowls, then ladle in the curry and throw on the basil...and don't forget the rice. (See image on page 75.)

Lamb korma

Lamb in an orgy of cream and spice, I can't say no.

1kg lamb, from the leg or shoulder
6 cloves garlic
3cm piece fresh root ginger
60g unsalted cashew nuts
60g unsalted peeled almonds
1 extra large onion, quartered
vegetable oil
12 cardamom pods
6 cloves
1 stick cinnamon
2 tsp each cumin and coriander seeds, ground
2 thin green chillies
150ml each of single cream and Greek yoghurt
1 tsp garam masala

Trim off any excess fat from the lamb, then slice it into large chunks – but not bigger than a mouthful. Put the garlic, ginger and most of the nuts, plus a small splash of water into a processor and whizz to a coarse paste – you may need to stop the machine a few times and push the mixture down from the sides. Add the onion, but pulse it, so that it remains finely chopped, not mushed.

Heat a shallow puddle of oil in a heavy casserole, then brown the lamb, a few pieces at a time, until tinted brown all over and lightly crusted on the edges, sprinkling with salt and a few twists of pepper as you go. Keep the browned lamb in a bowl. Leave the fat in the pan and then throw in the cardamom, cloves and cinnamon and allow to fry until you can smell the spice – only a few seconds, mind, for you don't want to burn it. Then tip in the contents of the processor and the ground spices, stir through and allow to fry, constantly scraping the base of the pan and turning through to avoid anything catching, until the onion has softened and started to brown. You may need to add a little more oil.

Now tumble the meat and its collected juices back into the pan, along with the whole chillies, then pour in the cream and stir everything together. Stir in 150ml water and the yoghurt, bring to a bubble and season. Put on the lid, and pop the pot into a 180°C/350°F/Gas 4 oven and leave to gently murmur away for an hour. Once removed from the oven, spoon off the puddle of fat that will be sitting on the surface – it's okay to leave a bit – and stir in the garam masala. Serve scattered with a few saved nuts that have been dry-toasted in the oven.

Curry-house chicken tikka masala

Honed here to perfection, my tandoori-roasted chicken in a creamy tomato curry-ish sauce is pretty damn wonderful. Another curry, up there in the comfort zone with Mum's. Eat with fragrant steam-boiled basmati rice. (There again, if you fancy just making chicken tikka, do that, and ignore the curry – then stuff it into split naans with some leafage, yoghurt and sweet mango chutney.)

4 large chicken breasts, preferably on the bone,
   skinned
juice of 1 lemon
8cm piece fresh root ginger, finely grated
8 cloves garlic, crushed
4 green chillies, deseeded and chopped
4 tsp garam masala
4 tbsp plain low-fat yoghurt
1 x 400g can chopped tomatoes
3 tbsp tomato purée
8 cardamom pods
3 cloves
1 tbsp runny honey
125g butter, plus extra for basting
250ml single cream
2 tsp ground fenugreek (optional)
2 good handfuls coriander leaves

Cut each chicken breast into three with kitchen scissors. Slash the meat about three times in each chunk, without going to the edge, then pile into a dish, and sprinkle with salt and lemon juice. Massage in the salt and lemon, then leave for 20 minutes. Put half the ginger plus any juice, half the garlic, 1 chopped chilli and 2 tsp garam masala into a largish bowl. Tip the yoghurt in and beat together, then add the chicken along with its juices. Rub the mixture into all its slashes. Cover and refrigerate overnight or for a good 24 hours in its tenderising yoghurt bath, like Cleopatra in her milk tub.

Make the sauce now, for this can be reheated the next day, and tastes better for it. Tip the tomatoes into a saucepan, then fill the empty can with water and tip this into the pan too. Add the tomato purée, remaining ginger, garlic, chilli and garam masala, the cardamom pods, cloves and some salt. Stir the lot together and bring to a gentle bubble. Allow to splutter away for a good 20 minutes, stirring occasionally. Beat in the honey, then the butter, then the cream, and if using, the fenugreek. Taste, and add a touch more honey or salt if it needs it. I like it sweetish. Leave to cool, then refrigerate.

To cook, turn the oven to its highest, then remove the chicken from its yoghurt bath. Lay the pieces across a baking sheet, then roast for 20 minutes (if it's off the bone, 15 minutes). Melt a little butter and brush-baste the pieces about halfway through. Reheat the sauce and add the chicken. Throw coriander leaves over each serving – and it's nice with a few toasted flaked almonds scattered over, too.

Thai fried egg rice

In Thailand they'd eat their rice and egg with cool slices of cucumber and tomato. I like mine with stir-fried shoots on top that become all eggy once you've forked or chopsticked into the yolk. In Indonesia, they'd scoop and wolf it with prawn crackers.

vegetable oil
6 small shallots, finely sliced
5 cloves garlic, finely sliced
1 tbsp fish sauce
3 large mild red chillies, deseeded and chopped
1 tbsp sweet chilli sauce
1 tbsp dark soy sauce
250g cooked long-grain rice (see page 72)
handful of beansprouts
4 large eggs
handful each of slender asparagus, mangetout
   and fine beans

Heat 2 tbsp oil in a wok or large frying pan and fry around two-thirds of the shallots and garlic until the shallots have frazzled at the edges. Add the fish sauce and chopped chilli and fry for a further 30 seconds. Add the sweet chilli sauce and soy sauce and splutter together for a further 30 seconds.

Next, tip in the rice and stir-fry the mixture for about 3 minutes until it reaches a good deep colour, adding the beansprouts toward the end. Add salt to taste, then tip into four warmed plates or bowls. Wipe out the wok. Fry the eggs in a frying pan, in a puddle of oil, keeping the yolks soft. Meanwhile, stir-fry the remaining garlic in 1 tbsp oil in the wok, until it looks light gold, then throw in the vegetables and stir-fry for about 45 seconds. Sprinkle the rice with the reserved shallot, and top each with stir-fried veg and a fried egg.

Mum's curry

This is comfort curry, the way my Mum and all mums make it. An anglicised hybrid of something distantly Indian – with ex-pat roots in countless officers' messes, hill stations and country clubs. Forget fresh spices, and let the old-fashioned curry powder and paste do all the work for you – just as Mum did, in the garam masala dark ages. You could stir a tablespoon of flour in at the end of the onion-frying stage but I find the apples thicken it beautifully. This is one that my Mum wheels out on Boxing Day or the day after, with all the last of the turkey bits and bobs thrown in – and a tray of fruity extras to heap on top. The extras are all unauthentically Indian – but of course – desiccated coconut, salted peanuts, sliced banana, chopped cucumber and tinned – yes, tinned – mandarin segments are de rigueur. If you haven't had turkey, use cooked chicken, duck or goose in$\underline{stead}$. Serve with plain boiled long-grain rice – and some fried pappadoms. Fresh chutney wouldn't go amiss. Makes loads for four, or feeds a polite six.

2 onions, chopped
2 tbsp sunflower or vegetable oil
2 tsp curry powder
2 tbsp curry paste (a balti or Madras is good)
2 cooking apples, peeled, cored and chopped
1 tbsp sweet mango chutney
approx. 600g cooked turkey or chicken, thickly
  shredded
500ml chicken stock (see page 47, but a stock
  cube is fine)
juice from canned mandarin segments (optional)
1½ tbsp sultanas

In a wide low saucepan or casserole, gently sweat the onions in the oil until they're softened but not too coloured. Stir in the curry powder and cook for a further minute, then add the curry paste and gently fry, stirring repeatedly for about 2 minutes (you may need to add a dash more oil). Stir in the apple, chutney and turkey until well coated. Pour in the stock, plus a dash of the tinned mandarin juice (if using on serving), then add the sultanas, bring to a low bubble, and season.

Allow to splutter away for a good 30 minutes or until the apple is very soft, the sultanas are plump, the liquid has turned nice and gloopy and everything looks fused with curry colour. Stick in your finger and taste, adding more salt if necessary. It will keep – and improve – like this in the fridge over two or three days. To dish up, spoon into bowls or on to plates of boiled rice and tip with all the bits and pieces mentioned above. Everyone will love you.

Perfect pappadoms Home-fried pappadoms are a must with any Indian in my house. Prepared well ahead, they'll stand in as a first course too. Once you start, they come fast. Use a wok to deep-fry in, as it concentrates a depth of oil where you want it (and without using too much), and have a pair of tongs and a wooden spatula at hand. Pour in enough vegetable oil to make a pool slightly wider than an uncooked pappadom, then heat it until fairly hot – but not smoking. The first pappadom in is always to test. Toss one in, dunk it in the middle, and within a split second it will writhe and its edges will curl in. Then, immediately as it curls, grasp it with the tongs and flip it over, dunk quickly, and the curling edges will sweep out flat. After a second or two whip it out, allow to drip over the pan, then place in a colander, edge down, to drain. It should be pale and crisp. Then carry on with the rest.

Fast fresh chutney I always make two quick fresh chutneys, an onion one and a yoghurty raita to soothe. For the onion one, I finely shred a medium onion, then toss with lemon juice, a chopped tomato, 1 tsp toasted cumin seeds, a touch of salt and a good wodge of chopped fresh mint. Or I might shred up a piece of fresh coconut and toss this in too with a few fried mustard seeds. For the yoghurt, I beat a big cupful of it with a crushed clove of garlic and more chopped mint. As simple as that.

Fragrant Persian chicken pilaff

This is basmati rice at its best, and you get this gorgeous spice-buttered crusted base on the rice. It's almost a chicken biryani – there again the Persian Moghuls brought the biryani to India, so no wonder. Leave out the chicken if you want and serve with boiled eggs.

400g basmati rice
a thumbful of saffron strands (optional)
8 small chicken thighs
vegetable or sunflower oil
butter
12 cardamom pods, squashed
3 cloves
2 cinnamon sticks, broken
2 dried bay leaves, torn
handful of whole blanched almonds or toasted
    pine nuts
1 onion, sliced
handful of large sultanas

Put the rice in a sieve, then stick it under a cold tap and give it a good rinse, gently shaking it about a bit. Tip it into a bowl and cover with cold water, then leave it to soak for a couple of hours, then strain again. Slip the rice into a pan of gently burbling water, add a dash of salt, cook for 4 minutes, then strain. The rice won't at all be cooked, should retain a little moisture and be quite damp for its next stage.

Meanwhile, pop the saffron (if using) in a dinky dish with 2 tbsp of warm water. Next, salt and pepper the chicken thighs, then gently fry them in a heavy saucepan or casserole in 2 tbsp of oil and a knob of butter, until they're golden all over. Then chuck in the spices and bay, and fry for a few more seconds or until fragrant. Lift out the chicken thighs and put them on a plate, leaving the spices in the pan. Stir the almonds and onion into the spices and gently fry, adding a touch more oil, until the onion starts to caramelise. Remove from the heat, tip in the rice and sultanas, and turn everything through.

Next, bury the fried chicken deep into the rice – leaving a good layer of rice at the bottom of the pan – then level off the top and dribble over the saffron water or 2 tbsp water. No, you're not adding any water at this stage – so, no frets, nothing is missing from the recipe. Cover the pan with its lid, which should be nice, heavy and tight-fitting, so that everything beautifully steams inside. Then set over a minuscule heat – and I mean *really,*

really low, for anything merely 'low' will end up burning the rice at the base of the pan. Leave to gently steam-cook for about 30 minutes. To serve, lift out the chicken, then stir a good knob of butter through the rice and pile into bowls or on to plates.

Old-fashioned kedgeree

I like my kedgeree uncurried. For me kedgeree is about the simple repetition of mouthful after mouthful of delicious smoked haddock and eggy buttery rice with a ton of good-old curly parsley. If you prefer it curried, then add a teaspoon or two of curry powder at the onion-frying stage. Kedgeree is also rather good made with flaked kipper – and I don't mean a tired-out one.

500g smoked un-dyed haddock, cut into pieces
1 medium onion, chopped
60g butter
250g long-grain rice
4 large eggs, hard-boiled, shelled and roughly
    chopped
1 good bunch curly parsley, finely chopped

Put the fish pieces in a wide saucepan, then pour in water to cover. Bring to a bubble then gently cook for around 8 minutes. Turn off the heat and lift out the fish; keep the water. Once cool enough to handle, pull off and discard the skin, then flake the meat into large chunks.

Gently fry the onion in half the butter with a little salt and pepper, until it has softened but not coloured, then tip in the rice, and stir through. Pour in enough of the reserved poaching water so that it comes about 3cm above the rice. Now, turn up the heat and bring to a bubble, then down to low, cover with a good-fitting lid, and very gently cook for about 10 minutes. Turn off the heat, fold in the flaked fish, eggs, parsley and remaining butter, and replace the lid. Leave on one side for a good 5 minutes. Taste, adding some salt and pepper if need be, then serve.

The ultimate mushroom risotto

The ultimate risotto for me is risotto con i funghi. *I give it the Italian nomenclature here for Italy is the homeland of good risotto. Once you know how to make this, you can make any risotto. Make sure you choose meaty mushrooms: fancy frail specimens won't hold up or add much flavour in this, so no oyster mushrooms please. Most would sling some fresh wild mushrooms in but there's no need to, for the full thrust of a ripened forest floor can be got by simply adding a few slices of dried porcini (ceps) and their soaking water. If you're a strict non-meat eater, use vegetable stock. It's gorgeous too made simply with fresh shiitake mushrooms.*

400g mushrooms, such as chestnut, small portobello, shiitake or wild mushrooms
6 pieces dried porcini (cep)
1.5 litres fresh chicken stock
100g butter
1 tbsp olive oil
1 small onion, finely chopped
1 clove garlic, very finely chopped
400g risotto rice (see page 73)
freshly grated Parmesan

Truly wild mushrooms – a lot now are cultivated – contain unwanted bits of forest, so will need a clean and trim. Rinsing under water is not forbidden, so a quick dunk and drain will do the job. Jettison anything that looks unwell and pasty about the gills: mushy watery bits mean the mushroom is on its last legs – i.e. it's rotting, and will not be pleasant. Larger mushrooms will need reducing to 1cm thick slices, medium ones in half, and smaller mushrooms can be left whole. You're going to have to spend the next 20 minutes or so at the stove, so, if you need jollying along, get set up with the radio or TV.

If you're using dried porcini, put them in a cupful of warm water as they'll need a good 10 minutes or so to rehydrate. These should be added to the mushrooms or to the chicken stock. I prefer the latter as they're there to punch in flavour – for once cooked they go to soggy cardboard and all their goodness is spent. Select a large pan with a heavy bottom to make the risotto in – this'll give even and maximum heat distribution. In another pan, put the stock with a ladle and bring this to a gentle blipping bubble.

Heat three-quarters of the butter with the oil, add the onion and gently fry it until it looks translucent and has softened, using a wooden spatula or spoon to stir it occasionally. Stir in the garlic, the mushrooms, a dash of salt and pepper, and turn up the heat a fraction. Fry for about a minute or two, turning the mushrooms occasionally to give each a turn at the heat source. Add the rice and stir through – without bashing it about too much – so that the grains are evenly mixed with fat, mushrooms and onion. Knock down any grains stuck to the sides of the pot, then add the porcini soaking water – if using – and enough stock just to cover the grains. Adjust the heat so that the rice burp-bubbles rather than racingly splutters.

As soon as the stock level drops below rice level add another ladleful of stock. Stir through and across the bottom of the pan every now and then, so that the grains cook evenly and don't stick – treating them carefully, as damaged grains will mess things up. Keep adding ladlefuls of stock and stirring every minute, until the rice is ready (see page 73). Then remove from the heat, fold through the remaining butter and 30g grated Parmesan and leave it to sit, lid on, for a couple of minutes before serving – making sure it's quite wet as it will want to absorb more liquid as it sits. Serve with or without more Parmesan showered on top.

Leftover heaven Make **mushroom risotto cakes** with leftover risotto. Mould the chilled mixture into flattened burger shapes then dust each in flour, dip in a little beaten egg and smother with breadcrumbs. Fry – like fish cakes – on both sides until golden and gorgeous. Serve with a fried egg slipped on top and with a few salad leaves. These great little cakes will cover brunch, lunch, supper or dinner.

sunday lunch beef

Sunday lunch roast beef. When was your last? And I mean a proper roast lunch. That full-on glorious works that steeps the house and fugs up the bedroom windows: a hunk of crisped beef all melty-pink in the right places, that demands a crusted tin of the best roast potatoes and a pan of glossy rich gravy.

It's those potatoes and that gravy that do it. You won't get these from any other roast. The roasted beef spuds at my prep school were unbelievable – as in brilliant, not refectory daggy. Better than home. They'd wallowed in gargantuan tins around a field of beef joints, drinking up all the beef concentrate they could stomach, and were then wheeled out of furnace-fired ovens, all crusted to perfection. However, they were not for us. The domestic, Peg, hovered with bread knife and would thwack the steel counter if we dared get near. Our potatoes came from tins that had not seen the joint. The specials were for the staff. I helped serve – it was the only way in.

Roast beef has to be the most grown-up of all the roasts and it's the one we all pick if eating out on a Sunday. Maybe we've lost our way at home with it, thinking it too tricky to get right ourselves. But I can assure you it's as easy as a chicken to get right – if not easier, and here I am going to take you by the hand and show you how.

Perfect roast beef

Good roast beef starts life, naturally, with a good bit of beef. And there are various cuts to choose from. These are my top choices: a rib roast – an on-the-bone joint; rib-eye – the same cut but off the bone; and sirloin – also called strip loin. You can use topside but I think it always a tad chewy. I go down various different routes to get my joints. I order organic, properly husbanded meat from smaller producers by e-mail or phone; sometimes I'll buy from my local butcher; and then there's the supermarket joint. They all turn out a treat – but the well-cared-for meat always gets the gold for flavour.

Which joint? Buy a joint that's at least 2kg or more and strapped with a fine blanket of fat. Apart from feeding a houseful, the meat will be pinker and more velvet-like in the middle. Plus you'll have plenty left over for sandwiches and a bonus pot of dripping – great smeared on to hot toast with a smattering of sea salt. A rib joint, bones on or off, is my top choice. Its flesh is marbled with fine threads of fat, which not only inject flavour but also act as a sort of self-lubing irrigator throughout the muscle as it roasts. If you go for one on the bone, the sawn ribs will ooze extra goodness into the sticky beef bits in the roasting pan – just the kind of delicious gunge you want for your potatoes and gravy. Sirloin or strip loin is lean and very tender, if not so flavoursome as a rib, and will be happier than the rib if caught on the very rare side. A 2kg joint or a three-rib roast, will feed eight with some seconds.

What's the knack for the perfect beef roast then? Similar rules apply to all joints. The secret behind a good roast – meat that's tender pink in the centre and caramelised to a crispy rich crust on the out – is accurate timing. And this is gauged by its weight. So make sure you note it, before slinging its wrapper. The other trick to success is to give the thing plenty of space, which will make for perfect roast potatoes too. And don't get too clever with the veg – you won't have time. Boiled roots, one perhaps mashed, and some blanched greens are an appropriate two-veg to add to the line-up.

Leftover heaven Use up slices of rare roast beef either in a **green salad** flaked with Parmesan (see page 45), an **Asian-style salad** or a delicious **Asian slaw** (see page 28). Or make **rare roast beef sandwiches** – layering up fine slices of beef, sprinkled with a little sea salt and then stacking with rocket and chunky shavings of Parmesan. A smidgen of mayonnaise beaten with a dash of lemon juice is nice slicked in too, and pastes the whole glorious thing together.

Perfect roast beef

For the beef, take a look at the notes on page 85, and then get stuck in.

2kg beef joint or a 3-bone beef rib
2 tbsp beef dripping

Whip out a big roasting tin – or make that two tins, if your oven is small – and set the oven to 220°C/425°F/Gas 7. Next, after noting the weight of your joint, sit it in the tin, rub it with a generous amount of sea salt and freshly ground black pepper, then smother it with about 2 tbsp dripping. Roast it for 20 minutes, then turn the oven temperature down to 190°C/375°F/Gas 5 and roast it for about 13 minutes per 500g for rare. For instance, if you were roasting a 2kg joint, after its initial 20-minute blast, you'd then roast it for a further 50 minutes or so. Basting is not that necessary. A three- to five-rib roast – that's one on the bone – will weigh in much heavier and is thicker and will therefore need extra time (see Rib roast for a crowd on page 89). To maximise succulence, shift the meat from the roasting pan, loosely wrap with foil, and leave in a warmish spot to rest for a full 20 minutes before carving. Don't fret if the meat cools too much, for the hot gravy and hot plates will warm it up.

Glorious beef gravy

1 tbsp beef dripping
2 tbsp flour
vegetable cooking water, or water with 150ml red
  wine
⅛ beef stock cube, beef bouillon, or 2-3 tsp Marmite

Shift the potatoes from the roasting pan (the joint will have departed) and make the gravy in this. Scrape up all the bits, add the dripping and the flour to the fat in the pan and set over the burner. Fry the flour until it turns brown then gradually incorporate enough hot vegetable cooking water or just water and red wine with half a beef stock cube or some bought beef bouillon, to make a gravy, adding any of the resting beef's collected juices. Bubble over a fierce heat until reduced and thickened. Rather than use a stock cube, my Mum always puts in 2-3 tsp of Marmite in all her gravies. It's an instant hit on thin vegetable water and with a spoonful of flour turns the lot into a thick dark gloop of gravy goodness.

Home-made horseradish cream

2 shallots, very finely chopped
2 tbsp white wine vinegar
4 tbsp soured cream
1 clove garlic, crushed
3-4cm fresh horseradish root, peeled and grated

Mix the shallots with the white wine vinegar and bubble down in a pan until evaporated. Next, remove from the heat and spoon into a bowl, then mix with the soured cream, garlic and fresh horseradish root. Season with salt and a few twists of black pepper.

Perfect dripping roast potatoes

**1.35kg Maris Piper or King Edward potatoes
about 3 tbsp beef dripping**

Par-boil potatoes in their skins for 8 minutes, then drain, leave to cool, and strip off and discard the skins. Next, cut them in half and add them to the roasting pan with the meat at the begining of the cooking, adding salt and pepper and melted beef dripping. Then toss them in everything, spreading them out around the joint – not more than one layer deep – slide into the oven, turning them over once halfway through their time. If cooking something larger, like a rib roast, slip them into the roasting pan with the meat for the last 1½ hours of the joint's cooking time: move the joint to one side, scrape up all the caramelised sticky bits in the pan, and toss the potatoes in it all, adding salt and pepper and a drop more beef dripping if necessary. If they refuse to take on a crunchy crust because they're sweating, transfer them away from the meat to a low-sided tin, giving them a turn on the top shelf of the oven. They'll be fat gorged, so the extra heat should do the trick.

Lightest Yorkshires

I prefer my Yorkshire pudding light – using just water, and no milk. You can use half water and half milk, if you prefer. Try to bake your Yorkshires on their own, while the joint is resting, as they perform best in a very dry oven – humidity is their enemy. Animal fat here please, not oil.

**2 large free-range eggs
1 tbsp vegetable oil
100g plain flour
300ml water
60g dripping or lard**

Put the eggs, vegetable oil, flour, water and a shake of salt into a liquidiser or processor and blend, or whisk the ingredients together by hand, adding the water a little at a time, then leave to stand for a short while. Meanwhile, divide the dripping or lard between the wells of a multi tart tin or muffin tin or pour into one large deep tin (roughly 30 x 20cm), then put in a 230°C/450°F/Gas 8 oven until very hot and smoking. Remove and immediately fill each with batter and put back on the top shelf of the oven. Bake for 20 minutes or until the batter has risen, puffed and done its thing. Eat the Yorkshires with the gravy poured over

Rib roast for a crowd

A 5-rib roast, to serve 20 plus, sure is a hunk of carcass. My first one came mail order, so I hadn't had a chance to gauge its size until it landed, ice-packed and polystyrene-boxed, on my doorstep. It looked more ready for the Saatchi Collection than my oven. If you can handle it – literally, it's heavy – it'll feed a houseful and, if you buy it from a reputable butcher, it will give you the best roast beef in the world. It's far superior to your top or silverside roast. Follow the gravy and Yorkshires instructions opposite. You'll need a big brutish roasting tin for a 5-rib.

Beef on the bone is big bold stuff. And so is cooking it. There's no messing about, no fancy stuff. Bits and pieces with bones still attached bear immediate anatomical i-d and there's no way of prettifying them. Neither should you want to. A roast rib of beef is a thumpingly handsome chap, and he needs little to show him off. The last thing you want though, when doing something on this scale, is to have to heave-ho it all to the table. So to save the washer-up whingeing over a stack of serving dishes, and things congealing before they make the table (including person on pans), turn your kitchen into a carvery and let everyone dive in to what they want. Leave everything in the cooking pots and tins – with all veg drained, lining them up on the work surface with spoons, ladles, a stack of hot plates and a sheaf of napkins. The hot pans will keep it all warm and it looks dead homely too. For the roast potatoes etc. follow the instructions opposite, but increase the amount of potatoes.

1 x 5-bone beef rib
3-4 tbsp beef dripping

Set the oven to 220°C/425°F/Gas 7. Rub the oven-ready rib of beef joint with a generous amount of sea salt and freshly ground black pepper and smother with the dripping. Roast in a large sturdy roasting tray for 20 minutes per 500g for rare with a crisp crust. Turn the oven temperature down to 190°C/ 375°F/Gas 5 after 1 hour and then turn back up for the last 30 minutes of cooking time. Leave the meat to rest, loosely covered with foil, for a full 20, or even 30 minutes before carving.

Fast rare blackened beef

1 x 500g piece beef sirloin
olive oil

Trim a sirloin joint of excessive fat, but leaving a little. Rub the joint all over with salt and twist over some pepper and rub in. Sit it on a preheated smoking-hot heavy chargrill pan, griddle-pan or heavy frying pan and leave it to sizzle, smoke and splutter for a good 3 minutes or so – *without* prodding it. Shift it slightly on to a new side and continue to sear. After another 3 minutes shift again, and continue until all sides are done. This will take about 12 minutes and the joint should end up looking nicely blackened all over. Next, sit it on a roasting tray, rub with olive oil, then roast for a good 12 minutes in a 220°C/425°F/Gas 7 oven. Leave to rest until cooled, a good 20 minutes or so, then wrap in clingfilm and refrigerate until needed. Finely slice, then leave the slices open to the air to develop their rare red colour. Serve with salad or slaw.

Roast chicken dinner

Roast chicken, now here we go. I need say nothing to sell it. It's the one we do most often. Its portability makes it so attractive. It has ready-to-roast package appeal. It's home food and the niftiest little number I can have at the ready.

Now, years ago when I worked for Habitat, they sold a thing called a chicken brick. This was a rounded clay pot made up of two halves that neatly slotted together and entombed the bird. It looked more sarcophagus than pot. The brick sealed in all the juices and kept the bird very succulent as it roasted, plus you got a salt-crisp skin on top and a stock-rich pool below. Pot-roasting, along with poaching and regular roasting, is the best way to cook chicken. We all know how sometimes a nice fat hen, once roasted, can turn into a bit of a wasted old bird. A pot roast prevents that – and you can forget about it. Apart from the convenience of it all, you cash in on all of the bird's flavour, as the pot holds a sauna-like microcosm of chickyness that'll sop into anything that's nestling alongside. And remember, a roasted bird once cold, with perhaps a glorious bit of jellied deliciousness clung to its undercarriage, is sublime too.

Perfect roast chicken

Roasting a chicken is straightforward, but getting it right? Easy. Read the following to get a grasp of everything but then when you come to cook, follow the abbreviated recipe – with everything on board.

Which chicken do I use? A battery-farmed bird costs the same as a bag of fancy supermarket salad. Hmmm, no more than a bag of air and green bits, and worse still, it's not had a life. Not great. And for that reason alone – forgetting flavour and whether or not it's organic – I will not buy those poor things. So even if you can't taste the difference between a battery or a free-ranger, please champion the latter, albeit to campaign toward a not so poultry life.

If you haven't had much luck with the chickens you've hunted down in the shops, try phoning for one. I've roasted up some fantastic mail-order birds. I haven't had great successes with the more expensive French free-rangers – you know, the ones with all the authenticating insignia of coquettish rosette labels and metal tags. These gastro-fed fowl may have been leading the good life but are a bit too lean for my liking and can be tough, no matter which way I cook them. All that French hen strutting doesn't make tender meat. And all those labels, per-lease.

What tin do I use? If you're roasting your chick in with the potatoes make sure you use a big tin that's not high sided. A deep and too small tin won't do the job, as once the chicken is ensconced, all the spuds will have to shunt up tightly together – or worse still, jumble on top of each other – and the whole lot will sweat it out rather than roast. The dry oven heat needs to get at the outer fat sopped layers of the spuds to get them to a deep crisp. The alternative is to roast the spuds in a separate tin.

Where do I start? Turn the oven on high, in readiness for a good roasting. Next relieve the chicken from its bondage of clingfilm and elastic harness and let it breathe while you turn your attention to the spuds. If you want cracking good roast potatoes, you'll need to par-boil them first. That means peel them, then if they're medium sized (around 6cm long), cut them in half lengthways. Larger potatoes cut into three. This way the surface area to volume ratio errs in favour of plenty crisp outside to well-done fluffiness inside and you'll get good crunchy edges. Next, simmer the cut spuds in salted water for 5 minutes, no longer. Tip them into a colander to drain and then back into the pan in which they were cooked. Salt and pepper them, add a wodge of butter and a splash of olive oil – and any herbs, like rosemary, if you wish – and turn them through, so that they get coated and their edges rough up. Salt and pepper the bird inside and out, and then it's hands-on lavishment: smear all over with butter, plus dab a wodge inside. If you have an odd bunch of twiggy herbs stick these in too. Sit it breast up in the roasting tin, then squeeze over the juice of a lemon, then stick the used fruit inside the bird's cavity and tie the legs together. If you're not a fan of lemon, leave it out, yet some swear that it helps the skin crisp.

Juicy breast, what's the knack?
Some like to roast their chickens upside down, to let the juices flow into the breast meat, then turn it back upright for the final browning. However, there's a danger the skin will rip and then the juices will pour out. If doing the upside-down way, lean the chicken on one breast first, then shift to the other breast later, and to avoid rips, stick a whole peeled carrot under the breast to support it. The deliciously roasted carrot can then be eaten too. If you're roasting your chicken without potatoes, add a puddle of white wine and water to the tin – around 100ml of each, just enough to send up a steam and allow the bird to roast rather than soak in a hot bath. This vaporises the air around the bird and will help keep the breast meat moisturised and juiced.

When do the spuds go in? Right at the start, with the chicken. Distribute the par-boiled potatoes around the chicken – they can touch each other but shouldn't crowd each other out – then season them again. If you want to add vegetables, too, do so now – and raw: peeled small carrots, quartered parsnips, quartered red onion, Jerusalem artichokes (unpeeled), large chunks of pumpkin etc. If some are done before the bird, they can always be removed and kept warm.

Once the bird is in can I just forget about it? No. Sorry. This is make-or-break time for the perfect roast. Slide the assembled tin on to the middle shelf of a 220°C/425°F/Gas 7 oven, then roast for 20 minutes. Next, turn the oven down to 190°C/375°F/Gas 5 and roast for a further hour – but don't wander off. Make sure you spoon the juices over the bird about three times while it's roasting and turn the potatoes over at the same time, too. Use a metal spatula, so that you don't lose all their crusts to the tin.

My potatoes still aren't crisp. That's fine. Because all is not finished yet. The chicken needs plenty of time to rest – and that means valuable time spent sitting out of the oven so that its flesh relaxes which will allow the juices to beat a path back into all the right places. Essential for juicy breast meat. While it's resting, the potatoes can be finished off. So lift the bird from the tin and on to a warm serving dish. The easiest way to do this is to slide a fish slice underneath with one hand and, with the other, stick the handle of a wooden spoon right into the bird's cavity and lift. Cover it loosely with some foil to keep it warm, then it's back to the spuds: turn the oven up to high, turn them over again,

giving them more room by filling the space where the chicken sat, and put the tin back in for about 10-15 minutes.

Now for the gravy…and the rest. I like a thin un-floured gravy with chicken: a gravy made from a reduction of cooked vegetable water (carrot water is good) emulsified with all the heavily seasoned and sticky goo that's stuck to the bottom of the roasting tin. Now, there's quite a lot to think about at this stage, I know. The chicken's been out for a good 10 minutes – that's absolutely fine, so no worries there – and the potatoes need to come out so you can get at the tin. Turn off the oven, then tip the potatoes into their serving dish and keep warm in the oven. Next, drain some vegetable water or kettle boiled water – enough, by eye, to make gravy for four – into the roasting tin. Then drain the veg and tip it back into its still hot cooking pan and leave, lid on. Don't worry about the chook, she's improving with the wait. In fact, even after a half-hour stop-over, she'll still be warm, and extra delicious. Next, set the gravy tin over a good heat on the stove and as the contents bubble, scrape up all the bits and let bubble for a few minutes. Taste it and add more salt and pepper, until it's how you like it.

Perfect roast chicken dinner

Read pages 91-2 for the complete low-down and for some tips, then follow this with ease.

1 chicken, around 1.5kg
1kg potatoes such as Maris Piper or King
  Edwards
a big knob of butter
olive oil
1 small halved lemon (optional)

Turn the oven on to 220°C/425°F/Gas 7, then sit the chicken breast up in a good-sized roasting tin. Prepare it and the potatoes as described on page 92. Slide the assembled tin on to the middle shelf of the oven, then roast for 20 minutes. Turn the oven down to 190°C/ 375°F/Gas 5 and roast for a further hour, spooning the juices over the bird about three times during its roast and turn the potatoes over at the same time, too. Remove from the oven and lift the bird on to a plate, loosely cover with foil and leave to rest. Now, if your potatoes aren't quite crisp enough, turn the oven up to high again, turn them all over and spread them out, and then put back in for about 10-15 minutes. Drain the potatoes and keep warm in the turned-off oven.

Tip up the tin and spoon out excess fat (if any), then add about 500ml drained vegetable cooking water. Set the tin over a reasonable heat on the stove and as the contents bubble, scrape up all the bits and let bubble for a few minutes. Taste it and add more salt, until the thin gravy is how you like it.

Leftover heaven Where do we start? Gosh. Chicken, crisp bacon and salad sandwiches glued together with mayo is one way. Then check out all the options on chicken salads in the second chapter. And don't forget to use the carcass to make a stock (page 47 will show you how), and this can then be frozen.

Herby stuffing

If you want to stuff the bird, then it will need a few minutes' longer in the oven to be cooked through properly. I'm more a crumb 'n' herb mix man when stuffing a bird (a bunch of herbs to four thick slices bread, blitzed with an onion and a clove of garlic). Sausagey things can be too rich and fatty and interfere with the light pan juices but this is a very quick sausage stuffing that can be baked separately. More adventurous stuffings can be knocked together using couscous pre-soaked in stock, mixed with toasted nuts, fried onions, mint and chopped dried apricots.

4 herby sausages
fresh breadcrumbs
1 shallot, finely chopped

Squeeze the contents of the herby sausages into a bowl, mixing in a pile of fresh breadcrumbs and the shallot, plus some salt and pepper. To make fresh breadcrumbs, just whizz up chunks of white bread in a processor.

Bake separately in a lightly greased gratin dish or small tin for around 45 minutes alongside the bird.

Fast-roast tarragon butter chicken with pan-roast potatoes and greens

Fast because we're using two baby chickens here, and the roasting is over in half an hour.

2 poussins (baby chickens)
4 cloves garlic, crushed
150g butter
4 tbsp chopped tarragon
800g-1kg potatoes suitable for chipping
olive oil
500g greens, such as cabbage, spring greens,
   broccoli or dwarf beans

Take the elastic off the little birds, then rub them, inside and out, with salt and pepper. Then mash half the garlic into the butter with the tarragon and some seasoning. Next, slip your fingers between the flesh and the skin of the birds' breasts (oo-er), so that the skin is released from the meat. Then stuff these pockets with about half of the butter mixture. Tie together their legs with string and place the chickens in a large shallow roasting tin, well apart, and roast for 30 minutes in a hot 220°C/425°F/Gas 7 oven, then leave the pair to rest, covered with foil, for a good 15 minutes.

Meanwhile, peel and cut the potatoes into rough 2cm cubes, then tumble them into a large frying pan or two pans, toss with sea salt and pepper, adding enough olive oil so that they sit in a very shallow pool, then slowly fry for about 20-25 minutes, occasionally turning, until golden all over and very tender. Finish them by tossing through the remaining crushed garlic during their last few minutes in the pan. Meanwhile blanch the greens in boiling salted water (about a minute for cabbage and spring greens, and 3 for beans and broccoli florets), then drain and plunge into cold water, then drain again.

When ready to serve, toss the greens in a pan or wok with the remaining herb butter over a fast heat, then cut the chickens straight down the middle and into halves (I use a serrated bread knife). Divide between four plates with the greens, and pour over the herbed buttery juices from the greens pan.

Pot-roast herby bird with melting garlic potatoes

This is completely fail-safe. Even if you over-roast everything the breast won't have dried up – and the potatoes, well, they may even have got better. It's one that you slam in and forget about, almost. Do it with or without the garlic potatoes.

1 chicken, about 1.5-2kg
butter
olive oil
2kg potatoes
1 bulb garlic, separated into cloves
bunch of mixed herbs, such as thyme, rosemary, savory or flat parsley, roughly chopped

To get the chicken looking golden, you need to launch it in that direction first. So, salt and pepper the bird all over, inside and out, then smear it all over with about 30g of butter. Heat a wide heavy casserole until warm, add about 2 tbsp olive oil, then the bird and brown all over. To get the chicken perfect without scorching it and tearing its skin, do this on a low heat over 15 minutes, and make sure you turn it on all sides – preferably using wooden spatulas. Then take it out and get the potatoes on the go. Peel and slice them into discs about 5mm thick, then layer the slices in the base of the pot with the garlic cloves, salt, pepper and some herbs and then pour in around 150ml of water (or chicken stock if you have it) and douse with around 3 tbsp olive oil.

Next, put the chicken on top of the potatoes, breast up, smother with herbs and a further smear of butter and put the lid on the pot. Pot-roast in a 190°C/375°F/Gas 5 for 1 hour. Then whip off the lid, turn up the oven to 220°C/425°F/Gas 7 and open-roast for a further 20 minutes. Take the chicken out and leave it somewhere warm, covered with foil. Put the pot back in the oven, turn up to 230°C/450°F/Gas 8 and cook for another 15 minutes or so. This will brown up the potato discs and set their starchy edges deliciously chewy crisp.

Honey-roast drumsticks

This one evolves at home constantly – and every family has their own version. You can add some grated ginger if you have some.

8 chicken drumsticks or thighs, skin on or off
4 cloves garlic, crushed
1 tbsp runny honey
2 tbsp soy sauce
1 tbsp roughly chopped rosemary
1 tbsp vegetable oil

Lay the chicken across a roasting tin, then salt and pepper it. Next dribble, spill and sprinkle over the remaining flavourings and oil, and then jumble the chicken pieces around a bit so that they become well coated. Leave them like this until you're ready to cook. Jumble through again just before you roast them.

Roast the tray of chicken in a 220°C/425°F/Gas 7 oven for 35 minutes, remembering to turn the pieces over midway. Then remove the tin from the oven, cover with foil and leave on one side for 10 minutes: the meat will carry on cooking a little and will have time to relax and become succulent. I know they're only legs but this relaxing time makes all the difference.

Weekend roast lamb

If Desert Island Discs became Desert Island Dinners, then a roast lamb lunch would be my number one. Its Englishness is as patriotic as *the* Desert Island disc, 'Jerusalem'. Total pastoral heaven. Be it sheep – gambolling or roasted; mint – rampantly growing or sauced; new potatoes – in soil or in the colander; or the cauli, tucked up in a blanket of milky-white sauce in my best friend's mum's tureen. The holy lamb of God that is in England's pleasant mountains seen, tastes so much better than it hymns.

That roast lamb lunch, of the sort we do at the weekend with all the traditional trimmings, is unique. For not only is it about the lovely lamb, sauces and gravy or the veggies on their own, it's about a marriage – a glorious togetherness on the plate. Once side-by-side they do magic in a way no other roast does: the gravy laps and the wobble of mint jelly ebbs to melt-down; the spooned-on vinegared-mint sauce dutifully deltas; and the slices of just-carved lamb – now spattered with a bit of this and that – act like magnets on it all, sopping everything up. My fork can now patter around contentedly, in a delicious quagmire of minted meat, gravy and plundered potato, and can get to work on the cauliflower and its white sauce, turning it all into an unctuous slurry. Meat, cauliflower, sauce, gravy and potatoes all minted up. Roast lamb dinner proper. You get the picture.

Perfect roast lamb

Lamb is best in early summer, when the spring-born lamb has had some time out on the grass and developed a bit of character. My joint for roasting is shoulder. It stays more tender and holds a fuller quota of crispy fat than leg – although leg is delicious too.

Where do I start? To get the fat on the move and things crisping, lightly prick the fatty side of the shoulder all over with the tip of a knife, without piercing the meat. I'm not into stabbing the lamb all over and sticking it with rosemary and garlic, for it may have that look of I-know-what-I'm-doing and sit pretty before it's roasted, but it will be peppered with frazzled bits when it's roasted and the meat will have poured out its juices through its slashes and succulence dealt a blow. If you like your lamb with rosemary, then tuck some sprigs in with the potatoes – or just stick the lamb on a raft of it and roast it on that.

What's the secret of succulence? Roast lamb does things to me, especially the crisped bits of skin with their attached seams of melting fat. Yes, I eat it, and too much. But even if you're not keen, avoid removing too much fat before you roast, for it's there for the meat's sake too. Flavour comes from fat and it keeps the meat fed while it cooks – it's an automatic built-in baster. It's this delicious combination of perfectly rendered fat, along with spring-grass-fed meat, which makes – in true carnivore speak – eating a young piece of sheep so, so good.

Leftover heaven Often at the end of a lamb joint, roasted leg in particular, there's a batch of meat that hugs the bone, too pink for words or digestion. Rather than waste it, it can be slivered off and used in a **big doner kebab**. Dip the slices in a mint jelly marinade made from beating 1 tbsp mint jelly with the same of balsamic vinegar and lemon juice, adding 2 cloves of crushed garlic, a good pinch of cinnamon, salt and pepper and a shake of Tabasco Green. Then you quickly sear them in a hot pan. Stashed with lots of finely shredded lettuce, white cabbage and onion into warmed pittas, and dolloped with yoghurt and wolfed down – can you think of anything better? Make a **salad of cold sliced roast lamb tossed with mint, parsley and lemon tabbouleh** (a herby cracked wheat salad). Rub thick slices of undercooked lamb with dukkah – an Egyptian blend of crushed toasted hazelnuts, sesame seeds, roughly crushed coriander and cumin seeds – and some salt and pepper, then brush with oil and pan-grill. Eat with rice stirred with yoghurt and freshly chopped herbs.

My best friend's mum's roast lamb lunch

My best friend's mum, Pam, who never made a song-or-dance over her cooking, cooked the best lamb roast in the world, and served it with mint sauce and cauliflower in white sauce. It was the stuff of Sundays. No fancy stuff. And hers was delivered, Sunday after Sunday, with all the right trimmings, without fail, and with pin-point roast perfection. Pam made her gravy with Bisto granules, and that's how we loved it. I've used the pan gubbins here. Hers was always shoulder – use a leg if you prefer. Make your mint sauce and your cauli's white sauce while the lamb is roasting. All good classic stuff.

1.6-2kg shoulder or leg of lamb
vegetable or olive oil
1-1.5kg potatoes suitable for roasting

First make a note of the joint's weight before binning its wrapper. Then lightly pierce the skin and fat all over with the tip of a very sharp knife, making tiny little prick marks – no deeper than the fat itself. This will help the fat to run and crisp the skin. Next sit it in a large low-sided roasting tray and massage it with both sea salt, fine salt (the latter will slip into the prick marks) and pepper, then rub with oil, and move to one side.

Next, peel the potatoes, cut them in half and boil them for 5 minutes, then let them drain and tip them back into their pan. Slop over a little oil, plus shake over some seasoning and then shake the pan a little to roughen up their edges and coat them in the fat. The roughed sides will help them become crisp. Carefully tumble them into the roasting pan and around the joint, and spread them. They shouldn't be piled on top of each other, so if your roasting tray is too small, then shift most of them into a separate tray. If you've had to do this, it's a good idea to swap the isolated potatoes with the lamb's potatoes halfway through the roasting, so the spuds all get their fair share of the good meat juices and fat.

Now, roast on the middle shelf of a 230°C/450°F/Gas 8 oven for 20 minutes, then turn down to 190°C/375°F/Gas 5 and roast for 20 minutes per 500g, swinging the oven back on high again for the last 10 minutes if it hasn't browned up enough. For rare roast lamb, roast on high for the first 30 minutes, then roast for 15 minutes per 500g. Make sure you shift the joint to one side three-quarters through the roasting time and then, using a fish-slice type utensil, turn over the potatoes. When the lamb is done, shift it from the roasting tray and leave it to rest, loosely covered with foil in a warmish place for about 20 minutes. If the potatoes haven't browned and crisped enough at this point, spread them out over a new baking tray or baking sheet and pop them back in the oven on the top shelf, as you'll now be needing the lamb's tin to make the gravy.

Delicious redcurrant jelly gravy

2 tbsp butter
1 tbsp flour
600ml vegetable cooking water
1 tbsp redcurrant jelly

Put the lamb roasting pan on the heat, and get rid of any surplus fat. It's unlikely there will be a lot of fat as the potatoes will have drunk up the lot, so add the butter to the pan. Next, set the pan on the hob, add the plain flour to the fat and fry, scraping away, until lightly browned, then slowly add the cauliflower or other vegetable cooking water, bring to a fierce bubble and then stir in the redcurrant jelly. (If you want your gravy plain, leave out the jelly.) And scrape the bottom of the pan to incorporate all the good gunky bits. (See image on page 102.)

Fresh mint sauce

I know the jar is easy temptation but it scores nul points *next to a freshly made. You've lavished love on your lamb, so win the contest by serving it with your own mint sauce – and so, so easy to fling together. Bought mint jelly – the wobbling blob of radioactive green – is totally allowed. Of course. Okay – so is jar mint sauce. But do give this a go with a bunch of mint. Once mown to shreds by your knife and swirled with the vinegar, you'll have a sauce that sings as loud, as green, and as demanding as 'Jerusalem'.*

3 tbsp chopped mint
½ tbsp caster sugar
2 tbsp white wine vinegar

In a small bowl, stir the chopped mint and caster sugar with 2 tbsp boiling water, then stir in the white wine vinegar and a pinch of salt. That's it. As simple as that.

Gorgeous cauliflower and white sauce

500ml full-fat milk
1 small onion, halved
1 tsp black peppercorns
2 bay leaves
2 pieces mace or chip of nutmeg
30g butter
30g plain flour
1 cauliflower, quartered

Pour the milk into a small saucepan, then throw in the onion, black peppercorns, bay leaves and mace or nutmeg. Heat until it foams up, then take off the heat and leave to one side for about 30 minutes. Melt the butter in another small pan and, using a wooden spoon, stir in the flour. Allow to gently foam without browning for about a minute or so. Then strain the flavoured milk, discarding all the bits and pieces, into the hot flour paste, stirring all the time until you have thick white sauce, then season with salt and white pepper. If it looks lumpy, just beat it harder or, failing that, sieve it. Leave in the pan; it will gain a skin but once reheated and stirred, the skin will go. Cook the cauliflower in bubbling salted water until just cooked – test it with a knife, this could only take about 3 minutes or so. An overcooked cauli is not a good thing. Pour the reheated sauce over the cauliflower and serve.

Fast-roast lamb with salsa verde

This uses a leg but off the bone. It's butterflied, which means opened out – and your dear butcher will do this for you – and then it's marinated. It's one I've thrown on the barbie over the years with fabulous results. Barbecues aren't kind to individual portions of meat and this being one large piece – the slimmed-down version of your usual joint – makes perfect barbecuable sense. The outside gets that lovely barbecue-blackened crust, while the inside stays lovely and pink. And carving? Well, it couldn't be simpler, as you just slice, working your way from one end to the other. Turn it Moroccan by rubbing it with ras-el-hanout, a Moroccan spice pedlar's special house blend, that wafts of the souk, and is now – as is most of the world – available from a supermarket near you (Seasoned Pioneers brand being excellent). If not available, use the pungent trio of lemon, cumin and coriander. If you want it ultra tender, then soak the butterflied lamb in milk overnight first, then drain and proceed as below.

1 large onion, cut into chunks
4 cloves garlic
grated zest of ⅛ lemon
2 long sprigs rosemary
1 butterflied leg of lamb
4 tbsp olive oil

Put the onion into a processor, along with the garlic and lemon zest, then strip the rosemary needles in too, discarding their stems. Pulse-blast to make a coarse mushy paste. If you don't use the machine, then finely chop everything to something mush-like. Lay the lamb out flat in a tin or dish, skin side up, and rub with salt and pepper and some of the olive oil. Turn over, flesh side up, and using the point of a sharp knife, slash the chunkier areas of flesh to make gashes that penetrate about halfway through the meat – and space them widely. Rub all over with salt and pepper and the onion and rosemary mixture, making sure some of it gets wedged down into the gashes. Next, slop over the remaining oil and rub this into everything too, then leave it to bathe for as long as you want. Overnight or 1 hour, it's up to you and your time.

To roast, place on a rack set over a roasting tin, flesh side up, and spoon over the collected oil in the dish. Then pop the lamb into a 230°C/450°F/Gas 8 oven and roast for 20 minutes, then turn over and roast for another 20 minutes. Test it for doneness, by sticking in a knife at a thick part and pushing the meat apart. If it's too pink for your liking, then roast it for 10 minutes more. If barbecuing, it will need around 15 minutes on each side. Let it rest for a good 10 minutes or so, loosely covered with foil, before cutting into nice thick slices. Serve with a green salad or a bean salad, and couscous (see page 135) is good. And so is the salsa verde below. Anything, actually.

Salsa verde *Salsa verde* – Italian for green sauce, nothing scary – is an easily made olive-oil-based green relish bunged full of soft herbage and capers, and is made for lamb. In spring I make mine with wild garlic leaves, again excellent with the lamb. It's a mere flick-of-the-switch processor job. So rather than cook veg to go with the roast, have this and a simple green salad instead.

Drain off half of the oil from 1 x 50g can anchovies in oil then tip the fillets and a drop of the oil into a processor or liquidiser. Stuff into the processor 1 big bunch each of flat-leaf parsley and basil or wild garlic, 2 cloves garlic, 1 cup fresh white breadcrumbs, 2 tbsp white wine vinegar, 1 tbsp rinsed capers or cocktail gherkins (cornichons) and 200ml extra virgin olive oil. Season with salt and pepper, then whizz up for about a minute or two. Don't overfill it. If it doesn't all fit, blast some, then stuff in more – it will all eventually mulch down. Decant into a bowl and put on the table with a spoon for everyone to take what they want of it.

Olive and rosemary lamb with tomato and roasted garlic beans

This could stretch to serving a less hungry six. For ultra-tidy-looking chops, get your butcher to trim off the excess fat and bits that run up the bones. Rather than roast my own tomatoes, I sometimes resort to chucking semi-dried tomato quarters in this – had from supermarket deli counters.

2 bulbs garlic, divided into cloves, unpeeled
olive oil
2 racks of lamb, 12 ribs in total
2 large sprigs rosemary, finely chopped
16 stoned black olives, finely chopped
1 red onion, sliced lengthways into narrow wedges
6 plum tomatoes, quartered
2 x 400g cans butter beans, drained and rinsed
300g green dwarf beans, tops trimmed

Scatter the garlic cloves over a very shallow roasting tin, jumble with a dash of oil and some salt and pepper, then roast in a 190°C/375°F/Gas 5 oven for 20 minutes. Rub the lamb with salt and pepper, then press the rosemary needles and the olives on to the fat side of each rack. Turn up the oven to 220°C/425°F/Gas 7, then place the racks of lamb in the roasting tin, olive crust side up. Tuck the roasted cloves of garlic and the onion under the lamb, and scatter the tomato wedges around the outside. Spoon around 2 tbsp olive oil over all, then roast for 25 minutes, keeping an eye on it all. And if the oven proves a little fierce, turn it down to 200°C/400°F/Gas 6 halfway.

When the lamb is cooked but rare, remove from the tin, cover with foil and leave to rest for a good 8 minutes or so. Spoon out excess fat, leaving about 1 tbsp, then pop the garlic cloves out of their skins and back into the tin with the tomatoes and onion. Next, tip in the drained beans and about 4 tbsp water, twist over some seasoning, then gently fold together and heat through on the hob. Pop the green beans into a pan of salted boiling water and cook for 3 minutes.

To serve, slice the lamb into cutlets, drain the dwarf beans and serve two to three chops per person with green beans and a pile of tomato and roasted garlic butter beans.

A delicious lamb and mint salad

This is a great one for using up the joint's leftovers – especially when you want a switch in flavours and something with a bit of smack. This niftily hoovers up the rare bits and chunks that hug the bone, plus the mint and any odd runner beans.

sliced rare lamb – whatever you have left over
6 tbsp Asian dressing (see page 18)
3 small shallots, finely sliced
4 large stringless runner beans, or 10 mangetout, shredded
1 mild red chilli, deseeded and finely shredded
2 big handfuls each large mint and coriander leaves
1 small fresh coconut
2 tbsp toasted or salted peanuts, crushed

Toss the lamb with the Asian dressing (see page 18) then chuck in the shallots, runner beans or mangetout, red chilli, and the mint and coriander leaves. Next, crack open a small fresh coconut – keeping its water if you can – and remove the flesh. Using a swivel peeler, peel off and discard the brown casing, then finely shred the coconut flesh and chuck this into the bowl too. If you managed to catch some coconut liquid, add a tbsp or two. Then chuck in the crushed toasted or salted peanuts, toss everything together well and serve.

crackling pork

Come on, it's the crackling, isn't it? That's the reason for roast pork surely. Yes, the meat is sweet and good but it's the pork-scratching bit with it that makes it so. I can't see the point to a pork roast if there's no crackling to be had. Then there's the pan of apple sauce – yes, must have that too – and it's also the place for a good dollop of mash, for mulching with all that piggy-sweet gravy. Gosh, got my trotters out already.

Roast pork and apple sauce is the classic, but I'm also a pig and garlic fan. I have a particular memory of this – my honking hand luggage at Nîmes airport, en Provence. In the bag were two long chunky plaits of fat bulbs, with bulging hips and pink derrières, elbowing for space between a tub of oily-black tapenade, nobbly plum tomatoes, and some funky squat cucumbers – all bought from an old lady in an apron at her farm door in the middle of nowhere. I'd roasted the pork and garlic and now on top of my bag were the results: a stack of wrapped pork sandwiches with their full complement of crackling. And no ordinary ones at that. For they hummed roast garlic: sourdough loaf, all squished together with a good trowelling of yet more garlic-rich jellied stock. The in-flight picnic was good.

Now, a quick word on the pig front. Here's a meat that's suffered from intensive rearing. Modern farming methods have done it no favours, stripping it of its fat and flavour. Pork roasts can be so disappointing. So when picking your pork, plump for a free-ranger, a pig that has been allowed to rootle about in a field and grow naturally. For the unfortunate ones are penned between bars, with no room to move, and their little trotters never feel anything as glorious as mud.

Perfect crackling pork

A loin will give you a good roast with very good crackling, and is a handy size for four people. A large piece of belly pork with ribs attached will roast too, but as it's much fattier, it needs a long blast in the oven to render out its fat and get the skin puffed and crisp. The best way with belly, is to roast it the Chinese way (see page 113). Shoulder is another, and good if boned out and rolled up with some stuffing inside. And then there's leg, a nice big chap, and rack – a pork chop roast – my favourite. All need exceptional crackling as standard, so let's kick off there.

Exceptional crackling Good crackling requires the skin around the pork to be well slashed at regular and narrow intervals. And you'll need a very sharp blade to do this. I use a Stanley knife (a very sharp craft knife), so raid the tool box or dig out something from your model-making days. Or go and buy one. It's a must-have in today's pork batterie de cuisine. Make deep score-like parallel cuts across the skin. Some would say they should be 1cm apart, I go for something nearer a 5mm gap, to guarantee a quicker crackle. When you buy a pork joint to roast, it's usually slashed for you, however it can be inadequately done if had from the supermarket. If you can't do it, then get the butcher on to it before you leave his shop. The next magic behind crackling is salt. Rub it well with plenty of salt, making sure you massage the grains into the slashes on the fat. If using sea salt as well as regular table salt, the smaller grains will penetrate and make the fat puff as it cooks, and the sea flakes will encrust the outside beautifully.

To roast a leg If you want to roast leg on the bone, you want a piece around 2-2.5kg, which will be enough to feed a good six to eight. The skin and fat should then be slashed with cross-hatched effect, so that it ends up diamond patterned (like when doing a ham). Rub it well with plenty of salt, making sure you massage the grains into the slashes on the fat, then set it in a roasting tin and roast it in a hot 220°C/425°F/Gas 7 oven for about 25 minutes. As it's a large cut, it has a tendency to want to dry out a touch, so to stop this, now pour around 300ml of dry white wine or cider into the tray. You can chuck in some finely chopped carrot and a handful of chopped garlic cloves, too, which will provide a good self-making gravy to serve it with. Now, turn the oven to 190°C/375°F/Gas 5 and roast for a further 2 hours, allowing the joint to rest a good 15 minutes or so before carving.

To roast a loin Choose a boned 1.5kg loin with a decent amount of fatty skin strapped to its back. Using an ultra-sharp knife, slash the skin around the pork at regular intervals. Place the pork into a shallow tin, skin side up, then rub it well with plenty of salt, making sure you massage the grains into the slashes on the fat. Pop the joint in a 220°C/425°F/Gas 7 oven and roast for about 25 minutes, then turn the temperature down to 190°C/375°F/ Gas 5 and continue to roast for a further hour. If your crackling hasn't crackled sufficiently and is still a bit unpuffed and chewy looking, then remove it from the meat – it will detach easily. After covering the meat with foil to keep it warm and leaving on one side, place the fat, skin side up, on a rack over a roasting tray. Whack up the oven's temperature and slip just the skin back in on a high shelf, for 15 or so more minutes until crisped. The meat will need to rest a good 15 minutes before carving, so no worries. Carve the pork and serve slices with strips of crackling, cider gravy and apple sauce.

Leftover heaven Slices of cold pork with strips of crackling stashed with lots of rocket, some seasoning and stuffing or a good dollop of apple sauce, makes a very good meal of a sandwich. Dribs and drabs from the roast are handed a fresh zest of life when used in Pad Thai (see page 55 – no need for prawns) or resuscitate slivers with Asian dressing (see page 18), then toss with salad – something crunchy with shredded apple and mint would positively sing.

Garlic pork rib roast and cider gravy

Either eat the roasted garlic as it is – pushed from its papery skin – or squeeze it like toothpaste from its husk into a gravy as here, or fork into some mashed potato. Raw garlic is pungent, but once baked turns to a sweet paste – so don't be terrified at the amount required.

1 x 4-rib rack of pork, with skin
3 tsp fennel seeds, lightly crushed
2-3 large bulbs garlic with fat cloves,
   separated into cloves but not peeled
1 onion, finely sliced
1 bunch sage
olive oil
1 tbsp plain flour
300ml cider (or water or stock)

Make sure the pork skin has been well slashed and rubbed with salt (see notes above). Rub the fennel seeds into the slashes on the fat too. No oil. Roast the pork joint in a 190°C/375°F/Gas 5 oven for 45 minutes, then tuck the garlic, onion and sage underneath, splashing with a little oil. Turn the heat up to 220°C/425°F/Gas 7 and roast for a further 45 minutes.

Remove the roasting tray and turn the oven up to its maximum. Turn the pork now, so that it rests on its bones, then shunt it back in the oven for a further 15 minutes or so to guarantee perfect puffed crackling.

To make the garlic cider gravy, remove the garlic from the roasting tin and pop the garlic flesh out of its skins back into the roasting pan. Set the tin on the hob, sprinkle with flour, mix through and fry a little. Add the cider (or water or stock, if you have some) and bubble away. Scrape the tin a bit, to release the caramelised goo stuck to the base, and squash in the soft cloves. Serve with the pork, sliced through into chops. You'll need mash – and some cabbage is good with it too.

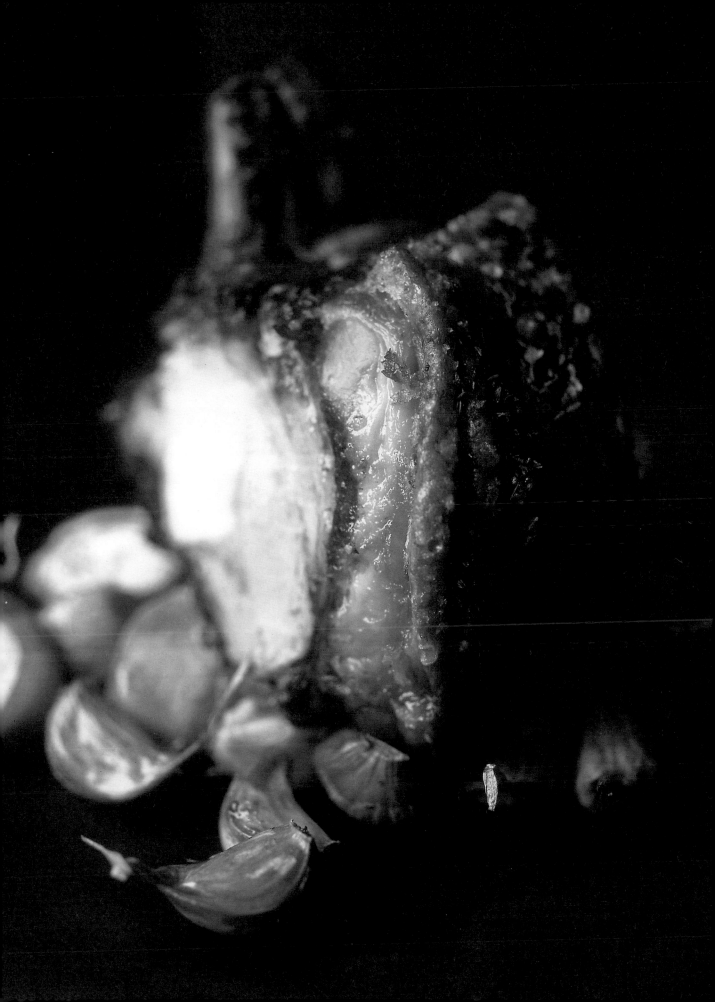

Apple sauce

2 big Bramley cooking apples, peeled, cored and
    finely sliced
1 tbsp caster sugar

Chuck the cooking apples into a saucepan with the caster
sugar. Add around 2 tbsp water and bubble until the apple
goes to mush, about 12 minutes. Of course, this can be
made well ahead, and left in a bowl ready for the table, as
it should be served cold.

Roast apples and beets

*Good with all roast porky things, plus pork chops and duck
too.*

4 medium uncooked beetroots, peeled and cut
    into wedges
2 tbsp olive oil
the leaves from 3 thyme sprigs
6 small Cox's apples (halved if large)
100ml apple juice or cider

Tumble the beetroot into a small deep roasting tin, then
jumble with the olive oil, some seasoning and the thyme
leaves. Roast for about 30 minutes in a 190°C/ 375°F/
Gas 5 oven. Add the Cox's apples and 3 tbsp of the apple
juice or cider, cover with foil or a lid and roast for a
further 20-30 minutes or until all is just tender but not
collapsing. Then pour in the remaining apple juice or
cider and reduce on the hob until faintly sticky.

Barbecue ribs

*The secret behind melting meat on ribs that are also sticky
and glazed without being chewy, is to simmer them in water
first before glazing and roasting. Normally this sort of rib is
cut from the lower part of the pig's rib cage, but if you go for
the American style spareribs – cut from the top – then you'll
have something much chunkier and meatier.*

12 pork spareribs
2 tsp five-spice powder
3 tbsp each of soy sauce and runny honey
2 tbsp each of hoisin sauce and tomato purée
2 tbsp vegetable oil

Bring the ribs to a low bubble in a pan of lightly salted
water, then allow to gently murmur away for about 30
minutes. Strain, leave to cool right down, then put in a
dish. Meanwhile, beat together all the remaining
ingredients, then brush this all over the ribs. They'll
happily sit like this until you're ready – in fact the
longer you can leave them the better. From time to
time, brush over any marinade that collects in the dish.

When ready to roast, salt and pepper them all over and
brush with the marinade again, then lay out over a
baking tray or sheet and slip into a 200°C/ 400°F/Gas 6
oven. Roast, brushing with more marinade after about 10
minutes, until glossy and sticky, about 20 minutes in all.

Chinatown crispy pork

The Chinese eat their crispy pork at room temperature – it's never served hot in Chinatown. The pork needs a good rest to become succulent again, then you can serve it simply with boiled rice and soy sauce, and perhaps a few stir-fried and simmered Chinese leaves, finished off in a dash of water and oyster sauce. Easy this, and lashings of oriental crackling.

1.5kg good fatty belly pork on the bone, with skin and in 1 piece
3 tsp five-spice powder
3 tsp fennel seeds, roughly ground
1 tsp caster sugar

Using the point of a very sharp knife, densely prick the skin all over right through to the fat. You need to make hundreds and hundreds of pricks, and they should be very close together, which can take up to 10 minutes of your time. However, once well pricked, all the work is nearly done…and you'll end up with perfect crispy pork. Pour a kettleful of boiling water over the fat side of the meat, then pat it dry. This will shock it and open up all those holes you've made. Now, if you have time, leave it in an airy place for an hour or two.

Next, rub with lots of salt, then rub in the five-spice powder, the fennel and sugar. Place the pork, skin side down, on a rack set over a roasting tray half filled with water, and roast in a 230°C/450°F/Gas 8 oven for about 30 minutes, then turn over and roast for 30 minutes more. Then turn down the temperature to 180°C/350°F/Gas 4 and roast for a further 1½ hours. The pork skin should have puffed beautifully, and turned crackling crisp. Give it a tap – if it sounds hollow, it's crisped.

Allow the meat to cool. This way it regains moisture and becomes unctuous again, yet the crackly bit remains crisp. Place the crackling pork, skin side down, and using a serrated bread knife, slice through the meat between each rib – sawing through the crackling – to make thick strips, then slice off each piece of bone, and cut the meat into neat chunks. Then, armed with a bowl of rice, some blanched or steamed bok choi, some soy and your chopsticks, you're away.

Crispy duck

We should cook more duck. Unlike chicken and the Christmas turkey, it's really difficult to bodge up. You'd have to be hell-bent on giving it your worst to get it to dry out. And if you're put off by all that fat, don't be, for it all vanishes from the bird as it roasts, leaving behind the most delectable layer of crisped mahoganied skin. The lightly gamey meat, offered up with the thinnest melt-in-the-mouth seam of fat on crunchy skin, makes a duck the sexiest beast you could ever have at the table. Wanton and licentious are the words to describe flavour and texture here. Ravaging territory.

This is a bird in desperate need of liposuction though. Its blubber layer requires much reduction before eating. So always prick it over well so that it sheds it when it roasts. And roast it on a rack, so that the pooling fat is not in contact with the roasting bird. Mum never got the duck right. Her poor bird floundered in an orgy of fat and never crisped up. But now she follows my way – and gets the duck right every time.

Perfect roast duck

Start by selecting a good bird. I'd choose a Gressingham duck (a cross between the bog standard Aylesbury and a mallard), for it has bags more flavour than most. More than likely because it's more humanely reared – daylight, straw bedding and allowed to keep its beak (you don't want to know). A contented duck makes good eating. One duck will serve four but only if two are happy to eat leg and the others just breast. The alternative is to cook two ducks, so that everyone gets a leg and a breast, which may sound ogreishly greedy but although they look bulky birds, they're a touch lean – and roasting off two will at least provide some seconds. Double up on quantities below if you opt for the twin roast.

Do I carve or quarter? The choice is yours. I lean towards quartering as the meat has more chance of staying hot and all crispy bits stay intact. It saves you eyeing up the crispest pieces of skin on everyone else's plates but yours. To avoid blobs of fat on the cloth and a skidding bird, it's best to quarter the bird in the kitchen on a chopping board. Poultry shears are supposedly the correct tool for the job, but are clumsy and unmanagable. A serrated breadknife is the answer. Stick a carving fork in the fowl, then – and with ease – saw the thing into four. I like to saw the backbone out too; makes for a less lumpen arrangement on the plate. The last option is to do it the Chinese way and cleave: chop the whole bird, bones and all, into thick slices.

Tradition dictates the breast of duck be finely sliced, as my dad does, just so. For it's thought you taste the light gamey flavour of the meat more when eaten thin. But this fastidious approach probably has its roots in Tudor banqueting, as Elizabeth I's wooden teeth couldn't chomp on anything that needed chewing. Chunky slices are okay in my house.

What do I do with all that duck fat? Duck fat fried potatoes, that's what. Parboil some potatoes, cut them into smallish chunks, then gently fry these in some of the collected duck fat with a crushed clove of garlic and some sea salt, until all are crisped and gorged with fat, then toss through some chopped parsley just before serving.

And to serve? You'll want something green, like French green beans or Savoy cabbage to cut through all the richness of the duck, or some braised chicory. Make plenty of mash – if you're not fat-frying the spuds – and a delicious gravy or sauce, made well in advance. And if you're not doing the full-works roast, a simple green salad would be delish.

Leftover heaven Encase leftover shreds of Chinese duck in warmed **tortilla wraps** with shredded cucumber and spring onion with a smidgen of bottled hoisin or oyster sauce – just like crispy duck pancakes. Or use the Real McCoy Chinese pancakes if you can get them.

Perfect roast duck with orange gravy

Check the notes on page 115 before starting on your bird. Serve with lots of mash.

1 Gressingham duck, about 2 kg, with giblets
½ orange
½ small bunch thyme
vegetable oil

Orange gravy:
the giblets saved from the bird
1 stick each celery, carrot and onion
1 tbsp caster sugar
1 tbsp white wine vinegar
a few sprigs thyme
200ml white wine
1½ oranges
1 tbsp corrnflour mixed with 1 tbsp cold water

First relieve the duck of its clingfilm bondage, making a note of its labelled weight, then leave it out in an airy place to dry off for a good 2 hours or so – this will help the skin crisp up when it's roasting. Preheat the oven to around 220°C/425°F/Gas 7. Then, using the tip of a sharp pointed knife, prick the duck all over (but don't stab it as you might your enemy – as apparently Fanny Cradock once instructed). Pay special attention to any particularly lardy blubbery parts, so that the fat will ooze and trickle out when it roasts.

Next, massage the duck with plenty of salt, then some black pepper and finish by rubbing it all over with the cut side of the orange. Then stick the spent orange with a tuft of thyme inside and tie the legs together.

Set a roasting or grill rack in or across a roasting tin, and put the duck, breast up, on top. Rub it with a little oil, then stick it in the oven on the middle shelf and roast for about 20 minutes. Once mahogany brown looking, turn down the oven to 180°C/350°F/Gas 4 and roast for about an hour – or 45 minutes if you wish to keep it rare. Bear in mind, meat that's cooked beyond pink here has more flavour: red may be juicy, but tastes more of blood. If the bird is heavier than 2kg, calculate its roasting time at 20 minutes per 500g or 15 minutes per 500g for rare (I strike somewhere between the two) – and remember this timing starts after the initial 20-minute high-heat blast.

After the bird's been roasting for about ½ an hour, chop up the neck (that's the unfortunate-looking long thing found in the plastic bag), then fry with the vegetables in a tablespoon of the duck fat – collected from the roasting tin – until everything is well browned. Then add the liver, kidneys and heart (that's the rest from the little bag), sugar, vinegar and thyme, stir through and allow to caramelise, then pour over the wine and allow to bubble away fiercely until almost all gone. Peel the zest into large strips from 1 orange and add to the pan, cover all the bits with water, season well, then leave to gently bubble for a good 20 minutes. Finally, sieve it and return to a clean pan. Juice all the orange halves and add to the pan, then bring to a bubble and stir in the cornflour water and bubble for about 5 minutes or until thickened and cooked through – and taste again. Reheat when needed.

Once the duck is cooked, loosely cover the bird with foil and leave it somewhere warmish to rest for about 10 minutes. This allows the muscle to relax and the juices to redistribute, which gives back succulence. Serve with bags of mash and the reheated gravy poured over.

Juniper, port and cranberry gravy

A Christmasy gravy for duck. (See image opposite.)

5 shallots, chopped
60g butter
10 juniper berries, lightly crushed
2 bay leaves
250ml port
400ml chicken stock (see page 47, or made with the giblets)
3 tbsp cranberry jelly
1 tbsp cornflower mixed with 2 tbsp cold water

Fry the shallots in the butter with the juniper berries and bay leaves until the onion has softened. Add the port and reduce down by half, then add the remaining ingredients and cook until thickened. Sieve, discarding all the bits and pieces, and reheat when needed.

Fantastic Chinese crispy duck

If you're scared of duck, this is for you – completely failsafe and fabulous every time. The duck is first simmered – keeping it succulent – then roasted, which de-fats it further and puffs its skin to a crisp. I use an old-fashioned oval roasting tin with a lid to make this, as it fits the shape of the bird perfectly. If you want to cook two birds, poach one first and then use the same poaching stock to do the next. The stock can be frozen after use and used several times.

1 whole duck
6 shallots, chopped
1 litre chicken stock (see page 47, but a cube is
    fine)
500ml dark soy sauce
400ml Chinese rice wine
3 tbsp honey
4 star anise or 2 tsp ground star anise
1 strip orange peel
vegetable oil
spring onions, sliced, to serve

Sit the duck, bottom up, in a colander in the sink, then pour over a kettleful of boiling water – aiming inside as well as out. Leaving the duck to drain, dig out a pan that the duck will fit in snugly (something oval is ideal). Chuck the shallots into the pan with all the remaining ingredients, plus some salt – minus our duck, oil, and spring onions – put back on the heat and bring to a bubble, stirring to dissolve the honey. Next, place the duck in the pan, breast side down – the liquid should almost cover it – cover with a lid and gently braise on the barest of bubbles for about 1½ hours. Turn it over for the last 20 minutes or so. Once it has cooled a little, lift out the bird (an easy way is a lift with a wooden spoon handle slipped up its rear) and drain off the delicious gravy, then leave the duck in a cool place to dry for a few hours or overnight. Refrigerate the gravy, then skim off and discard the fat. All this can be done the day before, for the bird will sit happily overnight refrigerated.

When you want it, rub the poached bird all over with a touch of oil, set it on a roasting tray and roast in a 200°C/400°F/Gas 6 oven for about 30-40 minutes, or until it turns a lovely, deep polished brown and is crisp. Then pull off the meat and the delicious scrunchy skin with forks (just like they do at the Chinese) and eat scattered with shredded spring onion on a mound of rice and sauced with its reheated gravy. Fabulous, fabulous, I guarantee you.

Duck pot noodle

A homemade pot noodle in a delicate broth is bliss after appetites have been bludgeoned with too much. This is a flexible soup, designed to take all on board and recharge all that's left over. Use disposable cups, and there's no washing up. Fried crispy shallots can be bought by the big bagful from Asian supermarkets: they're always handy for chucking on this sort of soup, and last for ever in the pantry, but aren't essential.

150g dried noodles (I use rice noodles)
leftover roast duck, Chinese crispy duck or
    chicken
1 litre Asian stock (see page 48)
4 spring onions, chopped into small sections
handfuls of greens to taste (celery tops, iceberg
    lettuce or watercress)
4 quails' eggs, hard boiled
fish sauce
fresh coriander leaves

Cook/prepare the noodles according to the packet instructions, drain, refresh and divide between four mugs, beakers or bowls. Throw flakes of leftover meat into the Asian stock (see page 48) and reheat. Pile the spring onions on top of the noodles, along with the handfuls of greens to taste and some hard-boiled quails' eggs. Then pour the steaming stock into each bowl. The hot stock will reheat everything and wilt the greens. Then splash with fish sauce, toss on some coriander and eat, slurping from the cup and delving with chopsticks.

christmas dinner

Christmas dinner. We love it, although not quite so much if we have to cook it. For many it's a bit of a number. However, once you're in the groove, on the sherry, then it all goes with a swing. Now, Christmas screams tradition: the Turkey, the Roast Potatoes, the Trimmings, the Gravy. And, if you can manage it, the Pud. You want the traditional works but, in truth, not quite the way it was 50 years back. Most of us buy a Christmas pudding these days, and follow the packet instructions, so I leave that one with you. I go for making a trifle, as it's soaked in Christmas spirit and is the antidote to too much of big bird and her offspring of trimmings. Sure, I'll have the pud on top, if it's on offer – shop bought or not. Then there are all the leftover meats and cuts that do fantastic things on Boxing Day and beyond. Leftovers are mighty fine things and go well beyond the potential turkey-lurking sandwich.

I'm not suggesting you beaver away at the complete works I'm about to launch in to. Just pick out the-things-that-make-you-go-oooh. And I'm going to give you a countdown to blast off, a handy timetable to follow. A timetable? Hello? I know. So, if you're turned-off by tables, don't look at it. I don't blame you. The tyranny of the *Woman's Weekly* timetable (forgive me, *Woman's Weekly*, you're all gorgeous) is hardly the spirit – but for some it helps.

And PS. Ginormous birds? No. Just don't. You're not competing for the *Guinness Book of Records* on the size of bird you can cram into your oven (it's not as big as a Mini). I know largeness is all very Christmassy and everything, but it will exhaust you and set up roost in your oven, allowing nothing else in. One of about 5kg is quite big enough, and perfect. And buy a proper free-range bird; yes, it will cost £50, but it will have walked, and will taste of everything you remember once-long-ago turkey tasting. After all, it's the one day in the year you push that boat out. Let's not rock it.

Perfect roast turkey, potatoes and gravy

Read all this through to pick up all the tips and dos and don'ts that you might need (without yawning), then follow the abbreviated recipe that follows so that you're not floundering in a load of wordage while juggling pans with your foot stuck up the bird's bottom. Heaven forbid.

What tin do I use? You'll need two tins. One for the bird and one for the spuds. I like to circulate my potatoes between the two tins, so all get a spell tucked under her wings. This way they all get a fair share of the delicious goo that comes from such a lengthy roast. Make sure you use big tins, and for the potatoes, one that's not high sided. Deep and too small tins won't do, as once the turkey is ensconced, there won't be room for any spuds, and if the potatoes have to shunt up tightly together, or worse still, jumble on top of each other, the whole lot will sweat it out rather than roast.

So, where do I start? Obvious this may sound – but kick off by turning on the oven. So easily forgotten, until it comes to putting the bird in. Turn it on at its highest setting. Next, remove the bag of giblets found inside, then make a note of the turkey's weight – I go for something manageable around the 5kg mark. Then relieve the bird from its bondage of clingfilm – I leave it in its elasticated harness, for it holds it in shape – and then let it breathe on the side a while. All the bird needs now is a good salt and peppering – inside and out – and then an all-over smear with butter, plus a dab inside. Sit it breast up in the roasting tin, then squeeze over some orange juice. If you're not a fan of orange, leave it out.

How long do I roast it? Over-roasting is so often the turkey's fate. So timing and monitoring are key. Initially, calculate the roasting time by allowing 20 minutes per 500g. Then roast at 220°C/425°F/Gas 7 for the first 40 minutes, uncovered, then turn down to 190°C/375°F/Gas 5, and loosely cover with foil. This means that a 5kg turkey will take 3 hours and 20 minutes. However, I'd always check it for doneness at the 3-hour mark – just to catch it at possible perfection stage. To do this, pierce the leg meat to the bone with a skewer or sharp knife – the juices should run clear. If there's any trace of blood, continue for another 20 minutes or so. If it's not buffed-up and burnished looking near its last half-hour, remove the foil.

Juicy breast meat, what's the knack? A loose covering of foil and an occasional baste will help keep the breast meat moisturised and juiced. Some like to roast their birds upside down, to let the juices flow into the breast meat, then turn it back upright for the final browning. And it works. But turkeys can be a bit of a handful to heave-ho. However, if you wish to do it this way, and are handling a smaller bird, roast it on it each breast – propped on two whole large carrots (to prevent the skin from catching) for most of the cooking time, then turn it breast up for the last hour, to brown up. The carrots can be used to make the gravy.

Once the bird is in, can I just forget about it? No. Sorry. You can wander off for an hour or so, but that's it. Make sure you spoon the juices over the bird about three times while it's roasting – and remember to turn the potatoes. Everything should come gloriously to perfection by the end of the bird's cooking time.

But my potatoes aren't crisped. That's fine. Because all is not finished. The bird needs plenty of time 'to rest' and that means valuable time spent sitting out of the oven so that its flesh relaxes which allows redistribution of its juices back into all the right places. Essential for juicy breast. While it's resting, the potatoes can be finished off – and the gravy made. The easiest way to winch her majesty out, is in one hand to slide a strong fish slice underneath, and with the other hand, stick the handle of a wooden spoon right into the bird's cavity, and lift it straight on to its serving platter. Then cover it with some foil to keep it warm. Now back to the spuds: if they need to crisp up more, turn the oven up, and turn them over again, adding them all now to the potato roasting tin, and slip them back in for another 20 minutes or so. Keep the turkey's tin for the gravy making.

Time for the gravy. Keep it simple. Nothing fancy, as there'll be lots of other roasted flavours vying for attention on the plates. I like a thin gravy with turkey: a gravy made from a reduction of the cooked vegetable water (or you can use a vegetable stock cube), emulsified with all the heavily seasoned and sticky goo that's stuck to the bottom of the roasting tin. Turkeys come with giblets, and if you want, you can fry these up with some onion, then bubble them in seasoned water to make a different stock base – if not using vegetable cooking water. Dishing up at the making-gravy-stage can turn nasty – if you don't have a plan of action. There's quite a lot to think about and the hob's going to vanish, I know. The bird's been out for a good while, which is absolutely fine, so no worries there; yet the veg has to be ready so that you've got its water for the gravy. And all has to stay piping hot. Answer: cook the veg now, then drain, keeping a good jugful of its cooking water for gravy-making, then put it back in its hot saucepan, lid on.

Tip up the now vacated turkey's tin and spoon out excess fat – if there is any, leaving about a tbsp, then slide it on the hob and stir in the tbsp of flour. Scrape it about and fry it until it browns, then tip enough vegetable water into the tin – about a litre – and bring to a rolling bubble, continually scraping across the pan base to release all the gorgeous gunge into the gravy water. Don't worry about the chook, she's improving with the wait. After her half-hour stop-over, she'll still be hot – and extra delicious. Let the gravy reduce a little, then tip it into a smallish saucepan ready for reheating and for easy pouring. Taste it and add more salt, until it's how you like it.

Fantastic roast turkey Christmas dinner with all the trimmings

Read pages 121-2 first, then proceed with this summary. Feeds eight with seconds.

1 quality turkey, around 5kg
125g butter
1 orange, halved (optional)
4 tbsp vegetable oil
2kg potatoes, such as Maris Piper or King
   Edwards (or other suitable for roasting),
   peeled and parboiled
1 tbsp plain flour

Get out two large roasting tins – one for the turkey and one for the spuds. Turn the oven on to around 220°C/425°F/Gas 7, then sit the turkey in one of the tins. Next, salt and pepper the bird inside and out, and then smear it all over with butter and put a dab inside, and squeeze over some orange juice, if using. Allow 20 minutes' roasting time per 500g. Then slide the bird into the oven and roast for the first 40 minutes, uncovered, then turn the oven down to 190°C/375°F/Gas 5, and loose-cover the turkey with foil, but not to the edges of the tin. Then roast for a further 2 hours and 40 minutes. But check for doneness about 20 minutes before the end of the cooking time as above. Remove the foil for the last 30 minutes, if not gorgeously browned.

Tip the potatoes into a colander to drain and then back into the pan in which they were cooked. Salt and pepper them, add a wodge of butter and a good splash of oil and turn over to give them all a good coating and rough up their edges. Scatter them around the bird and across the extra tin, for the last 2 hours of the turkey's cooking time. Turn the potatoes over after an hour and swap the ones from the turkey tin with some in the spud tin. And remember to baste the bird from time to time.

When the turkey is cooked, lift it on to its warmed serving platter and leave on the side (somewhere warmish), covered well with foil to keep it warm – and keep its tin on stand-by for gravy making. Then turn the oven up to 200°C/400°F/Gas 6, put all the potatoes into the potato roasting tin and put back in the oven for 20 minutes to crisp up, if they need it. At the same time, put the stuffing meatballs in to roast, if making (see page 127). Next cook the vegetables, then drain, keeping about a litre of the cooking water for the gravy.

Leaving about a tbsp of fat in the turkey's tin, stir in the flour and fry it until it browns, then tip in the veg water slowly and while stirring, bring to a rolling bubble, continually scraping across the pan. Let the gravy reduce a little, then tip it into a smallish saucepan ready for reheating, and taste. And there you have it: perfect turkey, perfect potatoes and perfect gravy.

Fast roast turkey One Christmas I came face to face with one big bird and one too small roasting tin. Being in a tiny cottage holiday home, I'd neglected to forecast that all would be scaled down to match. However, dilemma brought about drastic measure – and discovery. There was nothing else for it but to dismember the old dear and make her smaller: I cut off the legs and roasted these with the potatoes and trimmed back the backbone (which I chucked in with the potatoes as a flavour enhancer) and roasted the breast meat on its own. It literally halved the cooking time and gave fantastic breast meat. It makes turkey sense: such a large mass takes hours of thumping heat to cook it through to the bone and so can play havoc with delicate white meat. Dividing it up before cooking is therefore absolutely logical – that's if you can bear missing out on her majesty's full glory.

Cooking know-how here is to judge the length of the cooking time from the weight of the breast meat alone. So, weigh the breast and then calculate the roasting time at 18 minutes per 500g, then roast everything uncovered in a 190°C/375°F/Gas 5 oven – kicking off on 220°C/425°F/Gas 7 for the first 30 minutes. Season, dress and baste it as above, putting the breast with some potatoes in one tin and the legs with the rest of the potatoes in another.

Leftover heaven Mum's curry scores brilliantly with leftover turkey. It's such a tonic at this time of the year, so see page 78. For a turkey **Cordon Bleu panini**, sandwich cooked turkey with slices of Stilton and ham between buttered semi-baked baguette, then grill on a ridged grill pan, squashed flat (by placing the base of a heavy pan on top of the baguette), until the bread looks toasty and the cheese is on the ooze. For a **toasted turkey sandwich**, layer turkey between toast with cranberry relish, watercress or rocket and mayonnaise that has first been beaten with crème fraîche and grain mustard. For **turkey tortillas**, lay a tortilla in a hot pan to warm through and crumble over Cheddar or mozzarella, lay on a rasher of crispy bacon and shreds of cooked turkey, then chuck on a few chucks of ultra-ripe avocado and coriander leaves, if you have them. Sauce with Tabasco, and roll up. Combinations are endless.

COUNTDOWN TIMETABLE

Make stuff beforehand to create space to breathe on the day – and then use these timings as a help. We're talking through a 5kg turkey here. And relax, we're not ticking off the procedure on a clipboard. Lunch is at 2pm, say.

DO AHEAD
The Parma ham stuffing meatballs; the cranberry relish; the bread sauce… and lay the table.

CHRISTMAS DAY

9am	**Get in there!** Remove the turkey from the fridge and unwrap.
9.30am	Preheat the oven to 220°C/425°F/Gas 7. Smear the bird with butter and season.
10am	**Turkey time** Pop the bird in the oven.
10.15am	Prepare the vegetables.
10.40am	Turn oven down to 190°C/375°F/Gas 5, baste the bird and cover loosely with foil.
11.00am	**The potatoes** Peel, parboil and prep them for roasting, and set on one side.
11.30am	Put the prepared spuds in to roast – some around the turkey and the rest in another tin – and baste.
12.30pm	Swap the potatoes round the turkey with some of those in the other roasting tin, and baste.
1pm	Test turkey for doneness.
1.20pm	Turkey out, testing for doneness again, and cover with foil. Turn the oven up to 200°C/400°F/Gas 6. Put all the potatoes into the one tin and put back in to crisp if needed. Put the stuffing meatballs in to roast.
1.40pm	Put the water on for the greens, and cook.
1.45pm	Shift her majesty from the tin and make the gravy.
1.55pm	Start to bring the turkey and all the trimmings to the table.
2pm	Everyone to their places – lunch is up.

Parma ham and cranberry stuffing meatballs

Oven-juggling birds, potatoes and stuffings can be difficult and is not helped if a ton of stuff is to be cooked together. Apart from things not browning up when there's too much in the oven, most ovens simply can't stomach the overload. Here the stuffing moves in, once the bird has flown. If you want to cheat a little, these can be pre-roasted, then oven reheated. These stuffing thingies are fabulous – and any leftover balls are great reheated and eaten with green salad. Makes 16.

1 x 340g bag fresh cranberries
6 tbsp caster sugar
6 shallots, finely chopped
4 cloves garlic, crushed
30g butter, lard or dripping, or 2 tbsp olive oil
1 small bunch sage, finely chopped
6 sprigs thyme, leaves finely chopped
1 x 500g tube quality sausagemeat
400g streaky bacon, finely chopped or minced
200g fresh white breadcrumbs
4 tbsp lightly crushed cooked chestnuts or
   walnuts
finely grated zest of 1 lemon
16 large slices Parma ham

Put the cranberries and sugar in a small pan, pour in around 200ml water, stir, bring to a gentle bubble until the sugar has dissolved, then turn off the heat and leave to go cold. The berries will soften and deflate slightly. Fry the shallot and garlic in the fat until the shallot has softened but not coloured, then stir in the herbs, and season. Mix in the sausagemeat, minced bacon, breadcrumbs, nuts and lemon zest. Using your fingers, make sure everything is squished together well. Drain away the syrup from the cranberries, then stir the berries into the stuffing mix.

Press the mixture into sixteen balls – each the size of a large golf ball – and wrap each one in a slice of Parma ham, lining them up on a tray. You may get a few tears here and there – just make sure there aren't any major gaps. Cover with clingfilm and put in the fridge to firm up – overnight, or for as long as suits you. When the turkey has finished roasting, remove the clingfilm, place the balls across a shallow roasting tin, leaving lots of space between them, then dab them all over with a little extra oil and roast for 30 minutes or so at 200°C/400°F/ Gas 6, or until crisped and gorgeous.

Tangerine cranberry relish

1 red onion, finely chopped
1 tbsp olive oil
8 juniper berries, lightly bruised
2 tangerines, clementines or satsumas
250g fresh cranberries
3 tbsp caster sugar
2 tbsp Grand Marnier or Cointreau

This can be made a day or two before. Fry the onion in the oil with salt and pepper and the juniper berries until softened but not browned. Pare off just the zest from the fruit in thick strips. Add to the pan with the squeezed fruit juice, the cranberries, sugar and liqueur, then give the panful of fragrant Christmas fruitiness a good mix. Allow everything to bubble and splutter a bit – for about 5 minutes or until the berries have softened, become sticky but not totally collapsed. They should hold a little pre-burst tautness but be cooked – so try one, and if you feel it's too tart, add another tbsp sugar. I like it sharp – remember all the other things you are going to be eating it with. Serve at room temperature.

Proper bread sauce

450ml full-fat milk
15 cloves, very lightly bashed
1 tsp black peppercorns
1-2 bay leaves
1 onion, halved
100g crustless white bread (use an old loaf, if
   you have one), made into breadcrumbs
good knob of butter
dollop of mascarpone cheese or double cream
   (optional)

Pour the milk into a pan and throw in the cloves, peppercorns, a sprinkling of salt, the bay and the onion. Bring to a bubble, then allow to gently murmur away for a few minutes, then turn off the heat and leave overnight – so that all the flavours marry together. Strain the infused milk into a saucepan and discard all the flavouring bits and bobs. Tip in the breadcrumbs and stir over a gentle heat to make a thick sauce. Give it a lick and add more salt if it needs it, then beat in the butter – and a splodge of mascarpone or cream will enrich it further. Serve warm or cold.

chilli con carne

and one-pot suppers

What's happened to us? In this fast-cook age, we've forgotten our long-and-slow pots of wonderfulness. Now, the five-minute variety of cooking – I have to say popularised by magazines and books to encourage sales – requires almost chef's skills; it's last-minute stuff that needs quite a bit of dexterous handling, attention and know-how, and then a lot of fiddle to get it presentable on the plate. A pot of slow-cooked food, however, has to be planned, yes, but it's the easiest form of cooking going. Kitchen skills are nil really. Timing can be as clumsy as you like. And the results? Always fabulous.

Think on this scenario, you may know it: you get in from work midweek, and your chums are coming round for a bite to eat. They may well be bundling through the door literally an hour after you. So, it's in the shower and chuck on something fresh; see to child, pet, whatever, and if time, clear debris and things. Time-up comes quick. So you do the frantic hit-and-miss last-minute work-out at the stove or it's a shop-bought ready-made with a bag of salad tipped out. Now, if you'd made something in advance, that will have improved with its overnight wait, then you could have had a beautiful supper ready in the time it takes for you to please yourself: that's very casually throwing something gorgeous together including you. A something that's delicious and fail-safe, that won't rely on any last-minute cooking or cheffy presentation, yet will have that wow factor. Sound food to be proud of, I reckon. And I'll kick-off with one of our most loved – chilli con carne.

The perfect chilli con carne

Chilli con carne. YES PLEASE. Even the food fashionistas succumb to this one – if on the quiet. As with spag bol, chilli con carne has a hold on us – and is there when all the food in the world won't do. Chilli con carne has to be one of the most unsung heroes of our family kitchens. It's *the* great storecupboard dinner: mince from the freezer and everything else out of packets, bottles or cans. Home food, adored by everyone. Take my friend Shaun, he dines out in posh restaurants on the most recherché of foods, then at home knuckles down to a vat of chilli. In fact it's all he ever cooks. And his tips have now become mine. Rarely seen is a recipe for chilli con carne - it appears to be one of those things we should pluck from the air. So here it is, with a few important details thrashed out.

Is it Mexican? Chilli con carne has little to do with Mexico. It's Texan. They're near neighbours, yes, but a good chilli is born of the USA. A Chihuahuan wouldn't recognise it and no Mexican would wave for it, for like spag bol, it's a hybrid dish that doesn't exist in its country of so-called origin. In fact to some it's only a hair's breadth away from a spag bol. Imagine: switch to automatic pilot and – distracted by the telly and not looking at the pot perhaps – you forget the beans and cayenne, well, you arrive at a spag bol. Easily done if you are a New Yorker, for in Cincinnati they serve their chilli on noodles.

Now, spices. Do we? Do you cumin your chilli or not? Shaun's little joke, and it gets a laugh, just. He doesn't. He's Brit-Tex-Mex purist when it comes to making a good chilli. I put in a hefty smidgen – so it's in here. And I put in a little dried oregano and a dash of Tabasco, here and there. I'm treading carefully. I don't want to upset the chilli cart, as once when I added an extra bay leaf to my ultimate spag bol recipe in my column in the *Sunday Times* one reader wrote pages: I got it in the neck for being too posh, accused of whiling away my days at endless wine tastings around Chelsea, and living in Fulham. I couldn't see the relevance either. And all over a bay leaf.

So how much chilli? If there's not enough cayenne pepper (ground chilli) for your taste, then make it 4-5 tsp, but don't get frivolous or over-zealous, and start flicking in loads like some mad Muppet chef. Go in gently, adding a smidgen, leave it to murmur and return to taste – for the heat intensifies once it's been left to sit. I sometimes pop in some of those fearsomely hot tiny little dried chillies – for the unexpected ambush on the tongue heightens flavour. Stumbling on these, however, can leave you like Beaker post experiment – hair on end. Go too far, and you're into S&M.

The ultimate chilli con carne

There's nothing to this really. Once you've got out everything that goes into the pot, it's plain sailing all the way. You could add more tomato purée, but I think we've got enough here. Enough to turn it that gorgeous 1970s bistro wine-red. Reheated and eaten the next day, it will taste at the peak of loveliness. Serve with a grating of mild cheese. This will feed six.

2 large onions, chopped
3 cloves garlic, crushed
olive oil
2 tsp ground cumin
1 tbsp dried oregano
3 bay leaves
1kg coarsely ground beef
2 tbsp paprika
3-4 tsp hot cayenne pepper
4 tbsp malt vinegar
6 tbsp tomato purée (yes, that's 6)
3 x 400ml cans chopped plum tomatoes
2 x 400ml cans red kidney beans, drained and
   rinsed
300ml red wine
dash of Tabasco, to perk it up at the end if needed
mozzarella or mild Cheddar, grated

Gently fry the onion and garlic in about 2 tbsp oil in a big casserole or heavy saucepan, until the onion has softened. Stir in the cumin, some seasoning, the oregano and bay leaves, and cook for a minute more. Add the minced beef, breaking up any clods with a wooden spoon, stir through and brown all over – you may need to add a drop more oil. Mix the paprika with the cayenne and vinegar in a cup and stir this in, too – you may want to only add three-quarters at first and add more later, once you've tasted the chilli. Squeeze in and stir through the tomato purée. After a further minute, tip in the canned tomatoes, kidney beans and red wine, mix and season again, then bring to a bubble.

Then either put it in a 180°C/350°F/Gas 4 oven, or very gently braise over a low heat on the hob, for 1½-2 hours. If you do it on the ring, check up on it from time to time, giving it a stir through and adding a dash of water if things start to look on the dry side. Reheat through on the hob later, as and when you want it, but taste it again for each pot of chilli behaves quite differently: some need a perk up later in the week – a slap of Tabasco does the job. Serve over boiled long-grain rice and top with grated cheese. (See image on page 130.)

Hungarian goulash

Not sure how Hungarian it is, but it don't half taste good. Serve this with good bread and with a green salad, simply dressed with olive oil and vinegar. Some cooked waxy new potatoes can be popped in the pot toward the end of the cooking, or during reheating. The goulash is excellent if cooked the day before, then reheated for a good 45 minutes (at 180°C/350°F/Gas 4), with the soured cream swirled in just before serving.

1kg braising steak, cubed
3 tbsp plain flour
60g lard or 3 tbsp olive oil
2 red peppers, deseeded and sliced
2 onions, finely sliced
2 fat cloves garlic, finely chopped
2 big tbsp paprika
2 x 400g cans chopped plum tomatoes
a string-tied small bunch of fresh bay, thyme
   and parsley
750ml beef stock (a cube is fine)
1 x 250ml pot soured cream
handful of flat-leaf parsley leaves

Toss the meat with some seasoned flour, brown all over in hot fat in a casserole until it looks dark, then lift it out. Do this in batches – so as not to sweat the meat – and hang on to the remaining flour. Next, lightly blister the peppers by flash-frying them in the leftover fat, then remove and keep to one side. Add the onion and the garlic to the remaining fat in the pan, adding more fat if needed, and gently fry until well softened and touched with brown, then sprinkle over the paprika. Add the saved flour to the pan and stir through and cook for a few minutes more, stirring occasionally to prevent the floured onion from catching. Add the tomatoes, stir through and bubble up, then tip in the meat and any of its collected juices, along with the tied herbs and enough stock so that the meat is just covered, and bring to a bubble again. Put in a 150°C/300°F/Gas 2 oven and gently braise for 2 hours, stirring in the seared peppers halfway through the meat's cooking time. Tip in the soured cream, swirl through, allow to reheat a bit, then serve strewn with parsley.

Casserole beef with carrots and dumplings

A rummage through Oxfam in Cambridge landed me a cookery book that had two scribbled post-it notes stuck one on top of the other on its recipe for Burgundy beef. The top one: 'I think we need to eat that stewing steak we've got. Perhaps you would stick it in the slow-cooker with some mushrooms/onions and that red wine that we didn't finish last night? HURRAY it's Friday xxx Anne.' And then the post-it underneath read: 'You look gorgeous when you're asleep...can we go to bed when I get home from work?' I bought the book straightaway. I've added dumplings to slow things down a bit.

750g braising beef, cut into 4cm chunks
beef dripping, lard or oil
4 fat carrots, cut into thick wedges
1 stick celery, finely chopped
6 pickling onions
1 clove garlic, finely chopped
3 sprigs thyme, finely chopped
250ml red wine
2 tbsp plain flour
500ml beef or chicken stock (see page 47, but
   cubes are fine)
1 small onion, finely chopped
4 rashers bacon, finely chopped
60g white breadcrumbs
100g self-raising flour
60g shredded beef suet

Fry the beef all over in some fat and seasoning in a casserole until browned on all sides, and then keep on one side. Add a touch more fat to the pan and gently fry the carrot and celery for about 5 minutes, then keep on one side. Tumble the pickling onions, garlic and two-thirds of the thyme into the pan, then pour in the wine and bubble until reduced right down. Sprinkle over the flour and stir through, then tip the meat back in and ease it down to the base of the pan with the onions jumbled around and filling any gaps. Turn up the heat again, pour in the stock and season well, then cover. Slip into a 180°C/350°F/Gas 4 oven and leave to slow-braise for 1½ hours.

Meanwhile, make the dumplings. Fry the onion and bacon in a knob of fat with the remaining chopped thyme and some salt until just softened. Mix with the breadcrumbs, flour, suet and some seasoning, then bind the mixture with a little water to make a dough. Roll into walnut-sized balls, and leave on one side until ready to cook. After the meat has done its time, stir in the carrots and celery and then place the dumplings all over the top of the casserole. Cook for a further 40 minutes, occasionally ladling over some of the juices. If it looks a bit dry, add a dash more water.

Mum's pheasant in a pot

This is another one you can leave, set the timer, and forget about. Cooking a pheasant this way is pretty failsafe, as it keeps it juicy and tender. Timing is not the key – so don't worry if everyone's late for dinner. Reheat it, and the cider-drunk apples and creamy juniper juices will improve and the meat will fall from the bones – just as we like it. Excellent eaten with mash or fried potatoes, or with some wilted dark cabbage and boiled parsnips mashed with an egg yolk.

1 large hen pheasant or guinea fowl
3 tbsp olive oil
50g butter
8 pickling onions or shallots
2 cloves garlic, crushed
8 juniper berries, lightly crushed
200ml dry cider
4 Cox's apples, cored and quartered
150ml double cream

Salt and pepper the bird all over, then gently fry in the oil and half the butter in a large frying pan, on either side of its breast and on its back, until golden brown all over. Then lift it into to a deep casserole. Plonk the onions into the frying pan, add the remaining butter and gently fry all over for about 3 minutes. Add the garlic and juniper, and fry for about 30 seconds further, or until the garlic has coloured. Pour in the cider and 150ml water, plus some salt and pepper, and gently bubble for 5 minutes. Tip this around the bird in the pot, and stick in the apple quarters so that they fit snugly. Cover the pot, put in a 180°C/350°F/Gas 4 oven and braise for 45 minutes. Pour in the cream, return to the oven and cook for a further 15 minutes. Cut the bird into portions and serve with the apple, onions and all their creamy juices.

Moroccan lemon butter chicken

If coq au vin *was the chick dish of the 70s, then I reckon this is the one of now. If you don't want to make your own stock for couscous or indeed joint the chicken, then use a stock cube and use chicken pieces instead. There again, if you want to make the stock but you're not sure how to cut up a chicken, get your butcher to joint it: ask him to remove the backbone and wings and keep them for the stockpan. To make a stock – no panicking now, this is dead easy – sling the backbone and the winglets into a pan with a halved onion, salt and pepper and about a litre of water, and then gently bubble the lot together for a good half hour or so. Great fuel for your couscous.*

Please try to get preserved lemons – it makes a hell of a difference to the results (they're in the supermarkets) – but if not, boil a quartered fresh lemon in water for about 8 minutes and then use this instead. Raw lemon will be way too powerful.

1 free-range chicken, around 1.5kg, or that
    weight of chicken pieces
2 large onions
2 fat cloves garlic, crushed
4 bay leaves
1 tsp each of ground cinnamon and ginger
2 preserved lemons, cut into wedges (or see
    above)
100g butter, melted
water or stock
handful of green olives

Cut the chicken into leg and breast portions, cutting off the backbone and wings, then cut the legs into thighs and drumsticks and the breasts in half. Salt and pepper the chicken pieces, then put them into a shallow casserole or heatproof gratin dish in which they'll snuggle without too many big gaps. I find one of those old-fashioned enamel oval roasting tins with a lid works brilliantly, as in many ways it mimics a tagine pot (the conical lidded Moroccan stewpot). Grate the onions over the top of the meat, add the garlic and bay, and then push all this down and in between the chicken pieces. Sprinkle over the ground spices, and stud the gaps with wedges of lemon.

Gently pour the clear part of the hot melted butter over the chicken pieces, discarding the milky stuff at the bottom of the pan. Spoon a little water or stock around the chicken, so that it about half submerges the chicken pieces. Then cover, leaving a glimpse of a gap between pot and lid or foil, bring to a bubble on the hob, then stick in a 190°C/375°F/Gas 5 oven for about an hour. The liquid should have reduced. To brown the chicken a little, remove the lid or foil, turn up the heat to 200°C/400°F/Gas 6 and allow to cook for another 10 minutes or so. At the same time add the olives to the buttery-onion pan juices to warm through.

Serve the chicken with the pan juices and olives, with couscous or bread and a few fine slices of the cooked preserved lemon. Absolutely divine.

Perfect couscous

60g butter
1 tbsp oil
1 onion, finely sliced
2 heaped tbsp whole almonds, sliced, or pine
    nuts
handful of sultanas
400g couscous
hot chicken stock
fresh mint leaves (optional)

Heat the butter and oil in a frying pan, then throw in the onion and slowly fry until it looks browned on the edges. Add the almonds or pine nuts and a handful of sultanas and carry on gently frying until the nuts take on a bit of a glow. Drain on kitchen roll.

Next, bin the packet instructions – they're never right – and tip the couscous into a heatproof bowl, and level. Pour over enough hot chicken stock, so that the liquid barely reaches the top layer of grains. You'll need around 500ml (but no need to measure). It will absorb the water quickly, so be fast when you pour – a few dry patches left on top is your goal. Leave for about a minute, then fork through so that the top dry grains are mulched in. Leave for another 5 minutes, fork through, and taste – it may need a dash more salt. Mound into a dish and tip over the fried onions and nuts. If you wish to add mint, tear some up and chuck it over just before serving.

Melting shoulder of herby lamb

Slow-cooked shoulder of lamb is fantastic – and it's yet another you can shove in and forget about. This one is incredible, made delicious with a classic blend of dried herbs. Eat with lots of mash. Mint sauce or mint jelly is good with it, too. Herbes de Provence is an aromatic mix of dried wild thyme, bay, rosemary and savory, and is readily available from supermarkets. For once, only the dried will do here. And when the new season's young garlic comes in in spring, use three whole bulbs instead of the regular garlic here. Works very well with lamb shanks, too – but you'll need to braise shanks for an extra hour.

1 shoulder of lamb
30g butter
1 tbsp olive oil
1 bulb garlic, separated into cloves
12 shallots
300ml white wine
1 good tbsp dried herbes de Provence
6 baby leeks or 2 leeks

Slice off any excess fat from the shoulder – but leave enough to cover it – then place it in a shallow casserole or oval roasting tin. Lightly stab the fat of the lamb all over, then salt and pepper the joint and massage in. Brown the fat side of the lamb in the butter and oil, then turn fat side up. Tuck the garlic cloves and whole shallots around and under the meat, then pour in the wine and 100ml water. Sprinkle the herbs all over the lamb, and bring to a bubble on the hob, then put in a 220°C/400°F/Gas 6 oven, uncovered, and open-roast for 30 minutes. Turn the oven down to 150°C/300°F/Gas 2, cover, and slowly braise for about 2-2½ hours or until so tender that the meat will fork easily from the bone.

Meanwhile, trim the leeks, cutting large ones into sections, and give them a good rinse (they often hold trapped dirt in their upper stem), then pop them in with the lamb half an hour before the end of the cooking time. This will reheat beautifully the next day – and taste more glorious. If doing this, add the leeks to the pan when you reheat.

Easy lamb tagine

A tagine is a Moroccan stew gently perfumed with spice. Despite its exotic origin, it's an easy sling-it-in-and-forget-about-it casserole. Moroccans don't cook with fresh mint (it's for their tea) but we like to think they do, and we do, so it comes in here.

You can also change what's popped in the pot with the meat according to season. This one I've designated autumnal – adding squash and sultanas. In summer, I'd lay some thickly sliced tomato over the meat, and leave it at that. Eat with bread or couscous.

4 small lamb shanks, or 1 small shoulder of
   lamb, boned and cut into large chunks
1 tsp ground ginger
1½ tsp ground cinnamon
2 tsp each of ground coriander and cumin
pinch of saffron strands
3 tbsp olive oil
2 tsp runny honey
1 heaped tbsp sultanas
2 large onions, finely sliced
2 thick carrots, cut into chunks
1 small butternut squash or other pumpkin
   (around 500g), halved, deseeded, peeled and
   cut into large chunks
handful of mint leaves

Trim the lamb of excess fat – a little here and there is okay – and tumble into a wide casserole and sprinkle all over with the dry spices, some salt and pepper, the olive oil and honey. Then shoofty it all around, so that everything is nicely covered and gunked with spice, then spread out again, into one layer. Next, scatter over the sultanas and onion, then jumble the carrot around, fitting them down between any gaps. Salt and pepper it again, then pour over about 250ml water, cover with a lid, and bring to a gentle bubble on the hob. Then, slip it into a 160°C/325°F/Gas 3 oven and forget about it for about 1½ hours (2½ hours for shanks). Then unlid, sit the wedges of pumpkin on top, cover again and pop back in the oven for a further hour or until everything is meltingly tender and the meat almost forkable. Serve piled with its juices over couscous (if making), plus lots of torn-up mint leaves.

Fantastic *coq au vin* with rice

We like our coq *here with rice (so cook some long-grain as described on page 72), not the French way with fried bread – it's too much. Mum always uses those tiny little white button mushrooms in this, just the job for soaking up delicious juices, especially when slow cooked in* coq au vin *style braises. Swelled to gill-burst, they bob and duck in this one.*

1 good chicken, around 1.5kg, or that weight of
   chicken pieces, on the bone
250g pickling onions or shallots
plain flour
butter
1 tbsp olive or vegetable oil
250g bacon lardons
250g small button mushrooms
2 cloves garlic, crushed
tied bundle of fresh bay, thyme and parsley
500ml red wine, a Burgundy preferably
250ml chicken stock (see page 47)
handful of flat-leaf parsley leaves, chopped

Cut the chicken up into pieces, cutting off the backbone and wings (and keeping them if you want to make your own quick stock). Peel the baby onions without nicking off too much of their root end, so that they remain whole. It's a fiddly business, and the easiest way of doing it is to cover the onions in a bowl with boiling water and leave for about 5 minutes, then tip out the water and peel.

Salt and pepper the chicken pieces, then toss them with a little flour, so that they're coated, then gently fry them in about 30g butter and the oil in a heavy casserole until golden brown all over – you may need to do them in two batches. Then shift on to a plate.

Fry the bacon lardons all over until just beginning to look a bit crispy, then lift out and put with the chicken. After this, tip in the prepared onions, the mushrooms, a knob more butter and some seasoning into the pan, then gently fry all over until the mushrooms and onions have taken on a little colour. Again, you may need to do this in two lots. Toss the garlic through.

Now, put the chicken and bacon back into the casserole and snuggle it down, so that the vegetables are packed around it, tuck in the tied herbs, then pour in the wine and bring to a raging bubble for a few minutes. Tip in the stock, bring to a bubble again, then cover and pop in a 190°C/375°F/Gas 5 oven for an hour. When cooked,

give it a taste, it may need a tad more salt, and it will now need a further thickening.

In a saucepan fry 2 tbsp flour with a good knob of butter to make a paste then add a couple of ladlefuls of the casserole juices. Stir in, and let it bubble for about 5 minutes – to cook out the flour. Pour this thick sauce back over the chicken and vegetables, gently stir through, and reheat. Spoon over boiled rice and scatter with parsley.

Turkish lamb hotpot

In Turkey they do fantastic things with lamb. Here's my comfort version of their flavours.

½ shoulder of lamb, boned and cut into large
   chunks
1 tsp ground allspice
2 tsp ground cumin
1 large onion, quartered
2 cloves garlic
olive oil
1 medium aubergine, sliced into chunks
small handful each of mint and marjoram leaves
1 tbsp small raisins
250ml lamb stock or water
3 large roasting potatoes, peeled and finely
   sliced into thin rounds

In a casserole, toss the meat with the allspice and cumin and a good twist of pepper. Blast the onion and garlic to a mush in a processor, mix with the lamb and leave to marinate for an hour. Sprinkle with salt and 3 tbsp olive oil, then mix everything together. Briefly fry the lamb in its onion marinade to cook out the spices.

Chuck everything except the potatoes into the pan with the lamb, then turn through and bring to a gentle bubble. Cover the meat with an overlapping layer of sliced potatoes, season and brush all over with oil, then cover with a lid or foil, and bake in a 180°C/350°F/Gas 4 oven for a good hour. Remove the lid, brush with more oil, and bake for a further hour – uncovered – or until the potatoes have browned beautifully.

Alternatively, for dinner-party-smart servings, the hotpots can be baked in four individual ovenproof dishes, and then taken straight to the table.

perfect steak
on one-pan supper

There's something refreshing about knowing that you can whip out a pan, slap in a steak or chicken breast, then once you've chopped up a bunch of this and dressed a bowl of that, have something to-die-for on the plate. Especially when you're completely zonked-out and in need of all things quick. Yes it is. But. And it's a big but. Have you been to chef's school? We haven't, and it's all very well enthusing on TV programmes, on radio, in mags and in countless recipe books how easy it is to be passionate and spontaneous with your farmers' market ingredients, slinging this in, ripping that up, and then flipping and searing it all a bit, and hey presto – like a bunny pulled from a hat – you have the most divine thingy on the plate. Not. A sizzle to a frazzle more like. Some of us can, but most, no – and even the experts get it wrong from time to time. So, I've spelt out that one-pan fast-cooking thing here, so you know what to look for and – hopefully – how to do it well and get something good.

Strictly speaking, these are not all one-pan, as one or two of the recipes involve the pre-blanching of a vegetable or, say, cooking of potatoes first. I wasn't going to be pedantic, for few fast meals rarely come from just one pan, and I'd be compromising on things if – for the mere sake of a chapter heading – I left them out. Here I just want to capture the spirit of the thing – and get over the speed and ease in which a complete meal can come to the table, with excellent results.

The perfect steak

I want meat, and I want it now. That's how I feel when I want a steak. A steak supper is a meal that I want to come home to – time and time again. It reaches all the parts no other can reach. I'll have phases on steak, like girls do on chocolate. It's compulsive. Steak is about lust, sharp knives and red meat, and all that ballsy hunter-gatherer stuff. It's a thing you barely cook and then eat rare and bloody. It's carnivore stuff without nancy bits. So treat it simply and always take it big.

So, what makes a good steak? The beef and the cut. A good one will be carefully butchered from a piece of well-hung beef – somewhere around the three-week mark if you're lucky – and should be quite thick, around 2cm. For me it either has to be a sirloin or a rib-eye, as both behave and taste brilliant and the rib-eye is beautifully marbled with fat. Rump is pretty good too, but the others win. Fillet steak (cut from the centre of the loin) is the finest, but it goes hand-in-hand with restaurant food as it's bloody expensive – and actually rather bland, for there's no fat to be had. It's better eaten raw I reckon, and pumped with flavours: finely sliced as carpaccio and dressed with Parmesan and rocket and dribbled with a mayonnaisey dressing; or as steak tartare, finely chopped and jumbled with a mince of shallot, capers, Worcestershire sauce, Tabasco and raw egg. For me fillet isn't a scratch on the others when cooked as a steak.

And what about T-bone steaks – those great slices of sirloin with a nugget of loin and a chunk of bone? What about them – aren't they just big macho steaks for steak-house diners? Unfair, maybe, but they are ginormous. Too big for home. They'll never fit the grill pan if there's more than two of you. Oh, and I love the fat on a steak, but it has to be done to a crisp. I'm no Jack Sprat.

What's the secret behind the cooking? The pan. Use either a ridged chargrill plate or one of those heavy cast-iron frying pans. You have got to get one if you like steak. You'll never get truly good steak out of a flimsy frying pan. You see, it needs the fiercest of heats to sear it and caramelise it, yet keep it all juicy and bloody inside. A heavy cast-iron pan won't lose its heat to the steak but remain as fierce all through the cooking. You're not going to be frying it for there's no oil added to the pan: the meat is to be seared. And throw out all notions of 'grilled' steak – you're *not* putting it under the grill. No way – and ugh!

How do I start? Steak adores seasoning and so you should salt and pepper it well on both sides, and be generous with the pepper. Make sure you rub salt into the fat along the edge, as this will help it crisp and puff. If you like it really peppery, then roughly crush the peppercorns in a mortar and then smother both sides of the steak to make a rough crust. Next, splash it with a drop of olive oil, then rub that in too. Now, heat your heavy pan until raging hot – you'll see smoke rising from it – then cook the fat edge first. Sounds tricky, trying to stand a load of steaks on their edges on a throbbing hotplate. But not, here's how: gather up your steaks, one on top of the other, all fat edges side-by-side and grab a pair of tongs, then stick the steaks on their fat edges on the pan – all together – and hold them there with the tongs for a minute or so. Then go to cooking them either side, gently pressing on each one in turn with the back of the tongs, to ensure nice even contact with the steak and the pan's ridges.

When is it done? It will depend on how thick your steak is and how well done you like it. It's a heinous crime to hammer it until it's grey right through and drying out. We know that now. Well done in a restaurant is no-go – and if you ask for that, the chef may well turn primadonna and wipe it across the kitchen floor first, or do something too unmentionable to mention here. Medium is allowed, medium-rare is perfection, and blue (that's almost raw) is for zombie-flesh-eaters only. But if you must – do. It's allowed. The food police won't be knocking at your door. As a guide, to cook a regular thickness steak until medium-rare, you'll want to give it around 2 minutes on each side. Give it a prod with your finger, it should resist a little and spring back turgid and plump. For medium, cook it around a minute more on one side.

What do I serve it with? Oh, easy things. Enhancers – nothing involved. Leave the chef's béarnaise sauces to when you eat out. All it needs is a fantastic herbed and garlicked butter or some mashed Roquefort cheese slapped upon it, which will melt and delta all over the place and have each mouthful of tenderness swimming in gorgeousness. Some mild mustard dolloped on the side I'd want too. As far as things with, a good green salad and some boiled new potatoes are the withs. There again, if you're up for it, go to making chips…you'll be loved. Fried or chargrilled thick slices of flat-cap mushroom are another – milling around in more garlic butter. Particularly good if you were to cook a very thick piece of rib-eye or sirloin (almost joint size) on the barbie until blackened, then you could cut it into juicy rare steaks. You see, the great thing about a steak is – unlike nearly all other meats – its credentials are perfect when it's not properly cooked. You can't go wrong.

The perfect steak supper with thyme and garlic butter

Take a look at the notes on pages 141-2, then move in. Don't be scared at the amount of butter, you'll want it. I am not the snot-bag over garlic presses – I use one. It's the only way to get the garlic properly juiced. So if you have one use it, but always make sure you scrub it well afterwards. Freshly grated horseradish livens up the butter too.

4 sirloin or rib-eye steaks, around 2-2.5cm thick
olive oil
3 cloves garlic, crushed
6 good sprigs thyme, leaves finely chopped
150g butter
4 big handfuls rocket or watercress

Salt and pepper the steaks all over, then slosh with a little olive oil. Using your fingers, rub it all in, then leave the steaks on one side on a plate. Switch the heat on full-blast underneath your heaviest pan or – preferably – a chargrill pan or hotplate, of the sort with ridges (without the addition of oil) so that it becomes smoking hot. Add the garlic and thyme leaves to the butter and beat them in, along with a sprinkling of sea (or regular) salt. If you have a mortar and pestle, you could pound this mixture up in it, starting by crushing the garlic with the salt to a paste, then working in the rest. You want the butter mixture pretty soft, so that it melts immediately when plonked on top of the steak.

Now turn on the extraction – as smoke is going to pour – and sear the steaks' fat edges down first in the hot pan (as above), for a minute or so. Then spread them out, laying them all out flat and let them sear for around 2 minutes. Turn them over and cook for a further 2 minutes or so, until cooked to your liking.

Serve each with a good smack of the thyme and garlic butter on top and a pile of rocket on the side. Something in the potato or bread line will be needed too – unless you're on one of those no-carb six-pack-lusting diets.

Pan-braised chicken and Jersey Royals with mustard gravy

This was one of the Top 10 favourites of my Sunday Times readers. I know, because many asked for the recipe again, giving me the low-down on their lost page: the husband who threw it; the daughter who used it for the guinea-pig hutch; a dog who ate it...etc etc.

4 large chicken breast fillets or 8 thighs, skinned
plain flour
30g butter
3 tbsp olive oil
600g Jersey Royal or other new potatoes, scrubbed
4 good-sized sprigs rosemary, broken into bits
4 fat cloves garlic
200ml chicken stock (see page 47, but a cube is fine)
350ml white wine
4 heaped tsp Dijon or German mustard

Cut each breast, on the diagonal, into three pieces or, if using thighs, keep them whole. Season the chicken pieces all over and dust each piece well with flour. Heat half the butter and 2 tbsp of oil in an extra large frying pan (or use two), and fry the breasts on all sides until golden brown all over. Then remove from the pan and keep on one side, leaving the fat in the pan. Pop the potatoes into the same pan and fling over a generous shower of sea salt and black pepper, adding the remaining butter and oil if it needs it. Throw the rosemary into the pan of potatoes, along with the peeled garlic, and gently fry all over until faintly tinged golden.

Add the stock, bring to a gentle bubble and cover, and leave to cook until the potatoes feel almost tender when stuck with the tip of a knife. Watch the pan doesn't dry out. Then add the chicken to the pan, bedding it down amongst the potatoes, turn up the heat and pour over the wine. Allow everything to bubble up, then turn to low and let everything gently murmur for about 10 minutes or until the chicken is cooked. Blob the mustard between the gaps and into the juices, move things around a bit, then turn up the heat again and bubble until the mustard has dissolved into the pan juices. Eat with a simple green salad and good bread.

Coconut chicken with wok vegetables

You want dreamy chick? Do this. Okay, three pans come into operation here, but who cares when something so easy turns out so good. My veg selection is just a guide – use whatever you have, and try and give the breasts some time in their coconut bath: it makes a difference.

4 chicken breasts, skinned
finely grated zest of 1 lime (or kaffir lime)
2 tbsp fish sauce
1 small red chilli, deseeded and finely chopped
1 x 400ml can coconut milk
4 massive handfuls vegetables, from a mix of mangetout, green beans, carrot, beansprouts, spring onions, red pepper, baby corn, asparagus, shiitake mushrooms and so on
vegetable oil
3 fat cloves garlic, finely sliced
a handful of coriander or basil leaves

Plonk the chicken breasts into a container, then salt and pepper them, and tumble them with the lime zest, fish sauce and chilli. Tip over the coconut milk and leave to bathe for as long as possible, chilled. Now, overnight would be excellent but if pressed for time, an hour or so.

Shortly before you want it, prep the veg: you can keep things like mangetout whole but baby corn should perhaps be halved lengthways, spring onions roughly shredded and things like red pepper and carrot cut into fine strips. Put everything next to your wok on the hob. Lift the chicken out of its marinade and put on to a plate – a little of the coconut stuff should be left clinging – then spill each breast with a dash of oil. Heat a heavy grill pan or something cast iron until fiercely hot and smoking, then grill the breasts without disturbing them for about 4 minutes on each side or until just cooked through.

Meanwhile, tip the marinade into a small saucepan and add a ladleful of water (or stock if you have it). Bring to a bubble and leave to murmur and reduce while you stir-fry. Heat 2 tbsp of oil in your wok, then chuck in the sliced garlic, then throw in the vegetables at the point when the garlic is just beginning to colour. Stir-fry the veg over a high heat with some seasoning for about 2 minutes, keeping it a little crunchy. Remove from the heat, stir through the herb leaves, then serve piled with the chicken (cut in half on the diagonal, if you want to be arty) and with spoonfuls of the coconut sauce dotted about.

Chicken with cashew nuts

Once you've got all the meat and veg assembled here, it's an easy matter of just chucking things in the wok in some kind of order. Make your rice first, so that it's ready when you are – it will stay fine if kept covered in the pan it was cooked in.

4 chicken breast fillets, skinned
2 tbsp soy sauce (I use Kikkoman)
2 tsp rice wine (Chinese shaoxing) or dry sherry
2 big handfuls unsalted peeled cashews
vegetable or groundnut oil
3 tsp cornflour
1 tbsp rice vinegar or white wine vinegar
1 tbsp caster sugar
a splash of sesame oil
4 long mild red chillies, deseeded and cut into
    chunks
5 large cloves garlic, finely sliced
3cm piece fresh root ginger, shredded into
    matchsticks
1 big bunch spring onions, cut into large chunks
1 bunch coriander

Slice the small feather fillet from beneath each breast, then cut all the meat into large bite-sized chunks. Put these in a bowl and toss with salt, pepper, 1 tbsp soy sauce and the rice wine and leave to one side. Put the nuts in a roasting pan, add a tsp oil and shake, then pop them into a 200°C/400°F/Gas 6 oven. Keep an eye on them, giving them a shake once or twice, until they're evenly brown, about 15-20 minutes. Mix the cornflour with the remaining soy sauce and 5 tbsp of cold water, then stir in the vinegar and sugar.

When ready to cook, remove the chicken from its marinade, leaving any juices in the bowl, then fry it in batches in the wok in a deepish pool of vegetable oil (about 3cm deep) until golden, about 3-4 minutes. Then pour out all but 2 tbsp of oil from the wok and splash in some sesame oil.

Set the wok over your highest heat. Once beginning to smoke, throw in the chillies and stir-fry for about 15 seconds. Chuck in the garlic and ginger, and fry until the garlic has picked up just a touch of colour, then return the chicken and stir through, adding the spring onion. Tip any remaining chicken marinade into the wok along with the cornflour mixture and toasted nuts and bubble up until glossy. Chuck on some fresh coriander and eat with a mound of rice.

Oven-fried chicken Kiev

I thought chicken Kiev the most fantastic thing when I first had it. I went to an Italian restaurant in Burgess Hill with Pippa, my first proper girlfriend, and we had this – not Italian at all. There again, what did we care. It was great. She then went and married an Italian. These are short-cut Kievs and done in the oven, which saves on all that deep-frying. You could stuff them with slices of Emmental cheese and smoked ham instead – very 70s chicken cordon bleu.

4 thick slices white crustless bread, made into
    breadcrumbs
120g butter
finely grated zest of ½ lemon
3 fat cloves garlic, crushed
4 good sprigs parsley, finely chopped
4 large chicken breasts, skinned
plain flour
2 large eggs, beaten
4 tbsp vegetable oil

Scatter the breadcrumbs over a roasting tin and leave in a warm place (or low oven) to dry, then blend again until more finely crumbed. Beat together the butter, lemon zest, a little salt and pepper, the garlic and parsley, then turn on to a piece of greaseproof paper. Roll up into a sausage shape, flatten slightly and then refrigerate – the freezer will speed things up – then cut it into four pieces. Chill.

Using a rolling pin, lightly beat the breasts – enough to just flatten them a touch – then slice a small pocket in each lengthways and parallel to the the flat side of the breast. Season inside and out, and stuff a piece of the garlic butter into the centre of each fillet, securing the opening with a wooden cocktail stick if necessary. Roll in flour, then in the beaten egg, then straight into the breadcrumbs. To make a good crust, roll in the egg again and then back into the breadcrumbs, then put in the fridge for as long as possible to firm the coating up (overnight is fine).

In an ovenproof frying pan, fry the breadcrumbed chicken in the oil with a knob of extra butter for a minute or two, then turn over, and put in a 190°C/375°F/Gas 5 oven and 'oven-fry' for 15 minutes. Then turn over and cook for a further 10 minutes or until golden looking. Remove any lurking cocktail sticks and serve with a green salad and rice to mop up all the buttery juices.

Pan-roast duck breast with chilli greens

Easy-peasy and everyone will snaffle it up. The secret to proud success here is to very finely score – that's make fine shallow cuts through – the duck skin and fat without piercing the meat, like you would to make crackling happen on a pork roast. This will get the fat running once the breasts hit the pan. Use Barbary or Gressingham duck breasts – supermarkets sell them in packs of two, and one pack of something weighty will be big enough to serve four. But buy four if you're big on big-meat portions. You can do a mix of greens – or just use broccoli.

2 large duck breasts
3 sprigs thyme, leaves roughly chopped
1 tbsp honey
1 tbsp soy sauce
juice of 1 fat orange
1 tbsp white wine vinegar
½ tbsp caster sugar
2-3 large mild red chillies, deseeded and thickly
    sliced
2 cloves garlic, sliced lengthways
2 heads broccoli, separated into florets and
    blanched
1 tbsp vegetable oil

Using a very sharp knife, score fine cuts across the skin of the duck, then sit the breasts in a shallow dish, and rub with salt, pepper and the thyme leaves. Spoon over the honey and soy sauce, and rub in, then leave to one side for an hour or so – or overnight, if you've thought about it. But if you can only leave it for a minute or two, then it's still going to be fabby-do. Next, mix together the orange juice, vinegar and sugar, until the sugar has dissolved, and leave to one side.

Meanwhile prep all the veg. Heat a frying pan until hot, then remove the breasts from their honey and soy bath, and tip the marinade into the orange juice mixture. Put the duck breasts, skin side down, in the hot pan and then fry without any addition of fat. You'll see how the breasts start to pour forth their own fat and start to fry. They'll need about 4 minutes on this side, without moving them about, then you can turn them over. Now, don't panic, the skin will look charred, yes, but will not taste at all burnt. Now carry on cooking for a further 3 minutes. If they're small breasts and you are cooking four of them, then may be a minute less. You want the flesh pink in the middle. Then leave them to rest for 10 minutes, while you stir-fry the greens.

Stir-fry the chilli and garlic with some seasoning in the oil until the garlic is golden but not burnt, then toss in the broccoli. Stir around and season again, and then stir-fry until just beginning to wilt. Remove and pile on to pre-warmed plates. Tip the orange dressing into the wok and quickly bubble up, then pour it over the greens, and stick the duck breast (sliced, if you're being fancy) on top.

Lamb steaks with red onion broccoli

This is cooked to order – but will have you distracted for mere minutes. No lamb on the supermarket shelves? Then use pork chops, beef rib-eye steaks, kangaroo or even ostrich. Yes, it's amazing what you can't and can now find in supermarkets these days.

4 lamb steaks (from a leg) or chops
2 tsp caster sugar
4 tbsp balsamic vinegar
2 red onions
2 heads broccoli
olive oil

Scatter the steaks with the sugar and put in a dish or plastic sandwich type bag, then pour over the balsamic vinegar, making sure everything is evenly coated. Next, slice the onions lengthways into slim wedges, leaving a little of the stalk end on when peeling, to keep everything intact. Then cut the broccoli into florets – cooking it in salted boiling water for about 3 minutes, when you cook the steaks. Remove the steaks from their marinade, salt and pepper them, and splash them with oil, then sear them in a very hot heavy pan for about 2 minutes, then turn them over. At the same time add the onion, seasoning, a splash of the marinade and a touch more oil, and sear for another minute or so. Next, turn through the onion and add some more of the marinade and 2-3 tbsp of water, then reduce down. You should end up with onion that is seared and caramelised at the edges, and caramelised steaks that are pinkish within, and a soupçon per serving of gravy-like juice.

Sticky Asian chicken with chilli herb salad

That something so magical could come from so few things and in so little time excites me every time. You lust for Asian, you lust for chicken? Well, this it – and fast. Turn the chicken either gingery with root ginger or lemony with lemongrass – it's your call. To toast unsalted peanuts, scatter them across a baking tray and roast in a hot oven for about 10-15 minutes until golden, but keep an eye on them to catch them right. Use Thai sweet basil if you can get it.

8 chicken thighs, bone in
3cm piece fresh root ginger, grated, or 2 sticks
   lemongrass, trimmed and finely chopped
1½ tbsp caster sugar
3 tbsp fish sauce
1 tbsp vegetable oil
2 tbsp lime juice
1 tbsp rice vinegar
½ cucumber, finely sliced
2 long mild red chillies, finely shredded
4 spring onions, finely shredded
1 bunch each of coriander, mint and basil
3 tbsp unsalted peanuts, crushed and toasted

Lightly slash the skin side of the thighs, then rub all over with the ginger or lemongrass, and place in a strong plastic bag. Dissolve 1 tbsp of the sugar with 2 tbsp of the fish sauce and tip into the bag, then massage into the chicken and leave to marinate until ready to cook – 10 minutes, hours, or overnight. It doesn't matter.

Remove the chicken from its marinade, and then lightly fry in the oil in an ovenproof dish until golden on all sides, then pour over the remaining marinade left in the bag and slip the pan into a 220°C/425°F/Gas 7 oven and roast the thighs for about 15-20 minutes or until cooked through but still juicy. Mix the remaining fish sauce with the remaining sugar, the lime juice and rice vinegar, then toss with the cucumber, chilli, spring onions, herb leaves and half of the peanuts. Put two sticky thighs on to each plate, then pile the salad next to the chicken and sprinkle with the remaining peanuts.

Liver with bacon, onion and sage

Love liver. But it has to be all pinky in the middle. So, don't hammer it to death in the pan - too long in cooking and it will be grainy and dry. Onions with liver are usually slow-fried to melting point but this takes an age, so mine are fast and furious but achieve very good results. Eat with bread or mash, but I often go for rice on the carb front here. And if you're splashing out on calf's liver, there's no need to flour it or indeed make a gravy – and a mere 30 seconds on each side will do, if cut thin. The girlies amongst you can stick with chicken livers.

500g lamb's liver or chicken livers
2 onions, sliced
60g butter
3 tbsp olive oil
½ tbsp sherry vinegar or balsamic vinegar
1 small bunch sage
4 good rashers bacon
plain flour
500ml chicken stock (see page 47) or lamb stock

Wash the liver under cold water, then slice it into thin portions, around 1.5cm thick – and if there is anything tube-like lurking around, cut it out. If using chicken livers, leave them whole. Leave the liver(s) to drain in a colander.

Pile the onions into a large frying pan, then add half the butter and 1 tbsp of the oil plus some seasoning, and gently fry over a medium heat for about 10 minutes until softened and beginning to caramelise at the edges. Stir in the vinegar, then chuck in a few sage leaves, stir through and fry a little longer, then tip the onions on to a plate. Wipe out the pan, add the bacon with a tiny splash of oil and fry until crisp, then remove and put on one side.

Season the liver with salt and pepper on both sides, then dust all over with flour – it's best to roll the pieces about in a plate of it so that they become well crusted. Heat the remaining butter and oil in the frying pan (you may have to move into two pans here...read on to the end) and fry the liver for about 2 minutes over a high heat without moving it about. Add the remaining sage and then flip the liver over and fry for a mere 1 minute more. Now, tip the onions back into the pan and move them around so that they fill up any gaps, and keep frying for a minute more, then pour in the stock and let it bubble up well for about another minute, and you're done. Serve the liver with its sage and onions and gravy with a piece of bacon alongside. Yum.

Gravy dinners,
pies and mash

Big pork chops, apple sauce, mash, boiled cabbage and lots of gravy. That was the weekday meal at home. Mum's everydayer. One she did on auto-pilot after unloading the Sainsbury's shop and a quick snooze on the sofa. The steam from the kitchen would cut the air of a dining room that was always cold, and then get up the stairs; I'd smell it in my bedroom well before I was called. Mum was always the same, loving but kitchen tetchy, and the meal was always the same: a fat chop with its share of fat; the mash walloped big on the plate; a pile of boiled to just translucent, hastily cut sweet cabbage; and a very hot pale gravy, made from the cabbage water, lapping at the chop. And it was lovely. Really lovely, in fact. Gravy dinners have to be this. Big and bold and filling. Simple enough to be able to come together after that stint on the sofa.

Now, pies. I'd be pushed to pie it midweek. A little more aforethought and attention to detail is needed, more than I might be in the mood to give. They're more a weekend special. There again, a quick one can be knocked up by throwing the leftovers of a roast chicken dinner into a dish and sending it off for a re-bake, this time capped with a lid of bought pastry. It's the way to use up the bits left on the bird; the carcass for its stock; and uneaten peas and carrots. Once all the bits and bobs have had their quick spruce up, a last-minute make-over with some fresh herbs, and you have a pastry top on it, you are going to be in for a

great pie. Pastry is *the* regenerator, and a pie can cover up a carnage of sins. Put most things in or under pastry and they taste bloody good.

Pies are us. There's the quintessential British meat pie, the old East End pie & mash shop pie stuffed – if somewhat thinly – with a comfy gloop of thick dark gravy and threads of meat, and packeted in squidgy pastry. They're not bad at 4 am when you're really hungry and too tired to care – but make sure you're awake enough to avoid a slop of the shop's 'liquor' – a dubious dishwater-coloured gravy, that can kibosh the lot. Australian footy pies, sold from trailer vans to post-match post-pub tanked-up Ozzies are another sort, and come with a splat of mushy pea. Absolute trailer-trash, but fine if you're off your face. As are factory pies – the ones you get out of a tin. I was done in after eating three in a row once. Brain-dead at the time (well, you'd have to be). It's the home-made pies that save our institution's bacon, the ones from good pubs and home, and these are the ones I'm fanfaring here.

Perfect chicken pie

When I say pie, this is the sort of pie I mean. Big, round and generous and filled with good stuff. Nuggets of meat that are bound in just the right squelch of sauce and held together by good pastry; a flaky puff whose underskirts are deliciously sogged. There are many variants of chicken pie, and some are served hot and others cold. I'm talking hot pie here.

Two hot pies, to be precise. One holds poached chicken and flakes of ham in a velvet-cream sauce, with a flaky pastry case. The other that follows, my great-aunt Jo's recipe, is essentially chicken stew capped with a puff pastry lid.

Kick off by cooking the chicken
This can be done the day before. Put the bird into a saucepan in which it fits snugly, then fill with enough water so that it's just dunked under, then bring to a bubble and skim off any flotsam. Next, salt it well and twist in some pepper, then tuck in 2 halved onions, a rinsed quartered leek, and a tied mixed bunch of bay, parsley and thyme. Turn down the heat and let it gently poach for an hour. The water must just be blip-bubbling, not boiling. Turn off the heat and leave the chicken to cool in its stock. Remember, the stock is the all-important flavour-giver of the pie.

Do I have to make my own pastry? No, you can use shop bought – but don't buy the ready-rolled sort for the cased pie, as it may be cut too small. My home-made flaky pastry will taste the best, but a supermarket shortcrust works well too, although my version makes a stronger crust – ideal for enclosing a creamy filling, and keeping the pie intact when served. The recipe may make extra pastry, but better too much, than hopelessly struggle with too little. Bought puff pastry can be used to top a pie – as in Aunt Jo's. Pastry and pie fillings are best made well before putting them together.

Home-made flaky pastry For this, the fat is first hardened in the freezer, then grated into the flour, which makes it bubble and puff to a crisp when baked – a trick I've borrowed from our Delia. Put 330g plain flour into a bowl with a sprinkle of salt, then holding 220g chilled butter in its paper (pulled back), grate it over the flour. Using a wooden spoon, mix through, then slowly work in up to 120ml ice-cold water. Gently knead on a floured surface to make a pliable dough, without over-working, adding a drop more water as and if necessary. The butter should remain in gratings, which will allow the pastry to puff as it cooks – so don't bung this in the processor.

What sort of tin or dish do I use? You can make individual pies, a filled dish capped with pastry, or a large round pie completely encased by pastry. It's your call. My Great-Aunt Jo's pie (see page 156) can only be capped, as the filling is submerged in an unthickened broth-like stock. Pastry-enclosed pies should be made shallow, for – although fantastic cold – they're usually served hot, when the filling is pretty liquid, and if made too deep, once served and released from their tins, their hot soft centres could cause them to bulge and bust out.

My favourite creamy chicken and ham pie

If you're making a pie, you may as well make it big, as then there's seconds and plenty for later raiding – so this one will cut to eight. For a simpler pie, of the sort my mum makes, tip the filling into a large shallow pie dish and top with bought puff pastry.

1 quantity flaky pastry (see above)
1 medium egg, lightly beaten, to glaze

Filling:
1 x 1.5kg free-range chicken, cooked as on page 153, with its stock
200g cooked ham off the bone
80g butter
80g plain flour
150ml double cream
150g button mushrooms, halved

Once the chicken has cooled, lift it from the stock, then remove the meat – discarding all the skin and bones – and flake into chunks. Flake the ham into chunks as well, then put with the chicken in a large bowl. Sieve the stock, discarding all the flavourings.

Heat the butter in a saucepan, add the flour and cook together to make a paste, gently moving it about, so that it doesn't catch and burn. Then slowly pour in 450ml of the stock and the cream and cook to a thick sauce, while stirring. Season lightly, then stir in the mushrooms and cook for a couple more minutes, stirring occasionally. Pour this sauce over the chicken and ham and mix together. Allow to cool, then cover and chill.

Roll out the pastry until around 3mm thick and use to line a shallow 26cm diameter, lightly greased, loose-bottomed pie tin or tart ring – or something near to those dimensions. If using a ring, set it on a greased baking sheet. Trim the pastry off so that it leaves a lip-like edge around its rim, then fill the pastry case with the cold chicken sauce. Mould all the pastry scraps back into a ball and roll out again, into a disc large enough to cover the pie top. Brush the pie's pastry rim with beaten egg, then drape the pastry disc over the top of the filling, lightly pressing it to the pie's sides, then trim off. Make a hole in the middle (to allow excess steam to escape), then brush the top with beaten egg and bake for 1 hour in a 190°C/375°F/Gas 5 oven. If the top browns too quickly, move it to the lower shelf.

Great-Aunt Jo's quick chicken pie

My Great-Aunt Jo is an elegant 92. She's great fun and a great cook but has now hung up her apron, for bridge, reading and evenings out instead. Actually, she'd never be seen dead in an apron. I remember her chicken pie well. She'll call me a 'wicked creature' for popping it in here, but I must. All your veg comes in the pie, so no need for any other pans, therefore no need for after-supper washing up. So Aunt Jo.

1 x 1.3kg cooked chicken (or poach one as on
   page 153 and use the stock too)
300g young carrots, scrubbed
400g waxy new potatoes, scrubbed
1 onion, chopped
2 cloves garlic, finely chopped
40g butter
1 tbsp vegetable or olive oil
300g leeks, washed and cut into slim chunks
500ml chicken stock (see above or page 47)
200g peas (frozen are fine)
150g broad beans, shelled (frozen are fine,
   optional)
handful of chopped parsley or tarragon
350g bought ready-rolled puff pastry
1 medium egg, beaten, for glaze

Remove the flesh from the chicken. Discard the skin and bones, and flake the meat. Gently bubble the carrots and potatoes in salted water for around 8 minutes or so, or until they're just tender. If you've poached your chicken, then use its stock to cook the vegetables in.

Meanwhile fry the onion with the garlic in half the butter and the oil until softened, then season. Add the leek, a dab more butter and a dash of stock and sweat for a few minutes. Spoon the chicken and all the veg, including the peas and beans, into a deep china pie dish or rectangular tin (checking first it's the right size for your pre-rolled pastry), sprinkling in the herb and some seasoning as you go – the filling should reach the top of the dish. Next, pour over enough stock, so that it remains a good 1cm below the top layer. Unroll the pastry (or if it needs rolling, roll it out until around 3mm thick), then brush the rim of the pie dish with beaten egg and then place the pastry on top, pressing down the edges and trim off. Brush the top with beaten egg. Bake for 45 minutes in a 190°C/ 375°F/Gas 5 oven or until puffed and golden on top. Dish up with a good blob of mustard on the plate.

Sausage and mash and onion gravy

This is posh bangers and mash – not that a Beckham would know it. The guts of it is in the fantastic gravy. There's a lot of it, so make plenty of mash. You could add some mild or grain mustard to the pan when mashing the potatoes for mustard mash.

10 small red or regular onions, 6 finely sliced
butter
1½ tbsp plain flour
1 good tsp Marmite or Bovril
800ml beef stock (use instant)
1.5kg floury potatoes
4-5 tbsp cream or full-fat milk
8 sausages (your choice)

Fry the sliced onion in 30g butter with a dash of salt and pepper in a wide saucepan until well caramelised. Stir in the flour, adding more butter if necessary, and fry until the mixture has turned a good brown colour. Next, add the Marmite then pour in the stock and pop in the whole onions. Stir, cover and braise over a gentle heat for about 45 minutes or until the onions are tender.

Meanwhile make the mash. Peel then boil the potatoes in salted water until they're pretty soft. Then drain them and tip them back into their still warm saucepan. Splash with the cream or milk, add 30g butter and mash until nice and smooth, then cover to keep warm. (Mash will reheat beautifully in the microwave.) Next, fry or grill the sausages on all sides until well browned.

Pile the mash into four shallow bowls or deep plates and using the back of a large spoon make a well in the centre of each. Pour on the gravy and add a whole (or halved) onion, and some sausages. Put a pot of mustard on the table too.

Chef's mash If you want it extra smooth, mash 1kg cooked potatoes very thoroughly. Beat in 100g butter with some seasoning until it looks glossy. Heat 200ml full-fat milk with around 5 tbsp double cream until almost bubbling, then pour this into the mash slowly while heartily beating. And PS, on no account put it in the processor: it goes to a real glooperty-gloop glue.

Mustard kidneys with kale mash

What's the matter with us and offal? For God's sake. Yes. Yes, yes and yes – it's bloody delicious stuff, and we're a nation of wimps for being so pathetic about it. Come on, if you ate this you'd love it, so get down and cook it.

1 bunch curly kale leaves
1kg floury potatoes
120g butter
3 tbsp soured or double cream
6 lamb's kidneys
good pinch of English mustard powder
plain flour
1 onion, chopped
1 clove garlic, crushed
2 sprigs thyme, leaves only
1 tbsp brandy or a dash of balsamic vinegar
1 tbsp Dijon mustard
250ml stock (meat, chicken or vegetable)

Chop up the kale – cutting out any thick ribs first – then blanch the leaves in salted boiling water for about 2 minutes, and leave to thoroughly drain. Meanwhile, peel and boil the potatoes in salted water until tender, then mash with a third of the butter and a small splash of the cream, plus some seasoning. Beat in the kale.

To prepare the kidneys, cut them in half lengthways, then using scissors, snip out all the white inner veiny-looking bits. Season them with salt, pepper and the mustard powder and dust them with flour. Fry in about half the remaining butter, until brown all over, then remove from the pan, about 3 minutes in all. Gently fry the onion with the garlic and thyme in the remaining butter until soft, and season. Stir in a level tbsp of flour, add more fat if necessary, and fry until the onion roux has turned a light brown colour. Add the brandy and Dijon mustard, and stir through, then add the stock and gently bubble together for about 10 minutes. Add extra stock or a dash of water if the mixture evaporates too much – you want it sauce-like. Stir in the kidneys and warm them through, then stir in the soured or double cream, bubble up, and serve piled on to the kale mash.

Pub steak and kidney plate pies

This is an all-meat pie. Nothing more, nothing less. If making as one large pie, use a 1.2 litre pie dish.

800g braising steak
200g ox kidney, trimmed
40g beef dripping or butter
2 medium onions, chopped
2 tbsp plain flour
2 tsp each of Worcestershire sauce and tomato purée
450ml beef stock (use instant)
350g puff or shortcrust pastry
1 medium egg yolk, lightly beaten

Cut the beef and the kidney into bite-sized bits, then toss with salt and pepper. Brown the chunks all over – in batches – in about 2 tbsp of the fat in a casserole dish. Remove. Next, fry the onion in the remaining fat with some seasoning until lightly browned. Stir in the flour, dolloping in more fat if necessary, and fry until the now pasty-looking onion has turned a good brown colour. Then stir in the Worcester and tomato purée, beef stock and browned meat, and gently bubble together for about 5 minutes. Now turn the heat to very low, cover the pan and leave to gently braise for about 1½-2 hours or until the meat is nice and tender. Once cooled a little, spoon the pie filling into four individual ovenproof deep plates or shallow soup bowls.

If the pastry isn't pre-rolled, roll it out and cut out four circles to fit the tops of the dishes. You will need to gather up the scraps and re-roll the pastry to get the fourth probably. Then gather up the scraps again and using your hands roll out four thin long sausage shapes – like you did with play-dough at school – to fit the circumference of each plate. Brush the pie dish rims with egg wash, then flatten a sausage-shaped strip of dough around the edge of each plate. Brush this with egg and then place a pastry lid on top of each, using your fingers or tip of a knife to seal the edges to the pastry rim. Make a small hole or cross in the top of each pie (to allow steam to escape), then brush all over with egg yolk and bake in a 200°C/400°F/Gas 6 oven for 30 minutes or until puffed up and glossy brown.

Mushroom and potato pasties with Parmesan

The stuff of picnics – but snaffledom heaven when hot too. Been given a little bottle of truffle oil you don't know what to do with? Now's the place for it – slap it in here. Plate them with salad and you have lunch.

2 good handfuls mushrooms, cultivated or wild
2 largish potatoes
60g butter
2 cloves garlic, finely chopped
3 sprigs rosemary, thyme, savory or sage, roughly chopped
4 tbsp freshly grated Parmesan
truffle oil (optional)
350g bought shortcrust pastry

Trim the mushrooms if they need it and slice large ones into thickish slices. Boil the spuds in their skins in salted water until almost cooked, about 15 minutes, then once cooled peel them and chop them into little chunks. Fry the mushrooms in half of the butter with salt and pepper, then add the garlic and herb of choice, stir through and then fry for a few seconds more. Leave on one side to cool, then chop up. Mix the chopped potato and mushrooms with the grated Parmesan and a little extra seasoning (and a few drops of truffle oil, if using).

Roll out the pastry on a lightly floured surface until it's about 3mm thick, then using a large saucer or small plate as a guide, cut out as many 15cm diameter discs as you can manage to fit in – it doesn't matter if they are a bit bigger or smaller. Then gather up the scraps, knead together and re-roll the pastry, and then stamp out more, and carry on until the pastry is used up. You should aim for around six discs.

Place the discs of pastry on a lightly flour-dusted surface, then, leaving about a 2cm border, plonk a spoonful of the filling on to each, adding a dab of butter. Brush the border with water, then flip over to make semi-circular shaped little turnovers, and gently press the edges together. Make three short slashes acrosss the top of each one to allow steam out, then line them all up on a greased baking sheet. Pop into a 190°C/375°F/Gas 5 to bake for about 30 minutes or until the pastry is cooked and has the lightest of tans.

Pizza and the best oven bakes

'Opening hours: Friday nights only, and by invitation only,' says the sign on the door of Russell Jeavons' restaurant, a home to great tasting pizza. Not that an Italian would agree though. For this is not Naples, but Adelaide in Willunga, Down-Under, and Australians do things their way. Willunga is dead quiet at night, absolutely still and no-one about. Yet open the barn door of Jeavons' corrugated shed, and out booms the B52's 'Lurve Shack' and I step in to discover a humdinger of a joint, packed out. Long plank tables and a higgledy-piggledy collection of old diner chairs creaking with people. Everyone happy, everyone laughing, and giant pizzas bedecked with all things fresh flying this way and that. At its heart is a wood-burning oven, topped with a thatch of roughly hewn pizza boards, and it pelts out heat; and beside it is a bench upon a table, lined with heavy terracotta bowls, stacked with salads of crisp lettuce, carrots and beets, curling with snow-pea shoots and weighted with crumbled chunks of feta and goat's cheese. Further along, vast wheels of poppyseed cake sit, slicked with chocolate ganache, and a fat strawberry tart stares out, gleaming in its old tin.

I'm soon tucking in to a delicious pizza studded with oysters in the shell, and another, oozing mozzarella stuck with pancetta and wreathed with rocket leaves; and there are chunks of bread, lettuce and local halloumi to dip into bowls of olive oil and dukka (a ground spiced nut mix). More pizza arrives, all swirls of red onion, red pepper and courgette, quite deliciously over-the-top and as camp as a Pucci skirt. After polishing all the breadboards clean, tables and chairs are pushed back and we boogie the night away to 'We are family' with more pizza and pudding brought on for an interval. That's pizza. Food with joy.

Okay, so our home ovens aren't quite always so accommodating – neither are our neighbours with party noise – but we can still have a stab. Our ovens can't quite match the monstrous heat of the wood-fired oven, but if you make your bases as thin as possible – in other words, make an authentic Italian pizza – and turn your oven to its highest setting, then it's near possible. The idea is to get the base just cooked so that it's brittle around its perimeter yet chewily soft within. Now I know a true Italian pizza is sparsely decorated, but once in a while it's nice not be snot-bags and to pile on the topping and do the full works. So here's a selection, slim and thick. If you want to cheat, use an instant pizza base mix – it only needs a 5-minute work-out, and then more time to groove on down to Sister Sledge.

Perfect tomato pizza

After a home-made dough base, which is what I describe here, most pizza beginnings start life as the no-frills margarita, which is topped with tomato. This one I'll do hereafter – and the quantities here and there will make four big wheels.

What's the knack? Don't worry about it. You're not going to be faced with having to fly the dough on the point of your index finger like some circus act to make perfect wheels. But it will be hands-on and hands-in stuff, so roll up your sleeves and get stuck in. Be brave, be creative, flick on a CD and enjoy yourself – the prime reason to make pizza. Otherwise use a pizza base or packet mix or dial-up one – there's no crime in that. I adore biked pizza.

Do I need fancy flour? No. You could use the extra fine 00 Italian flour but only if you have it, as regular plain flour will work perfectly. So, pile your plain flour volcano-like on the work surface, make a well in the centre and sprinkle in the dried yeast, sugar and salt. Then pour in the warm (that's hand comfortable) water and olive oil, a small slop at a time, while mixing it in with your hands. If you want to use fresh yeast, dissolve it and the sugar in the water first and leave to froth for a few minutes before adding to the flour with the specified oil. Next, push it all together to make a dough and knead well for about 10-15 minutes.

How do I knead? Place the heel of your hand into the dough, then use your fingers to pull in the far edge, then push it down and away from you again, with the heel of your hand. Again and again. You'll build up a rhythm. Keep at it until it feels silky and soft, and not at all sticky. If it stays sticky, then dust down the work surface with flour and continue to knead a bit more. And if it feels too dry, then work in a tsp water – and then another, if it needs it. It should end up lovely and elastic. Next, dust with flour, put in a bowl, cover with a damp tea-towel and leave for an hour in a warm draught-free place to double in size.

How do I know when the dough is ready? Test it by giving it a small prod – the dough should spring back. Then, with hands flour-dusted, knock back the risen dough – this means give it a punch (to push out the air bubbles), then divide into four, and roll these into balls. Leave them for a few minutes to settle. Now – and before you forget – turn the oven on to its highest setting and lightly oil two large baking sheets. Preferably something heavy, that won't buckle in the hot oven.

And now for the cooking Using your hands, press the balls flat, then using your fingertips push them into round pizza shapes on the baking sheets, working from the middle and pushing out until you have about a 5mm thickness – leaving an undinted edge, which will puff and crispen in the oven and dam in any sauce. You won't be able to bake all four in one go, so only assemble two at a time. Spoon on the topping as described below, then slide straight into the oven and bake for around 12 minutes or until the edges have tanned and crisped a little.

What else can go on? Scatter over chunks of mozzarella cheese and bake and then serve scattered with torn basil or rocket leaves too if things are at hand. Just get lots of ingredients around you and your olive oil bottle, cap off and dying to

be slopped and poured. For a **Greek salad pizza** (yes, I know there's no such thing but it's glorious, and I'm not entering the Peking duck pizza realm – quite), smear your pizza base with a little of the passata, then scatter with sea salt, squashed tomatoes or sliced tomatoes, oregano, rings of red onion, black olives and then crumble with feta. Cramming everything on – but leaving a border. Season all over and dress all the vegetably bits well with olive oil, then bake as above. (See image on page 162.) And for something non-tomatoed, make a **sage and onion pizza**: season slices of onion, then brush liberally with olive oil and scatter over your plain pizza base. Next toss some sage leaves with a clove of crushed garlic and some seasoning in a dash of olive oil and scatter these over and around the onion slices, then bake.

Perfect tomato pizza

This is the foundation for all pizzas. Makes four large ones.

500g plain flour, plus extra for dusting
2 tsp dried yeast or 40g fresh yeast
2 tsp caster sugar
3 tsp salt
250ml warm water (hand comfortable)
extra virgin olive oil

Topping:
2 tubs cherry tomatoes, around 600g
2 garlic cloves, crushed
3 tsp dried oregano or other chopped fresh herbs

Pile the flour on the work surface, make a well in the centre and sprinkle in the dried yeast, sugar and salt, then pour in the water and 2 tbsp olive oil, a little at a time, mixing with your hands. If using fresh yeast, follow the instructions on page 163. Bring it all together to make a dough, and knead well for about 10–15 minutes as described above. Dust with flour, put in a bowl, cover with a damp tea-towel and leave for 1 hour in a warm draught-free place to double in size.
While the dough is doing its thing, make the tomato topping. Squeeze each of the tomatoes over a saucepan to rid them of excess pulp, then, keeping the squashed tomatoes on one side, heat up the tomato pulp. Pour in about 1 tbsp of the oil and add the garlic, oregano and some salt and pepper, and bubble up furiously. Let it splutter for a while until it has thickened and reduced, then turn off the heat and let it cool right down.

Then, with hands flour-dusted, knock back the risen dough (see page 164) and divide into four. Roll these into balls, and leave them for a few minutes to settle. Preheat the oven and grease two large baking trays. Next, using your hands, press the balls flat, then using your fingertips push them into round pizza shapes, working from the middle and pushing out until you have about a 5mm thickness with a little edge, which will expand and crispen in the oven and keep in any sauce on top. Put a pizza base on each baking tray (you're baking two at a time only, remember).

Spoon a quarter each of the tomato pulp over the pizza bases on the trays, scatter over the squashed tomatoes, then slop each one with olive oil. Slide straight into the oven and bake for around 12 minutes. Prepare and bake the remaining two pizzas in exactly the same way.

1970s lasagne

The 1970s was the mince decade. Dick Emery in big Elnett hair and white trouser suit was one walking mince, and the other was the stuff Mum had stacked in her chest freezer. I'm sure there was also a book doing the rounds called Marvellous Meals with Mince, *full of some quite unmarvellous grey-toned concoctions. We lived off mince – off the TV and off the plate; some very good things and some awful stuff. However, the dish that shone out and stayed with us for ever was our version of lasagne. Cheesy and meaty. We used more meat to pasta, and of course it should be the reverse. And instead of mozzarella we used Cheddar (go for it here if you like) and even cottage cheese (ugh!...please, no). As usual, not Italian, but bless it, its heart was in the right place, and that's how we adore it now. So here goes. This will serve six.*

olive oil
1 large onion, finely chopped
2 cloves garlic, finely chopped
100g salami or bacon, minced or finely chopped
1kg minced beef
2 tbsp tomato purée
3 tsp dried oregano
2 x 400g cans chopped plum tomatoes
150ml beef stock (use instant)
60g butter
70g plain flour
600ml full-fat milk
freshly grated nutmeg
250g no-cook lasagne pasta sheets
block of Parmesan
100g mozzarella cheese, grated

There are two sauces and some layering up to be done, so get everything made and cheeses at the ready and then you can assemble. You'll need a 20 x 30cm shallow baking dish (or similar), inside lightly greased with oil.

To make the *ragù* sauce, gently fry the onion and garlic in a wide pan in 2 tbsp oil until softened but not coloured. Tip the salami or bacon in along with the minced beef and stir through, breaking up any clumps of mince. If you've bought a pack of supermarket mince, watch you don't tip the blotting-paper-like wadding attached to the mince's underside into the pan. (How many times have I done that?) Let it fry, moving it around from time to time, for about 4 minutes or until it's faintly browned all over – it will, however, look more an unfortunate grey than brown. Next, season it, then add the tomato purée, oregano, chopped tomatoes and

stock. Bring to a good bubble, and let it gently cook for about 20 minutes. It should be thick, gorgeously red, and not watery.

To make the white sauce, melt the butter in a saucepan, stir in the flour and let it foam a bit, then slowly add the milk, stirring all the time. Keep stirring over a gentle heat until it thickens and bubbles. Grate in a good shower of nutmeg, add some salt and pepper and stir it through, then remove from the heat.

To assemble and bake, spread about a quarter of the meat sauce across the base of the prepared dish, then cover this with a layer of lasagne sheets. Spread this with the thinnest layer of white sauce and grate over some Parmesan. Cover this with more pasta, and do the same again with white sauce and Parmesan. Now, go back to the meat, and spoon in and spread out evenly another quarter of it. Top again with three pasta, white sauce and Parmesan layers. Continue to the top until everything is used up, finishing with a thicker layer of white sauce and then scatter the grated mozzarella all over the top. Slide the dish on to the top shelf of a 190°C/375°F/Gas 5 oven and bake for about 40 minutes or until the pasta inside is cooked and the top molten and golden. Eat with green salad.

Auntie Glad's cauliflower cheese

My Auntie Gladys – a great-aunt really – always bolstered up her cauliflower cheese with the lovely stumps of its trimmed leafage and a wedge or two of tomato. The tomatoes were popped on top, so to catch the heat of grill and not turn the cauliflower cheese slushy. Toast lay in the cheese topping too, stuck like fallen headstones. It all made sense: the crisp with the melty, the rich with the sharp. I've swapped toast for breadcrumbs, as naked toast can catch under the grill. This is no time for fancy Gruyère or Parmesan either, for this is comfort eating, without surprises. Here's dear old Auntie Glad's (as Mum calls her).

1 large cauliflower
30g butter
30g plain flour
½ tsp English mustard
400ml milk
freshly grated nutmeg
100g mature Cheddar, grated
2 tomatoes, quartered
2 thick slices white bread, made into
  breadcrumbs

Cut the cauliflower in half, then into florets, keeping them large, the size they naturally are. Keep the core too and any nice stubby bits of trimmed outer leaf. Then bring a pan of salted water to a boil and plunge in all the cauliflower. Once back on the boil, cook for about 3-4 minutes or until almost tender. Pierce a stem with the tip of a knife to test. Once ready, tip it into a colander and allow it to drain well, steaming freely until cool.

Meanwhile, turn on the grill so that it becomes nice and hot. Then melt the butter in the saucepan and stir in the flour, and let it gently foam for about 30 seconds without colouring. Stir in the mustard, then slowly stir in the milk and bubble up to make a thickish white sauce. Then stir in a good grating of nutmeg, plus some salt and pepper. Remove from the heat and stir in about three-quarters of the cheese, and keep stirring until it has melted in. Arrange the cauliflower across a heatproof low-sided dish or roasting tin, then pour over the cheese sauce, making sure you get to slick all the florets in cheesy gloop. Grate over more nutmeg, and then stick the tomatoes across the top in any natural chasms. Toss the breadcrumbs with the remaining grated cheese and sprinkle this all over, along with a touch more salt and a good grind of pepper. Now pop it under your preheated grill until beautifully bubbling and browned, about 5 minutes or so.

Fast tomato tart with pesto

Works, looks and goes like a storm. If you've had a pesto-driven week, eat with soft goat's cheese or goat's curd, or tapenade instead.

500g cherry tomatoes or other tomatoes
extra virgin olive oil
1 pack ready-rolled puff pastry
1 medium egg, beaten
2 sprigs rosemary or thyme, roughly chopped
4 tbsp fresh pesto

Cut all the tomatoes in half, put them in a bowl and jumble them with a generous splash of the virgin. Then unroll the puff pastry on to an oiled baking sheet, and trim off a 2cm strip of pastry from all sides. Brush each strip with beaten egg and stick them egg side down to make a border – a bit like a picture frame – along the edges of the pastry rectangle and trim. Brush all the frame part with the beaten egg, then sprinkle all the pastry with a little sea salt and black pepper and some chopped herb. Now fill the unbordered area of the tart with the oiled-up tomatoes and season them. Slip the tart into a 200°C/ 400°F/Gas 6 oven and bake for about 15-20 minutes or until well puffed at the edges and golden. To serve, slosh a little of the oil over the tomatoes again once cooked and blob portions with pesto. Get out the salad.

Easy cheese soufflé

Cheese scones and cheese soufflés were the two things that I grew up making. Not showing off, just underlining that a soufflé is kids' play really. Soufflés were weekday suppers. That's how ordinary they are – or were. Now we all run a mile from the dear old soufflé, thinking it the diciest thing to dare to cook. It really isn't. Don't do twiddly individual ones, like you see in so many recipe books and restaurants. You want a big chap, and then it's easy. Gooey soft at its core and burnished on top, perfect.

30g butter, plus extra for greasing
20g plain flour, plus extra for dusting
150ml milk
4 medium eggs, separated
60g mature Cheddar, grated
40g Parmesan, freshly grated
pinch each of cayenne pepper and English
   mustard powder

First, find a suitable dish to bake your soufflé in. Something around 1 litre in size, round, high-sided and ovenproof – a soufflé dish is what you really need. Lightly grease it inside with butter, then add a small amount of flour and tip this all around so that it coats the whole of the inside, emptying out any excess. This will help the soufflé rise and stop the eggy mixture sticking.

Melt the butter in a saucepan and get it foaming, then sprinkle in the flour and stir through, allowing it to gently cook for about a minute without browning. Then slowly stir in the milk until you have a thick white sauce. If you get any lumps, then beat it with a whisk and they'll disappear. Remove from the heat and beat in the egg yolks, then the cheeses, the cayenne, mustard powder and some salt and pepper. Give it a taste to check if you need to add more seasoning. Now, using an electric whisk, beat the whites until they form soft peaks (gauge this by switching off, then lifting out the beaters – little floppy but firm peaks will be left behind).

Using a big metal spoon, stir a heaped spoonful of the beaten egg whites into the cheesy white sauce. Then fold in the rest. This means that the whipped egg should be turned in, not beaten in, otherwise you'll knock the hell out of the whites and the soufflé won't rise so well. Airy mixture means high-rising soufflé. Spoon the mixture into your prepared dish, then bake in a 200°C/400°F/Gas 6 oven for 25-30 minutes, without peeking at it until its time is up (this could make it sink). Serve straightaway. Some salad will make it supper.

Asparagus and potato tart

This tart is a tasty old faithful of mine. Slice it into long portions so that everyone gets their fair share of asparagus tips and ends.

250g waxy new potatoes such as Jersey Royals, scrubbed
16 stems asparagus
60g butter
3 medium eggs
225ml double cream
5 sheets filo pastry (or use shortcrust)
freshly grated nutmeg
175g Gruyère or any Swiss hard cheese, grated

Use either a 23cm square tin or a 36 x 12cm tin, or if you don't have either, use a 24cm round tin (in which case you'll have to cut the spears smaller and scatter them over the tart or use asparagus tips instead).

Cook the potatoes until tender in salted water. Slice into 1cm thick rounds. Trim the woody ends off the asparagus (*not* the tips – just in case you didn't know) and then plunge the stems into a pan of salted boiling water for about 2 minutes. Drain and plunge into cold water, draining again once cool. Melt the butter in a small pan, and beat the eggs with the cream in a jug.

Now, for the pastry. Unroll your filo pastry out of its wrapper. It's funny papery stuff and loves to dry out, so keep it covered with a dampish tea-towel when you're not with it. Brush the tart tin all over with melted butter, then lay a sheet of filo pastry inside, gently easing it into the corners of the tin so that it neatly fits (don't worry about it sticking over the sides), then brush all over – bottom and sides – with melted butter. Lay another sheet on top, fit in and brush with butter as before and continue with the remaining sheets of filo pastry. Then, using scissors, trim off all the edges so that they stand around 5mm or so proud of the tin.

Next, assemble and bake the tart. Make a layer of cooked potato slices in the bottom of the pastry-lined tin, breaking up some to fill in any major gaps. Sprinkle all over with salt, pepper and a good grating of nutmeg. Follow with a layer of grated cheese and lightly season again, then pour in the egg and milk mixture. Line a bank of the pre-cooked asparagus – stems all facing in the same direction (as in the picture) – across the tart. Brush the edges of the pastry with more butter, then bake on the middle shelf in a 180°C/350°F/Gas 4 oven

for 35-40 minutes or until the egg has just set in the centre. If the spears show signs of shrivelling while baking, then cover them – but not the pastry – with a square of buttered baking parchment. Serve hot, warm or cold (thinking picnic here).

The best shepherd's pie

I like my shepherd's pie with carrots and peas in. I know it's not traditional but then...so what? It's meant to be a leftovers dish anyway.

1 large onion, finely chopped
2 tbsp vegetable or olive oil
500g minced lamb
2 carrots, cooked
1 tbsp chutney (optional)
250ml lamb stock
handful of podded peas
handful of parsley leaves, chopped
1kg floury potatoes
60ml full-fat milk
butter
Cheddar, grated (optional)

To make the filling, fry the onion in the oil with some salt and pepper until softened, then stir in the mince, breaking up any clods. Fry this further until the meat is no longer pink looking. Chop up the carrots into small little nuggets and throw these into the pan, along with the chutney (if using) and stock and stir through. Bring to a bubble and allow to gently murmur away for about 30 minutes or so. Stir in the peas and the chopped parsley and then spoon everything into an ovenproof dish – something quite shallow and around 1.2 litres.

To make the mash topping, peel and halve the spuds, then cook them gently in salted water for about 20-25 minutes or until a knife pierces without any resistance, then drain them. Mash the potatoes with the milk and 60g of the butter, and a dash of salt, until nice and smooth but not too sloppy. Leave to cool.

Spoon the mash over the meat, smooth down with a fork, then dot all over with butter (and you can sprinkle with cheese here if you want to, Cheddar really) and then bake in a 190°C/375°F/Gas 5 oven for about 40 minutes.

Easy fish, chips and more

Every time I go to Hastings, down on the Sussex coast, I, like the rest of my family, make straight for fish and chips at The Blue Dolphin. (Excluding Father, who I'm sure would like it known here he doesn't do chip shops.) It's not just for the comfort of its tile-patterned lino, squeezy condiment pots, Radio 1, and its chip-shop blondes we head for; it's for the outsized battered fishes – too big for their spilling plates of chips – the stack of floppy buttered sliced-white, and the mugs of tea. At its best, elbow room is nil. Sometimes we eat it in the car, and steep ourselves in vinegared newsprint, or we'll sit on the shingle in the shelter of a fishing boat hull, and scoff it amongst a desiccated litter of grinning crab carapaces and other attractive and whiffy bits from the deep.

Now, I don't make fish and chips at home – it's the chip shop for that. They can handle the smog. However, when I do get a nice piece of fish I am tempted to simply flour it – or dip it in beaten egg and then into breadcrumbs – and shallow-fry it. It's a fast, fabulous and fail-safe way of cooking it. A dollop of tartare sauce and you're away.

The times are tough for fish, I know, but I still encourage the eating of them. Just don't go gobbling up those having a bad time. Cod being one. Keep him for a treat. Pick others – many of which are much more affordable – like line-caught mackerel or sea bass, coley, dogfish (chalked up normally as rock salmon or huss)

and flatfish. And to know you're backing the right fish, look for the Marine Stewardship Council's eco-label of sustainability.

Then there's salmon, which we can now eat loads of. Good salmon, as with all good fish, needs little enhancement. Undercooked and melting with a few woody herbs is my preference. I'm not one for old-school creamy sauces: they do nothing for salmon, for it's rich enough as it is. A nice plump fillet, salted a good half hour before cooking to help firm it up, then rubbed in oil and seared in a smoking hot pan until lightly crusted makes perfect salmon. But which to choose, farmed or wild?

Okay, I look at it like this: we farm; we breed chickens, sheep, cows, the lot. Farming is here to stay. Penning rather than running around to find our food is the obvious route. So it's only reasonable that we should turn our hand to fish. Salmon became the farm pioneer, and the high-density pens produced flabby, fatty fish with genetic deformities, and some serious eco damage too. However, certain farms now appear to have pulled their socks up, and have gone organic, and that doesn't just mean feed. It's now more about how and where these pelagics – fish designed to ocean roam – are kept. Pens are now set out in tidal straits, such as up in Orkney. So, when buying farmed, look out for organic. It won't be as shrimp-pink, for there are no unnatural colours added to the feed, and it will be denser in texture and

less fatty than most. So more than just fancy feed behind the tired organic label.

One big step up from organic-farmed, comes net-caught wild. Alaskan wild salmon is fished in controlled amounts from sustainable sea stocks, before the fish migrate up river. They've been at it for 40 years, so they must be doing something right. Alaskan salmon is unique, for its rich unctuous meat is deep red-pink from the all the seafood it's gobbled on its travels. It's what my mum gets as canned 'red salmon'. Yet it's now also sold fresh through some supermarkets from June through to September – though Mum is still on the tinned (incidentally excellent in fish cakes).

Aaah, fish cakes. I can't think of any other food that turns us all more kitten-in-a-basket gooey than a fish cake. Even something out of a chip shop – a fish cake in name only – I'll eat with the same gusto.

Perfect fish

To pick out spanking fresh fish, look for bright eyes and blood-free pink gills. Then get your fishmonger to de-scale it if necessary (or fillet it for you, if you want portions). Back home, give your fish another rinse off under a cold tap, pat it dry with kitchen roll and cook it literally when you're ready to eat. And don't be embarrassed to ask any questions you like at the fish counter – most in the queue behind you won't have much of a clue either.

You can't stick fish bones? If there's one thing that puts some of us off eating things that swim, it's the idea of all those fiddly little bones to mess with. And the extrication of meat from a mass of pins can turn eating into a laboratory-like dissection. Kippers are brilliant at it. The way out is to buy fillets: fish off the bone.

How do I cook it – and for how long? Fish needs the simplest of treatment and the speediest of cooking. It's God's answer to fast food. I've given various ways on the cooking front below, from pan-searing and pan-roasting fillets, to steaming, frying and grilling whole fish, then baking poached fish in a classic fish pie. One other way is roasting. Nothing could be more dreamily effortless. You only have to rub your piscatorial friend inside and out with one or two things – say, salt, pepper, some herbs and olive oil – and set him proudly on a roasting tray, stuff more herbs in his belly, and give him moments in your fiercest oven. Any fish will do. A trout, plaice or 500g tuna joint will need around 8 minutes. Something large, like a sea bass, salmon or turbot, around a kilo or so, will need 12 minutes or more. When done, the flakes in the thickest part should no longer look opaque – so have a gentle poke and look with the point of a knife when you think all is ready. Then it's just a squirt with a lemon, and time to devour.

Things to go with fish

Big chips Chips are a comfort I can mindlessly shovel in. Normally I wouldn't make chips at home as the chip shop does it best, but if it's extra large chips you're after, then it's DIY time. Allow about 250g large King Edward or Maris Piper potatoes per person. Peel, then cut lengthways into fat chips, throwing them into a big bowl of cold water as you go. Drain and jostle them around inside a tea-towel to blot off excess moisture. Heat a third filled large pan of vegetable oil – or deep-fat fryer – until hot enough so that when a chip is tested in it, it bubbles very gently and not furiously. This is blanching temperature – around 120°C/250°F – and will cook the potato through without browning up the outside. Cook the potatoes in batches for about 5 minutes – they should be cooked through (test one with a knife) and still be pale looking. Then drain and spread over kitchen roll. When you're ready to eat, reheat the oil but hotter – 190°C/375°F – and fry the chips in batches until all are perfect chip-coloured and crisp. Drain and scatter with sea salt.

Olive oil and sage roast potatoes Cook this before the fish. Lay 1 sliced onion across the base of a roasting tin, then peel and cut about 1kg semi-cooked new potatoes into thick slices and fit on top of the onion, along with some sage (or thyme). Pour over about 5 tbsp olive oil, and salt and pepper everything. Bring to a frying heat on the hob, then slip into a 200°C/400°F/Gas 6 oven and roast for about 45 minutes or until the potatoes are roasted looking and fork-tender.

Lemon and garlic spinach Lightly fry 3 finely chopped cloves garlic in a dollop of butter and splash of olive oil in a big saucepan until beginning to frazzle, then empty in a big bag of washed spinach leaves. Add a pinch of sugar and stir through until nicely wilted (no water needed). Drain off excess juice and mound on to a plate and squeeze with a fist of lemon.

Fast parsley sauce Finely chop 1 bunch curly parsley (discarding the stems). Put into a saucepan with 300ml fish stock or seasoned water, heat until it bubbles, then pour into a jug. Wipe out the pan, chuck in 40g butter and heat until it foams, then stir in 2 good tbsp plain flour. Still stirring, gently start to pour in the parsley liquor. If it gets lumpy, whack up the heat and beat harder – and the lumps will vanish. Beat in 300ml full-fat milk and keep stirring until it starts to bubble and pop with steam. Season, cook and stir for a further 5 minutes, and it's ready. Good with gammon and slices of roast ham too. (See image on page 179.)

Tartare sauce Simply beat together 250ml mayonnaise (see page 17), a small bunch of parsley, chives or dill, chopped, a finely chopped shallot, and 2 tbsp each of chopped sweet-pickled cocktail gherkins and chopped capers.

Perfect seared salmon with pan-roast tomato salad

I showed my sister how to do this quick-sear way of cooking, and she now swears by it, and can cook a salmon fillet without thinking. Brilliant for every day, and for a dinner. Works well with tuna fillet too. Net-reared salmon needs some help, so it's ideal here, salted and seared – or with some extra flavours bunged on, like pepper and rosemary. Ask your fishmonger for middle-cut fillets from a sizeable fish – they'll be thicker and remain more succulent when cooked. This goes with anything, but here I've plumped for pan-roasted tomatoes and salad.

3 sprigs rosemary
1 clove garlic, sliced
3 tsp sea salt or 1 good tsp salt
1 tsp black peppercorns
750g thick-cut salmon fillet, skin on
   and in 1 piece
extra virgin olive oil
8 baby tomatoes or 16 cherry tomatoes
4 handfuls salad leaves
balsamic vinegar

Strip the rosemary needles from their stems into a mortar, then stick in the garlic, sea salt and peppercorns, and bash well until the garlic has gone pasty and the rosemary is well bruised. Alternatively, chop the rosemary a little, crush the garlic, use a pepper grinder, and mix all together. Sit the salmon fillet on a plate, then tip over the bashed-up salt and rosemary mixture and slop on about 2 tbsp olive oil. Use your finger to rub this all over on both sides.

Heat a heavy frying pan until very hot, then lay the salmon skin side down in the pan and fry, without nudging it around or peeking at its underside, for 4 minutes. Scrape any bits and pieces of herb, oil and things left on the plate over the salmon, patting it on, while it's cooking. Carefully turn the fillet over, then fit around all the whole tomatoes, and sear for a further 2 minutes – jumbling the tomatoes a bit so that they pick up some oil and blister evenly. The salmon will look blackened on its skin side but won't taste burnt – just deliciously salty crisp – and the flesh will be rare in the middle. Cook for a minute or two longer if you prefer it more done – but you'll regret it, once you've tried it rare. Now, slip the cooked fillet on a board, then slice into four wide fingers, serving each with roasted tomatoes and salad, dressing the leaves with olive oil and balsamic vinegar. (See image on page 178.)

Grandma's fish cakes

Talk of fish cakes, and I'm reduced in size and in thoughts, a boy again, legs swinging under my chair at my gran's table. Grandma, pink-faced in the kitchen, battling through a steam of parsley sauce; I in Alan Bennett land, in a sea of bone-handled fish knives and forks and antimacassars, staring out of a 1930s terrace bay window. Clocks tick. I wait. Then a plate of sauced fish cakes is set down on my place mat. Hers were like soft cushions, plumped up with the best flakes of haddock in loose covers of oozing crispness. Good fresh fish and an unhurried fry in lard were their making.

The secret to well-formed, non-collapsing fish cakes is to pre-chill the mixture or cakes before frying. Then to cook them in enough fat, without prodding them around, so that they crisp and hold tight at the sides.

350g smoked haddock, of the dye-free variety,
   or other white fish
300ml milk
about 100g butter
3-4 spring onions, finely chopped
500g cooked potatoes
1 tbsp chopped curly parsley
grating of nutmeg
2 tbsp plain flour
3 tbsp vegetable oil

Poach the haddock in the milk with a knob of butter for 5 minutes, then remove from the milk and leave to cool. Keep 2 tbsp of the milk and then finely flake the fish, removing any bones. Bring the spring onion, a big knob of butter and the kept milk to a gentle bubble in a small saucepan, lightly softening the onion for about 1 minute. Tip this over the cooked potato and mash the lot together, adding the parsley, nutmeg and some salt and pepper. Fold in the flaked fish, then cover, place in the fridge and leave to chill and firm up.

Mould the mixture into four large or eight small balls and press down to form cakes, then dust each in plenty of flour. Return the cakes to the fridge until you are ready to cook. Heat 60g butter with the oil, in a large, preferably non-stick, frying pan. You'll want a shallow pool so that the side of the cakes cook and crisp up too – too shallow and your cakes may fall apart. Fry the cakes until golden brown underneath, then carefully turn them over, and fry this side until crisp looking too. Serve just as they are with tomato ketchup or a poached egg on top, or with parsley sauce and runner beans.

Perfect pan-roast cod

Obviously you can use coley, pollack or haddock fillets here too. All the perfect pan-roast fish fillet desires is a dollop of mash and even a blob of tomato ketchup. Yet when friends come round, I'll make a little something extra special: putting it with deflated tender greens and a good wobble of rosemary aïoli – that's a garlicky herb mayonnaise; or I'll douse the fish in gorgeous parsley sauce, and serve it with some boiled runner beans alongside. Both to-die-for. These two saucings can be found on pages 17 and 176. Ask the fishmonger for the middle cut of the fillet – you want it nice and thick.

4 x 180g (or thereabouts) thick slices cod fillet, with skin
90g butter
olive oil

Rub the fillets with salt and pepper and leave on one side for an hour or so, if you have time. The salt will firm up the fish a bit. Melt the butter in a big ovenproof frying pan and add a good splash of oil (around 2 tbsp), which allows the butter to get hot without burning. If your pan isn't big enough to hold the four fillets, use two pans. Then slip in the cod fillets, skin side down and leave to fry – without titivating or touching them – for about 4 minutes. Slip a spatula carefully under each and turn them over, and then slip the whole pan into a very hot oven – 220°C/425°F/Gas 7 – and leave to roast for about 4 minutes only. Or, if your pan handle isn't ovenproof, once flipped over, carry on frying for a mere 2 minutes more. To test for doneness, slip the tip of a knife between the flakes of one fillet, parting the flesh a little, and things should be looking nice and milky inside and not at all translucent.

Frying-pan trout

I used to spin for trout with my father in mountain streams, while on family caravanning holidays in Germany. After a gut and a rinse, they'd be floured and seasoned, and then fried in butter on the camping stove. I can hear the Calor gas now – a comforting ssshhh that then delivered supper. Some flaked almonds would go into the pan too, and then the whole fish would be served simply with chopped parsley and a lemon wedge. This is it, with my favourite dilled cucumber salad. A farmed trout isn't a patch on a wild caught one, but there again, we can't afford to be fussy. Or maybe we should? Anyways, this turns any old trout into fabulousness.

4 small whole trout, gutted
plain flour
60g butter
2 tbsp olive oil
handful of flaked almonds

Dilled cucumber salad:
½ tbsp caster sugar
3 tbsp white wine vinegar
1 medium cucumber, quartered and shredded
small bunch of dill, chopped
4 good tbsp soured cream

Make the salad first. Beat the sugar with the vinegar in a mixing bowl, then toss in the cucumber and dill. The salad will sit happily pickling for an hour like this.

Give the trout a wipe over, then salt and pepper them and dust them well in flour. Heat the butter and oil in a large frying pan (or two), and then slide in the fish. Fry them gently without moving them for 3-4 minutes, then, armed with a spatula and perhaps a pair of tongs to steady things with, carefully turn them all over. Continue to fry on this side for another 3-4 minutes. At the same time chuck the almonds into all the gaps and let these brown a little, about 2 minutes.

Serve each fish on a plate with the almonds sprinkled over, plus some dilled cucumber blobbed with soured cream.

No-frills grilled mackerel with tzatziki

2 fat cloves garlic, crushed
6 good tbsp thick Greek yoghurt
½ medium-small cucumber
4 fat mackerel, gutted and rinsed,
   heads on or off

Beat the garlic with a small shake of salt into the yoghurt. Using the larger holes on a grater, coarsely grate the cucumber. Give it a squeeze to release excess juice, then stir into the yoghurt mixture and leave in the fridge to chill. Rub the mackerel all over inside and out with salt and pepper, then grill them either under a hot grill or over some hot barbecue coals for about 3 minutes on each side or until well crisped. Eat with a good blob of tzatziki and bread.

PS Cornwall's mackerel handline fishery is the sixth fishery in the world – along with the likes of Alaskan salmon – to be awarded the MSC's (Marine Stewardship Council) sustainability label. It's responsible for protecting the magnificent stock levels of the fish in this area today. Shoals can now reach a staggering 5 miles long and 30 metres deep – and have recovered from the devastation of the 1970s freezer trawlers, that back then, hoovered up 4,000 tons per boat per day.

Herb-grilled sardines on toast

If your sardines are large – like pilchards or small herrings – gut and lightly slash.

12 small sardines
bunch of parsley, most finely chopped
3 shallots, finely chopped
2 fat cloves garlic, crushed
olive oil
2 tbsp white wine vinegar
4 slices toast, buttered or olive oil rubbed

Line the fishes up in a dish, then twist over some pepper and sprinkle with salt. Then chuck the finely chopped parsley over the fish, along with the shallot and garlic. Slop over around 3 tbsp olive oil and then using your fingers shoofty the fish around with the flavourings. Splash with a tbsp of the vinegar and then leave, covered and chilled, until you're ready to grill. Lay the fish out on a foil-lined tray, with all their chopped stuff, put under a hot grill and cook them for about 2-3 minutes on each side, until they're deliciously blistered. Alternatively grill in a preheated heavy frying pan or over barbecue coals (sandwiched side-by-side in one of those wire racks). Serve on toast with a few fresh parsley sprigs, splashed with vinegar (or lemon juice) and a touch of olive oil and pepper.

My favourite steamed fish

Steaming fish is fast and easy, but the flesh needs pumping up with a good smattering of salty seasonings. It's best steamed on the bone, for the bone boots in flavour and holds the flesh in shape. Easy to assemble, it takes only 8 minutes or so to cook, and then takes centre stage in all its whole fish glory. You'll need a good-sized steamer: alternatively buy two small fish – it doesn't matter if the tails climb the sides a little – or cut a large fish into big sections. Another way is to steam-bake it: wrap the fish in an envelope of greaseproof paper, chuck in its flavourings and lubricators, then pop it in a very hot oven for 15 minutes.

1 whole sea bass, trout, mackerel or snapper
   (about 1 kg), gutted
4cm piece fresh root ginger
soy sauce
1 fat clove garlic, finely sliced
6 spring onions, white sliced, green shredded
8 fresh shiitake mushrooms, cut into chunky
   slices
1 tbsp sesame oil
1 large mild red chilli, deseeded and finely
   shredded

Give the fish a rinse under cold water, making sure you give its gutted belly a good sluice out, then drain it and pat it dry with a scrunched piece of kitchen roll. Rub the fish inside and out with a little salt, then place on a heatproof plate (that will fit your steaming tray). Finely grate over about 3cm of the ginger, then rub this all over, and into its cavity, too. Leave the fish on one side for about 30 minutes. While the fish is waiting, finely grate the remaining ginger and pop the pasty mush with its collected juice into a small dipping bowl, then top this up with soy sauce.

Tuck a few slivers of garlic into the fish's cavity, then scatter over the remaining garlic and the white parts of the spring onions, and then tuck the mushrooms around. Then sprinkle with salt, 2 tbsp soy sauce and the sesame oil. Assemble your steamer – half-filling its base with water – and place the fish on its plate in the steaming tray. Cover, then whack on the heat and once steam starts to puff out, cook for about 8 minutes. Serve the fish with all its juices and bits, and scatter it with the shredded green tops of the spring onions and the chilli. Remember the dipping sauce, and of course chopsticks all round. It's a communal plate. You'll need rice

Butter-grilled plaice

In the fishy scheme of things, there's nothing more English than flatfish. There are many, and plaice is the most popular, but you can use any flatfish here. Ideally serve this with parsley sauce (see page 176), or do the lemony herb butter that I suggest here, or if frying, anoint with a squeeze of lemon only. I can't think of an easier supper. Don't try and grill four small plaice – they won't fit in your grill pan – but do one big one instead, or use four fillets. If you want to fry the fish, dust with flour first, then shallow-fry in a mix of butter and oil. You'll need to get out two frying pans for the fillets (if you want everything dished up together) and they'll need around 4 minutes on the skin side, without being moved, then around 2 minutes on the flesh side.

1 large plaice (around 1kg) or other flatfish, or 4
   good-sized fillets
100g butter
good handful of chopped soft herbage (parsley,
   chives, chervil, dill or tarragon)
1 lemon

If you're not using fillets, get your fishmonger to strip the top dark skin off the plaice before you leave the shop. Remove the rack from the grill pan, then line the tray with foil and sit the fish, flesh side up, on the foil. Then melt the butter in a small saucepan, chuck in the herbs and remove from the heat. Salt and pepper the plaice, brush all over with the melted herb butter, and pop under the preheated hot grill and cook for about 5 minutes or so – depending on how fat the fish is. A single big one may well need a full 10 minutes. Brush with more butter again halfway through. Check for doneness by parting some flakes of flesh at a thick part with the tip of a knife – they should look white, not translucent. Serve with a squeeze of lemon and the melted herb butter poured over. Some boiled new potatoes and peas would be nice.

Salt and pepper crispy squid

Squid, we love it – but love it best disguised, like battered calamari. This way with it is my all-time favourite: fried till just scrunchy, then garlic and chilli gunged, with a fab Vietnamesy dip to dunk into. Like all frying, it's wok-to-plate eating, so don't be too ambitious – keep this for a supper served in the kitchen, so that everything is kept crisp and instant. Pre-prepared large squid tubes – beautifully white, skinned and ready to cook – can be had in 1kg bags from the freezers of oriental stores, and very cheaply. Frozen at source they're very good. Or buy the squid fresh from your fish man – who will prepare them for you – but they'll cost more. And nothing titchy. Once you've wielded your knife over squid and veg, and stirred a few liquids together, the cooking lasts mere minutes. And remember, it's done in no time: any longer and you'll be into rubber, and a fetishist's supper. On-yer-bike calamari.

1kg (about 4) prepared large squid tubes
4 tbsp fish sauce
3 large mild chillies, deseeded and roughly chopped
3 small hot red chillies, deseeded and finely sliced
6 spring onions, chopped
8 cloves garlic, 6 sliced, 2 crushed
2 handfuls coriander leaves
4 tbsp each of lime juice and rice vinegar
2 tbsp caster sugar
vegetable or sunflower oil for frying
4 tbsp cornflour
lettuce leaves (cos, batavia etc.)

Slice through the side of each squid tube, so that they're one flat piece of flesh, then cut each in half lengthways, and lay them inside surfaces facing up. Then using the tip of a knife score a cross-hatch lattice-like pattern of cuts across the flesh of each piece – without slicing right through. Cut the squid into wide strips and toss them in a bowl with salt and pepper and ½ tbsp of the fish sauce.

Meanwhile, assemble the chillies, spring onions and garlic in piles, along with the coriander leaves. Then make the dipping sauce: stir together the lime juice and vinegar, the remaining fish sauce, 1 tbsp water, the sugar and crushed garlic. Drop in a few bits of spring onion and the sliced hot chilli, and leave on one side.

When ready to cook, preheat the oven to 180°C/350°F/Gas 4. Lay some kitchen roll over a large baking tray and put a spider (basket spoon) or some tongs at the ready.

Pour oil into the wok, until it reaches around 8cm deep, and then heat it until it's hot – but not smoking. Meanwhile, chuck the cornflour into the bowl of squid and toss well together. Then take about a third of the squid bits and slide them into the oil and fry for around 2 minutes – giving them a little prod and a dunk halfway through to separate them. Lift out and drip-drain, then spread over the lined tray and slip them into the oven to keep warm, while you carry on with the rest.

When ready, tip the oil out of the wok and wipe it clean, then add 3 tbsp oil. Chuck in the sliced garlic and gently fry until touched gold, then add the mild chilli and spring onion and stir-fry for about 30 seconds or so, then strain. Serve the squid scattered with all the crispy things, set the leaves alongside and the all-important dipping sauce. Tuck straight in – folding the squid in the leaves, dunking each earth-shattering mouthful into the sauce first.

A proper fish pie

This is a no-messin' fish pie. One for all times and all occasions. A good fish pie is nowhere without a delicious sauce and that's a sauce made from full-fat milk, made velvety with butter, with its full quota of parsley dots and – most importantly – with its stock gleaned from smoked haddock. No matter how beautiful your cod and prawns, without a full-on flavoured sauce, the pie is a goner. Here's perfection. Yields six good-sized portions (and could stretch to eight).

1kg floury potatoes
450ml full-fat milk
120g butter
100g Cheddar, grated
500g haddock or cod fillet, large fillets cut in
   half
500g smoked undyed haddock fillet, large fillets
   cut in half
2 bay leaves
50g plain flour
handful of curly parsley leaves, chopped
250g cooked and peeled medium-sized prawns
4 hard-boiled eggs, shelled and roughly chopped
1 small egg, beaten

To make the mash topping, peel and halve the spuds, then cook them gently in salted water for about 20-25 minutes or until a knife pierces without any resistance, then drain them (save some of the water in case it's needed later). Mash the potatoes with a splash of milk (about 60ml), around 30g of butter, and a dash of salt, until nice and smooth but not too sloppy. Then mash in most of the grated Cheddar and leave to cool.

Meanwhile prepare the fish. Put the fish fillets in a wide pan that will hold them snugly and pour over the remaining milk. Tuck in the bay leaves and dot with a tbsp of the butter. Add some pepper but hold back on the salt at this point, as the smoked haddock will flood the milk with salt. Bring to a gentle bubble and poach for about 5 minutes or until the fish is just cooked through: the flakes should no longer look opaque, a curd will have formed on the surface of the milk and, if cooking cod, the same sort of curd will have formed between the flakes. Remember the fish will be cooked further once it has gone into the pie, so don't overcook it – better under than over at this point. Flake the fish into large chunks, discarding skin, bones and bay leaves, but keeping all the buttery milk.

Now for that perfect sauce. Melt the remaining butter in a wide saucepan over a gentle heat, then stir in the flour to make a thin paste – but do not let it brown. Then gradually, and stirring all the time, add the reserved fish milk to make a white sauce. Heat it and let it bubble for a few minutes to cook out the flour, stirring frequently so that it doesn't catch. Then chuck in the parsley and dilute with some of the potato water if it's too thick. It should be gloopy, not heavy. Now stick your finger in and taste it, and if it needs a dab more salt add some. Carefully fold in the flakes of fish and the prawns, and fold the hard-boiled eggs in too. Don't stir, as you want to keep the chunks of fish whole and not send them into a mush. Now leave everything to cool. Cooling solidifies the sauce and makes the whole pie assembly job much more manageable.

To assemble, spoon the fish mixture into a large shallow ovenproof dish, then spoon the mash in large blobs all over the top, gently forking the dollops down. Scatter over the remaining cheese and lightly fork it in, patterning it so that it can build a good crust. Finally, brush all over with the beaten egg and bake in a 220°C/425°F/Gas 7 oven for about 40-50 minutes, until touched with brown all over. If it starts to brown too quickly, cover with foil.

favourite tarts

When it comes to good fruit tarts, the French know best. They make them wheel-sized and then artfully pack them with neat spirals of precision-sliced fruit. Back in my previous incarnation as an antiques dealer, I used to make monthly trips to Clignancourt, the antiques quarter of Paris. At the end of a morning's haggling I'd dive into one of the many cafés and sit down to a gargantuan slice of apple, apricot or greengage tart; its base baked until wafer crisp, yet slightly floppy if I dared pick it up. The fruit was cooked to the point of collapse, and the whole wedge encased in a pectin- rich glaze, the shrinking ripple of sliced fruit kept luscious under a film of set syrup. The balance of sweet with tang and crisp with flaccid, so perfect. It gave me a bigger buzz than the bric-à-brac, hence goodbye antique-ing, hello cooking.

A fruit tart shouldn't be fancy, for it should taste of the fruit that it is. As the fruit cooks, it bubbles out nectar-like juices, which in turn poach and steam the fruit into shape. The sugars ooze, caramelise and blister. In short the fruit just gets on with the work. All you have to do is provide pastry, a little sugar and an oven.

Now, pastry. What are your thoughts? Flour-dusted hands, a silky blanket of doughy loveliness and a smile? Or perhaps white stuff all over clothes and floor, and a collapsed, misbehaving clag of ill-shaped something-or-other, topped off with a load of bad karma – or am I being over-generous? It either instils terror, is *the* no-can-do or it brings moments of blissful therapy and, more to the point, the beginnings of something rather good to eat.

I'm not going to prattle on about how making pastry is an effortless task. It isn't. But I reckon if you can drive a car, use a computer, send text messages, set the video or make the bed, you can make pastry too. Don't ask me why those. It's just a mind-set thing. Apply and you will achieve. If you don't want to, I don't blame you either. In cooking you should only do what you want to do. There's some great ready-made shortcrust and puff pastry in the supermarkets now – and you can buy it ready-rolled too. I'd much prefer you made something here than not. Domestic gods and goddesses always cheat, that's how they get to where they are.

Perfect shortcrust pastry

Look, I don't want to waste your time. It looks an absolute yawn but it's just to give you lots of tips, not turn you off. But don't read it if pastry really is not your thing – buy pastry and skip all this.

What's the key to making pastry? Keep cool. Everything you're working with – and you. Having all your ingredients, work surface, tins and any bowls that you use along the way, starting at a cool temperature, is really going to help. It's the butter that can play up. The butter holds the paste together and mustn't get too warm. Unfortunately the kitchen, being the kitchen, is not always the coolest place to make pastry, so try and do it before you embark on any oven or hob stuff.

Where do I start? First tip the flour on to a smooth surface, or if you fear the mess and prefer to keep things more contained, into a mixing bowl. There's no need to sieve it or shake it all over the place. Next, sprinkle over the sugar (if using). Then take the cold butter from the fridge and cut it into rough little chunks and let them plop into the mound of flour as you cut. Now, using your hands, you need to 'work' the flour and sugar into the butter: gently rub the flour-coated butter between thumbs and forefingers, letting it fall back again, while simultaneously scooping up more flour and squashed buttery bits. As you work, the lumps will become more crumb like, until eventually they become like fine breadcrumbs. This takes minutes. Next, make a dip in the pile of crumbs and add 2 tbsp water and work it in, compressing the mixture together to make a smooth pliable dough. You may well have to add up to another tbsp water to reach this but add it in dribs and drabs, working each extra splash in thoroughly before you add the next. If you have a processor, you can do all of this paragraph in it.

How do I know when the dough is right? The dough must be smooth and free of any lumps and it must also be a little elastic – too dry and it will crack and crumble when it comes to rolling it out. The best way to test this is to flatten it a little and if it splits and cracks, work in a dash more water. Then roll the dough into a neat ball, flatten it into a large burger shape, wrap in clingfilm, and refrigerate for a good 30 minutes. This resting helps the rolling out later and also helps prevent shrinkage when it comes to the baking bit.

What sort of rolling pin do I use? The simplest. The sort that's just a wooden pole – no revolving drum, no handles – and preferably a long one if making a large tart. This sort will give you perfect rolling control. Using anything fancy that rotates around a pole, made of marble or stainless steel, is a sure way to making life difficult. The simple wood pole allows you to gauge pressure and make friends with your pastry.

How do I roll? Unwrap the chilled pastry and let it sit for a while, so that it comes nearer to room temperature – a good 10 minutes. Then lightly dust your surface, dough and rolling pin with flour. Have a little pile of flour at hand to keep everything in motion. Start by rolling the dough quite firmly, applying a forceful but controlled pressure of equal strength through both hands. And turn over after every two sweeps. As the pastry thins, reduce the pressure and roll lightly, swivelling the pastry a little after each two sweeps and turn over after about ten sweeps, dusting it with flour before you turn. Always roll with the shape of your tin in mind – saves on any patching-up later – and reduce pressure slightly when you reach the edges of the paste as here it's at its weakest. Try and work deftly and quickly and

keep hand contact with the paste to a minimum, to prevent the butter in the pastry from over-warming and turning greasy. Remember: lightness of touch. Ideally, the pastry should end up around 3mm thick.

My pastry's got cracks in Cracks will always appear when you roll, especially in the early stages when the dough is stiff and especially if it is too cold. It needs a little working with the rolling pin. Press the cracks back together and for those that occur later, knock in the offending edges, to prevent the cracks deepening.

What sort of tart dish do I use? Use a metal tin, as this bakes and crisps the pastry better than a ceramic flan dish, and one with a loose base, so that it can be lifted out for serving. Plain or fluted, it doesn't matter, then lightly grease the inside with butter. Or use a metal tart ring (that's a band without a base) and set this on a lightly greased heavy baking sheet.

And the safest way to get the pastry in? Dust the rolled out pastry all over lightly with flour. Then, to get it in one piece into the tin – without it tearing on you – roll it up on the rolling pin and then unroll it again into the tin. Don't force the pastry into the tin but allow the sides of the circle to flop inward so that the tin's edges don't tear through. Next, ease the dough into the base, then press the flopped inward dough back out and into the sides of the tin, making sure it goes into all the concave ribs (if using a fluted tin). Trim off the excess pastry but not to the rim: leave about a 1cm overhang. The overhang helps prevent shrinkage of the sides in its first baking. You can trim it neat to the rim

of the tin if you want to, especially if the tart case is very shallow.

My pastry doesn't fit properly No problem. If the pastry doesn't quite make it up one side of the tin you can patch it in with an offcut. Stick it against the offending side and smooth together. A dab of water on the surfaces will help bond it. Now, if hell happens and your pastry collapses in half on its way into the tin, it's not war time, just patch and push it together once in the tin. Once the filling is in and the tart is finished no one's going to know anyway.

What's baking blind? Some pastry cases are baked without their filling first, to get the pastry part-cooked and sealed, so the filling doesn't turn it all soggy. A must for tarts with liquid fillings. The blind bit refers to the fact that the pastry is lined on top with greaseproof paper or foil which is then weighted with baking beans or uncooked rice to hold the sides up. I use rice, and I line my case with clingfilm: it fits more snugly than the paper, and is ovenproof. First, prick the pastry base all over with a fork, then line it as suggested and fill right up with rice. Now, set the tin on a baking sheet and slide on to the middle shelf of a 180°C/350°F/Gas 4 oven and bake for 10 minutes, then take out and carefully remove the rice and the lining (keep this rice for the same use – it will last for years). The pastry won't be cooked and will look pasty but will be set. If you opted for a pastry overhang, now's the time to carefully trim it off. Then bake the now exposed case once again for a further 10 minutes.

Phew. Now you're well armed – or asleep on the sofa perhaps.

Your everyday sweet shortcrust pastry

For a savoury shortcrust – for quiches, flans and pies – just leave the sugar out. Meat pie pastry is good made with half butter/half lard. For pastry-making tips see pages 189-90. Makes 250g pastry.

160g plain flour
1 tbsp caster sugar
80g cold butter (straight from the fridge)

Put the flour, sugar and butter into a processor and then pulse-blast to make a breadcrumby looking mix. Next add 2 tbsp of cold water through the feed tube and pulse in to make a dough, then have a look at it and see if it's pliable enough. If not, pulse in a ½ tbsp more, and so on. Knead it a little and mould it into a round ball, flatten, then wrap in clingfilm and refrigerate for 30 minutes or until it's needed.

The ultimate rich shortcrust pastry

The French call this pâte sucrée *– it's rich, sweet, short and crumbly. If you care to tune into old money – as in Imperial ounces – it's so easy to remember. It's 3,3,3 and 6: 3oz sugar, 3oz butter, 3 egg yolks and 6oz flour. You can take it in your head wherever you go then. Makes 350g pastry.*

80g caster sugar
80g butter (unsalted if you like)
3 medium egg yolks
160g plain flour

Put all the sugar, butter and egg yolks into a processor and pulse to a rough paste – not too much. Then tip in the flour and pulse again until a dough is formed. Next, knead it a little until it's smooth and then mould into a round ball, flatten it, wrap in clingfilm and refrigerate for 30 minutes or until you want it. If making this one by hand, put the flour in a mixing bowl and make a deep well in the middle, then cut the butter into small chunks, letting them drop in to the middle. Shake over the sugar and drop in the egg yolks then, using a fork, mash together the butter, sugar and eggs – it doesn't matter if some flour falls in too. Then slowly draw in the flour, and work to a dough.

Extra treacle tart

It couldn't be easier or more delicious. Slices into eight.

350g shortcrust pastry (1⅛ x either recipe on
  page 191)
butter for greasing
9 tbsp golden syrup
2 tbsp treacle
200g fine white breadcrumbs

Roll out the pastry on a lightly floured surface until
about 3mm thick. Then grease a shallow 24cm diameter
(or smaller if you want) tart tin or tin plate and line with
the pastry, trimming off the bits but keeping them. Put
the golden syrup and treacle in a pan and gently warm
through until runny, then tip in the breadcrumbs and
stir through. Spoon this mixture into the pastry-lined tart
tin and level over, so that the filling is evenly spread
without gaps. Now, if you want to get fancy, re-roll the
pastry scraps, cut into thin strips, and make a weave of
these on top, carefully pressing the ends on to the pastry
rim. Then bake in a 190°C/375°F/Gas 5 oven for 30
minutes or until the pastry is crisp. Serve while still just
warm – if you can – with loads and loads of custard or
double cream.

Exquisite lemon tart

*This is the big generous restaurant lemon tart. I don't see it
around any more, so let's bring it back – it's exquisite. All
the tips on how to roll pastry, line the tin and baking blind
can be had on pages 189-90. Slices into eight big deep
wedges.*

butter for greasing
350g sweet shortcrust pastry (1⅛ x recipe on
  page 191)
3½ unwaxed lemons
260g caster sugar
6 medium eggs
160ml double cream, plus more to serve

The quantity of lemon and egg cream three-quarter fills
a 4cm deep x 24cm diameter tart tin. Plain or fluted, it
doesn't matter. Lightly grease the inside with butter.
Next roll out the pastry on a lightly floured surface until
3mm thick and then line the tin with it, leaving a 1cm
overhang. Blind-bake the case as described on page 190.

Meanwhile, make the filling. Finely grate the zest of 1½
of the lemons into a big mixing bowl, then add the sugar
and the eggs and whisk together. Stir in the juice from all
the lemons, then the cream. Scoop off any froth from the
top of the mixture and pour into the pastry case as soon
as it's ready. The egg seals on the hot pastry, preventing
later sogginess. It's best to pour the lemon mixture into
the tart case while it's sat on the pulled-out oven shelf –
saves any slopping and spillage from work surface to
oven. Then turn the oven down to 150°C/300°F/Gas 2
and bake for about 50-60 minutes. If you've made a tart
smaller than mine, reduce the time to around 35-40
minutes. It should have the slightest wobble to its centre
when pulled from the oven. Allow it to cool slowly; too
fast and the custard can develop a fissure – but this can
add character. Eat while still just warm (if time allows)
and with lots of cold double cream.

Giving it a crunchy caramelised top is very much
optional, it's a cheffy thing and you'll need a blow torch
for the job: just dust heavily with icing sugar and give it
a blast all over until the sugar bubbles into dark glassy
beads and bobbles.

Emergency apricot tart

This is my emergency tart, a big tray of a tart. No matter how last-minute I am, treating it rough and tough, it's always a beautiful thing. The apricots get on with the tart-making, as they ooze a delicious concentrate which does wonders with the pastry. If you can't find apricots, use plums instead. Failing that, leave off the sugar and flour layer and cover the pastry in finely sliced apple – and brush with the glaze after baking. For those with time and a hammer: inside the apricot stone lies a marzipan-tasting kernel and if you thwack open the stone (they're brutishly tough), these can be strewn over the tart or ground up and used instead of the flour over the base.

18 apricots
1 x 425g pack ready-made pre-rolled puff pastry
1½ tbsp ground almonds or plain flour
3 tbsp caster sugar
1 medium egg, lightly beaten
4 tbsp apricot jam

Using a small stubby knife and holding an apricot in the other hand, slice the fruit lengthways into three wedges – allowing the tip of the knife to follow the stone. This is very easy, and your pace will quicken as you master this Jack-the-Ripper action. Next, unroll the pastry on to a greased baking sheet – something near the size of the pastry (and one with a small lip would be ideal) – then scatter with the ground almonds or flour and half of the sugar, avoiding the edge. Line the apricot wedges across the tart, each row overlapping the last, so that the pointy bits stick up a little. Scatter over the rest of the sugar, liberally brush all the exposed edges of pastry with beaten egg and bake on the middle shelf of a preheated 220°C/425°F/Gas 7 oven for about 30 minutes or until crisped around the edges. The apricot's tips should be lightly seared and the pastry cooked through underneath.

Stir the apricot jam with 2 tbsp of water in a small saucepan over the hob until blended and syrupy, then brush this all over everything once it has cooled for a few minutes. Eat cut into big squares – hopefully while still slightly warm – and go crazy on the crème fraîche or double cream (or both).

Exceedingly good Bakewell tart

That Mr Kipling, he did some exceedingly good Bakewell slices, I well remember. You see Mum didn't do tarts, they came in finger-form out of packets – and we loved them. I became tart maker. Again, if you don't want to make the pastry, no probs, use a bought packet of sweet shortcrust instead.

500g ultimate rich shortcrust pastry (2 x recipe on page 191), or bought
1 medium egg white, beaten
5 tbsp strawberry or raspberry jam
100g unsalted butter
120g caster sugar
3 medium eggs
½ tsp almond essence
150g ground almonds
granulated sugar

Roll out the pastry until about 3mm thick, and use to line a greased 24cm diameter shallow tart tin, trimming the pastry to fit the tin. Leave to chill in the fridge for a good half-hour, then prick all over with a fork and bake blind (see page 190) for 15 minutes in a 180°C/350°F/Gas 4 oven. Remove the liner and rice, brush with a little of the beaten egg white, and bake for a further 10 minutes. Cool a little.

Next, spread the jam over the base of the pastry case. Beat the butter with the sugar until pale and fluffy, then slowly beat in the whole eggs, one by one, along with the almond essence – a mixer will make light work of this. Next, fold in the ground almonds, then spoon the mixture into the tart case, and level. Beat the egg white until it's foamy and brush it over the tart, then sprinkle the top with granulated sugar. Bake the tart for 45 minutes or so on the middle shelf of a 190°C/375°F/Gas 5 oven, until cooked and lightly coloured on top. Serve while still warm, with floods of double cream. God, it's good.

Deluxe strawberry tart

Serves eight with some seconds – and you'll need them. Eat the day you make it – it won't keep, and neither should it have to.

500g ultimate rich shortcrust pastry (2 x recipe on page 191), or bought
60g caster sugar, plus 1 tbsp
250g raspberries
1kg strawberries
1 medium egg
1 x 250g tub mascarpone cheese

Lightly grease a shallow 28cm diameter tart tin – or something a bit smaller if you don't have anything so vast. Then roll out the pastry on a lightly floured surface, until about 3mm thick, and fit it into the tart tin. Next, prick all over with a fork, then blind-bake (see page 190) on the middle shelf of a 200°C/400°F/Gas 6 oven for 10 minutes. Then turn the oven down to 190°C/375°F/Gas 5, remove the liner and rice, and bake for a further 20 minutes until blushed light gold and cooked.

Put the 60g of sugar, the raspberries and 1 tbsp water in a saucepan and heat until the berries have broken down, then sieve, pushing through the flesh, discarding all the pippy gunk. Next, stir in the strawberries and leave the berry mixture to cool to room temperature. Meanwhile, beat the 1 tbsp sugar with the egg until pale, then beat in the mascarpone until well blended. Spread this mixture across the tart base and chill. Shortly before serving, remove the strawberries from their raspberry bath, then arrange them all over the tart, noses pointing up. Serve slices with pools of the kept raspberry sauce. Delicious.

Fry-pan apple tarte tatin

Tarte tatin is baked upside-down – fruit on the bottom and pastry on top – and then turned out, so it's served the right way up. But more to the point, it's the most glorious full-on thing you can do with apples. Here the apples are islands lapped by a dark caramel sea and the pastry edges lap it up too. I have to say, this is a tart to knock all tarts flat. It's just too gorgeous for words. Something creamy on plating up is compulsory. You can swap ripe pears for the apples. This will cut into six generous portions.

350g ready-made bought puff pastry or the pre-rolled puff
5 Cox's apples
200g caster sugar
100g unsalted butter
½ tsp ground cinnamon

First, select a suitable all-steel frying pan to cook the tart in – such as an omelette pan or preferably one with steeper sides, measuring a good 18cm across its base. Then, roll out the pastry until 3mm thick and cut out a pastry circle that's a good 3cm wider in diameter than the base of the frying pan – imprint the pan base on the pastry and then use this as a guide. The cut circle doesn't have to be perfect. Chill in the fridge until needed.

Next, core and peel the apples and cut them in half lengthways. Melt the sugar in the frying pan until lightly caramelised. Watch it, for it mustn't turn to a deep red wine colour and burn. If you can't monitor the colour because your pan is black, do it in a stainless-steel pan, then tip it into the frying pan. Stir in the butter to make a toffeed caramel sauce – watch out for splutters. Arrange the apples, cut side up, on top of the caramel in the pan, then sprinkle with the cinnamon. They should be packed tight with only a few gaps here and there. Then put the pan on the hob over a medium heat, cover, and bubble for about 5-8 minutes.

Place the pastry circle over the apples in the pan and tuck down the sides so that the edges of the pastry reach the bottom of the pan and are awash in caramel. If the pan is hot, use a fork or knife to ease the pastry down. If the apples are hogging the sides, shunt them around a bit. Don't worry if there are any rucks or folds in the pastry or if the pastry is splashed with caramel – it's all part of the charm. Just aim to get the pastry tucked down on all sides. Once cooked and inverted this will form a frisbee-shaped base to the tart, with deliciously goo-crisped edges.

Place straightaway on the top shelf of a 190°C/375°F/Gas 5 oven and bake for about 30 minutes or until the pastry is well puffed up, crisp and golden looking. Take out of the oven and leave to cool a little – just as it is. Then after a good hour or so, enough time for the apples to take on the caramel and exchange juices, gently reheat on the hob, then it's time to tip it out. Place a serving plate – one with a deep rim to hold any caramel spill – on top of the frying pan and, holding the plate firmly on the pan, invert the tart on to the plate.

Eat with double or clotted cream or a good spoonful of vanilla ice-cream. Heaven.

Toffeed baby apple tart with ginger

650g large cultivated crab apples or other baby apples
juice of 1 lemon
1 sheet prepared puff pastry or sweet shortcrust pastry, about 3mm thick
500g caster sugar
5cm piece fresh root ginger, peeled and chopped
100g butter
½ tsp ground allspice

Peel the apples and core if large, and place in water acidulated with the lemon juice. Cut the pastry into a 25cm round – or 3cm wider than the base of the ovenproof pan you have chosen to bake it in – then cover and chill. Meanwhile, put the sugar, ginger and 1 tbsp water into a small pan, melt over a gentle heat until golden and a light caramel colour, then stir in the butter – watch out for splutters.

Put the apples into a baking dish, stems upward, pour over the toffee sauce, cover loosely with foil and bake at 180°C/350°F/Gas 4 for 20-30 minutes or until the apples are nearly tender. Remove from the oven and increase the heat to 190°C/375°F/Gas 5. Pack the apples into a heavy-based 22cm round tin or ovenproof frying pan. Sprinkle with ground allspice, then strain over the toffee syrup, discarding the ginger. Next, lay the pastry over the top, tucking the sides down into the pan – not sealing it to the sides. Bake in the oven for 30 minutes or until the pastry is golden. Invert the tart on to a plate and serve warm with thick cream or crème fraîche.

Pancakes and proper puddings

One grandmother baked and boiled, producing steaming puddings and things on my every visit; the other smoked and watched *Crossroads*, pulling out a packet of jam tarts or a Battenburg cake. One was fat and cuddly, the other as skinny and as well-dressed as a Sobranie cigarette. Both were lovely and had lovely things to eat. Very good summer pudding was made by Mum's old schoolfriend Anne; it cut into thick cold wedges of pressed summer fruit, was heavy with raspberries and always looked the part, sat triumphant on its dish in the middle of her polished mahogany table. It looked fabulous and went down impressively, yet I now know it's so easy to make. Mum (who incidentally had her eye not on the pud but on the nice set of cabriole-legged chairs that matched Anne's table) made crumbles and apple pies, though mousses and meringues – anything stuffed with cream in fact – were more her thing. Around my birthday time (late September), we'd all go blackberrying, and back home we'd get out this apple-corer and slicer – a hand-turned contraption that made short work of an apple – and then pile sliced apples and blackberries into an oval green Denby pie dish and make a rich buttery crumble for the top. Then there were the boil-in-the-can sponge puddings – officially Dad's army compo rations – we had on camping holidays, saturated with golden syrup. Loved those. Home-made or packets, it was all good to me. Still is.

The perfect pancake

The secret of the perfect pancake comes down – well, pretty much – to the pan and its pre-preparation. It's not rocket science, so no worries. You want a carbon-steel frying pan around 20cm across its base – something you might make an omelette in. It should hopefully have seen a bit of cooking and therefore be quite black, with a nice sheen. A non-stick pan is fine too. To prepare the pan, it's essential to get it quite hot and well greased. You're not going to be frying but searing the pancake: a kind of hotplate sear-fry process. A dash of oil is poured into the pan, swirled all around to coat, then poured out again. This seasons the pan, impregnating it with a fat layer. The fat layer has to be replenished before each ladleful of your pancake mix is poured into the pan, so keep a little heatproof jug on the side, into which you can drain out the hot oil. The making of the pancake mix itself is a breeze.

How do I cook it then? I've added butter to the batter mix, as this further lubricates it as it cooks, and gives the pancake a lovely lacey golden touch – and a richer flavour too. So no need to add more oil as it cooks. Next, pour enough batter into the centre of the pan, so that when it spreads it covers the base thinly. Just under a standard ladleful is the measure. Too much and your pancakes will turn out thick and blubbery. The first one is always the tester – and usually bites the dust.

How do I swirl? The batter must coat the pan evenly. Initially I swirl it across by gently using the base of the ladle to move the batter out, and then pick up the pan and angle it about a bit, to send the floating upper layer of batter around the sides. After that, just let it be, over a not-too-fierce heat for about 2 minutes, giving the pan a little shake after about a good minute or so. If the pancake is loose it will probably be ready for turning; if it doesn't move, leave it longer. Then carefully, using a bendy-bladed knife (palette knife), turn the pancake over. If you can flip it, then do it – and I don't mean high antics with the pan, unless of course you want to eat your pud off the kitchen floor. Now cook its virgin side for the same amount of time.

My pancake isn't looking like the picture Hopefully, it will – but for me the first never does. The first pancake can turn out a bit bodged, even for the flashiest pancake maker. Ideally, before the flip, the batter will have set underneath and should be patterned with a lace of goldenness. Too black? Then you've got the heat too high or left it way too long. The first one in seems to let the pan and everything know what is wanted and then sets things in motion – you'll now be able to judge the fat quantity, the action, and the heat that's required – and then all that follow will be good. Once you're in the groove, it flows.

Perfect pancakes

This is plain and simple, the Shrove Tuesday version with lemon and sugar. Or do that Little Chef thing, and roll them up with a slice of vanilla ice-cream in the middle, then plop some canned black cherries on the side in a reduction of their own syrupy juice; wrap them around mascarpone cheese and then drench with maple syrup; and they're fantastic too when wrapped around a scoop of the easy lemon ice-cream on page 222. What you're after is something creamy and collapsing inside with something sticky sweet to say hello on the outside. Things must delta, slither and slide. If you want your pancakes plumper and less crêpe-like, use 200ml milk only and add 3 tbsp water to the mix. Swot up on the notes on page 201, then proceed with the recipe below.

120g plain flour
2 medium eggs
300ml milk
50g butter, melted
1 tbsp vegetable oil or a knob of butter
caster or icing sugar
2 lemons, halved

Drop the flour, eggs, milk, butter and a pinch of salt into a processor or liquidiser and then blend to a smooth batter. Alternatively whisk it all together in a bowl. Pour the batter into a jug and leave it to stand on one side for a good 20 minutes. Next, heat your chosen frying pan – something approximately 20cm across its base (but no rulers please) – add the oil and swirl around so that it coats the pan, then tip the excess out.

Next, pour in a ladleful of batter and swirl around so that the batter coats the pan evenly. Leave it to cook over a medium heat for about 2 minutes, giving the pan a little shake after about a minute or so. If it shifts, have a peek at its underside and turn the pancake over. It should be golden (but if it's blackened, chuck it and start again). Then cook the next side for around the same amount of time, until golden. After the pancake is cooked on it's other side, place it on a warmed plate, then carry on with the rest – you should be able to get about 12 pancakes from the mix (three each). Stack them one on top of the other as you go – covering with a tea-towel or foil in a low oven until you are ready to serve.

To serve the pancakes, roll them up, shake over some sugar (icing sugar if you prefer), then squeeze with loads of lemon. Want to take it one step further? Then follow the orange and brandy butter sauce recipe below.

Orange and brandy butter sauce

Time now to put your Galloping Gourmet hat on and flambé all the way to the table.

50g caster sugar
3 oranges
125g butter
2 tbsp each Cointreau and brandy

Put the caster sugar into the frying pan that you cooked the pancakes in and then very finely grate the zest of 1 orange over the top. Allow the sugar to melt without stirring it, over a medium heat. Once it starts to caramelise and darken, stir in the juice of 3 oranges and the butter – watching out for splutters for the sugar will be desperately hot – and then let it gently bubble together for a minute or two. Spoon in the Cointreau and brandy and bubble up for a minute or two – at this point you can ignite it if you wish. Pour this sauce over your warm rolled-up or folded pancakes (pre-wrapped with crème fraîche, mascarpone or ice-cream, perhaps?).

Sumptuous summer pudding

Bread and berries as a pud. It may sound like no-I-don't-want-to-go-there land, yet it's one of those screamingly British out-of-sorts combinations that turns up trumps. Along with its winter twin, bread and butter pudding, it's an absolute seasonal classic. A summer pud should be slightly tart, for too jam-sweet and it's cloying. Get it just right – as I've measured below – and it's to-die-for. And no strawberries – a true summer pudding holds the later berries of summer only. This pud must be made at least the day before, to give it time to set. Even the day before that is fine too. Serves six with some seconds. To make one for four, halve the quantities and use a 600ml pudding bowl.

And if you have any leftover, make a summer pud semifreddo (soft ice-cream). Briefly pulse in a processor and add, ripple-like, to a tub of part-defrosted vanilla ice-cream. Freeze again, and serve in scoops or slices.

500g raspberries
500g mixed berries, such as redcurrants,
  blackcurrants, blueberries or blackberries
180g caster sugar
1 loaf thick-sliced white bread (a good one)

Check over the punnets of fruit and turf out anything squashy. Next, using a fork, for speed and ease, strip the redcurrants and/or blackcurrants off their stalks. Then put these with all the other fruit into a pan, tip in the sugar, stir through and then stick on a gentle heat. As soon as the fruit begins to release its juices and all the sugar has dissolved, which won't take long, then gently bubble together for about 4-5 minutes. The fruit will have given up lots of juice and should be swimming in it, yet should remain distinguishable and not be a mush. Now leave it to cool a little.

Meanwhile, cut the crusts off 12 slices of bread.

Next, strain off about half the juice into a dish (I do it through a sieve to keep the pips out), then dip a bread slice into it, so that one side becomes saturated with pink, then lay this in a 1.2 litre bowl (of the Pyrex pudding-bowl shape), so that its juice-soaked side hugs the side of the bowl. Do the same with the rest of the bread, overlapping the last slice of bread each time, to make a spiral arrangement. You'll find that the overlap is greater at the base of the bowl – this is fine. Also the bread at this stage will not sit snugly, but don't fret, for as soon as you spoon in the berries and juice, the bread will flatten down and behave itself. Finish by placing a full slice of bread at the bottom. The thing to make sure of is that there aren't any gaps – it doesn't matter how higgledy-piggledy it all appears. Next, pile in the fruit with some of the juice, then blanket the top with more overlapping squares of bread, squishing their edges snugly within the surrounding perimeter of bread edges. You should have a good pool of juice and berries left over – to hang on to for serving. Fit a saucer over the dish so that the rim just fits inside the rim of the bowl, and squash it on, so that things squish out a bit, then weight it with something heavy, like a large can of food. Put in the fridge and leave to chill overnight. It needs time to set.

To remove the pud, trim off any overhanging squished-out bits, then loosen the sides with a bendy knife. Invert on to a deep plate, and pour over the remaining berry juices. Eat sliced wedges with a ton of thick cream.

Bread and butter pudding

Old-school bread and butter pud I find a bit too flabby to stomach, and I much prefer this way, where you make a proper rich custard with yolks only. Go even more up-market by adding 2 tbsp brandy to the custard or soak the sultanas in rum first.

12 slices white bread
butter
2 tbsp each of raisins and sultanas
8 medium egg yolks
100g caster sugar
300ml full-fat milk
280ml double cream

Remove the crusts from the bread and then cut each slice into two triangles. Then grease a 20 x 25cm baking dish or tin – or something of similar size – with butter. Next, butter the bread, then place it in an overlapping layer in the bottom of the dish and sprinkle with a few raisins and sultanas. Repeat with another layer and another, until the dish is full.

Beat the egg yolks with the sugar, then beat in the milk and the cream. Pour the custard over the bread and leave it to soak in for a good half-hour. It needs this time, for the custard must have time to soak into everything before it's baked. Next, place a folded tea-towel (or folded newspaper) on the bottom of a large roasting tin, and sit the pudding tin on top. Now, half fill the roasting tin with hot water, so that it comes halfway up the outside of the bread pudding tin, then slide on to the middle shelf of a 160°C/325°F/Gas 3 oven and bake for around 1¼ hours or until just set. If the top hasn't developed a few ears of golden crunchy bread, then dust all over with more sugar and finish off under a hot grill – but watch it doesn't char.

Christmas panettone pudding

This is bread and butter pudding made with the sweet bread-like Italian Christmas cake, panettone. The 1980s loved it. Time then to resurrect it, as it tastes fantastic. If using pandoro or a fruitless panettone, sprinkle the bread layers with sultanas as you assemble. I adore this cold – it brings out the vanilla flavour. The custard is only gently sweetened, so it relies on a good snowdrift of icing sugar on serving, and of course a good dollop of something creamy. Serves 8.

½ panettone or pandoro (about 500g)
butter
8 medium eggs
3 heaped tbsp caster sugar
400ml milk
280ml double cream
2 tsp vanilla essence
2½ tbsp brandy
icing sugar

Slice the panettone as you would a cake but a little more slender, buttering each slice on one side. Lay each one, overlapping and butter side up, in a greased 20 x 30cm ovenproof baking dish or tin until full.

Beat the eggs with the sugar and then beat in the milk, cream, vanilla and brandy and pour over the buttered slices. Leave to soak in for 30 minutes.

Next, place a folded tea-towel (or newspaper) on the bottom of a large roasting tin and sit the pudding tin on top, then slide on to the middle shelf of a preheated 190°C/375°F/Gas 5 oven and bake for around 50 minutes until set. Finally remove the dish from its bath, turn up the oven to 220°C/425°F/Gas 7 and bake on the top shelf until crusted.

Handsome apple and blackberry pie

This has a shortbread style pastry on top, which goes lovely and crumbly and gunky underneath. Use a bought sweet shortcrust pastry, if you don't want mine. You can make little pies if you like. Eat with double cream.

6 cooking apples, not too large
350g blackberries
5 tbsp caster sugar
squeeze of lemon juice
50g butter
granulated sugar

Pastry:
60g caster sugar
125g butter
1 medium egg yolk
185g plain flour

Peel and core the apples and cut them into wedges, then place them in a pie dish, in which they'll comfortably sit, allowing enough space for the blackberries to muddle in later. Rain the apples with 3 tbsp of the caster sugar and the lemon juice, then dab and smear with butter, cover with foil, and bake in a 190°C/375°F/Gas 5 oven for about 20 minutes or until nearly cooked but not collapsing. Mix the blackberries with the remaining sugar, and when the apples are ready, mix in. Leave to cool.

For the pastry, put all the ingredients into your processor and briefly blend until it comes together as a dough or do it by hand in a bowl, then knead on the work surface until smooth. Roll into a ball, pat flat, wrap in clingfilm, and refrigerate for about 20 minutes. Roll out the pastry on a floured surface to about 5mm thick. Cut out a rough shape that's bigger than the top of the pie dish, then cut some thin strips off the remaining rolled dough, dampen with water, and press these around the rim of the dish – these will make a perfect seal between dish and crumble pastry topping. Dampen the pastry-lined rim and place the pie-top pastry over the top, lightly pressing the pastry on to its pastry-lined rim, to seal. Then make a small hole or slash in the top for steam to escape. Sprinkle all over with granulated sugar and bake in a 220°C/425°F/Gas 7 oven for about 10 minutes, then turn down to 190°C/375°F/Gas 5 and cook for a futher 15-20 minutes or until the pastry looks just cooked and lightly suntanned rather than too browned.

Rhubarb crumble

Rhubarb crumble has to be absolutely what it is, without fancy twiddles or nonsense. No ginger either, as some would. I just love the unadulterated tongue-smarting flavour of the stem with the sugary yet splodgy crumb on top. The tarty-pink rhubarb of spring will make it sweeter, however my penchant is for the ruby-green stalks of summer – sharp and brazen, they take no prisoners.

900g rhubarb stems
200g caster sugar or light muscovado sugar
small squeeze of lemon juice
200g plain flour
100g butter

Trim the rhubarb and chop it up into short lengths. Put it in a wide pan with 100g of the sugar, a squeeze of lemon juice and about 4 tbsp water. Bring the water to a simmer, and shake the pan a bit so that it all settles down. Once it's bubbled gently for a couple of minutes, you will see a lot more liquid has started to appear. Then turn all the stems over, so that the top ones get into the juices, then bubble up again, pop on a lid, remove from the heat, and leave on one side while you prepare the crumble topping. It will carry on cooking under its own steam, literally. Too much time on the stove will send it to mush, and we want it in chunks.

Mix the flour and the remaining sugar together in a bowl, then drop in the butter, cut into small chunks. Using your fingertips, rub the butter into the flour and sugar until it resembles crumbs. Spoon the rhubarb into a shallow baking dish or tin, but if there's loads of juice only add enough to half fill the pie dish. The rhubarb will produce yet more juice as it bakes. Then cover with the crumble topping and bake in a 200°C/400°F/Gas 6 oven for about 25 minutes or until the crumble topping is looking delicious. Again, get out the custard or the cream for this one.

Baked rice pud

This is how my mum makes it and how my dad hates it. My sister and I love it: enriched with evaporated milk and crusted with a beautiful dappled skin, with some chewy bits along the edges, where skin meets dish. If you're in my dad's camp on this one, then move on to another pud. If not, you'll be tongue out, ready, and dying to make it.

60g round-grain pudding rice
350ml full-fat milk
150ml evaporated milk
knob of butter
1 tbsp caster sugar
¼ tsp freshly grated nutmeg

Stick the rice in a small shallow baking dish or tin – something around 1.5 litres – then pour over the milk and the evaporated milk, plop in the butter, stir in the sugar and then grate over some nutmeg. Bake on the middle shelf of a 150°C/300°F/Gas 2 oven for 2-3 hours. Just forget about it for a while. Take the dog out or something. Once you return, it will have plumped up into the creamiest of rice puddings under a blotchy crust, and there'll be some lovely baking-smell magic in the air. Excellent nursery stuff.

Classic lemon pudding and cream

This is the classic surprise pud, for the mixture does a magic trick as it bakes: a fantastic cakey crust forms on top while a smooth tangy lemon curd evolves underneath. Make it in one dish but if you bake it in heatproof individual bowls, it not only looks good but can be served up without having to serve it – if you get my drift. Make sure you down it with lots of double cream.

100g butter, softened, plus extra for greasing
180g caster sugar
finely grated zest and juice of 4 lemons
4 medium eggs, separated
60g plain flour
120ml milk

If you have a mixer, use it, as it means making this is a doddle. Beat the butter with the sugar until pale and creamy. Then beat in the lemon juice and zest. Slowly add the egg yolks, one at a time, then add the flour slowly, then the milk. Whisk the egg whites until they form soft peaks, then fold these into the pudding mixture. Butter a deep, flat-bottomed, round baking dish or four separate ovenproof serving bowls and pour in the pudding mixture. Place the dish in a roasting tin and half fill the tin with hot water, then place the tin in a 180°C/350°F/Gas 4 oven. Bake for 1 hour or until firm but springy to the touch. Eat while still warm with loadsa cream.

Sticky toffee pud with toffee sauce

This isn't steamed for hours in a basin but tray-baked and then cut into portions and poured with the sauce – so, easy really. A nursery pudding like this needs custard to nurse it along further, so don't forget it.

180g stoned dates (Medjool dates are good)
1tsp bicarbonate of soda
160g unsalted butter
180g golden caster sugar
2 medium eggs
1 tsp vanilla extract
180g self-raising flour
120g light muscovado sugar
4 tbsp double cream

Chop the dates roughly, then tip them into a saucepan with 250ml water and bring to a bubble, then add the bicarb and leave to gently bubble until the dates are softened, about 5 minutes. Beat half the butter with the golden caster sugar, using a whisk, until pale and creamy, then beat in the eggs, vanilla and flour. Then slowly beat in the date water and the chopped dates, until you have a nice slurry-like gloop. Line a 20cm round cake tin or 22cm square baking tin with buttered greaseproof paper (just lightly greased on the inside), then pour in the mixture and bake in a 180°C/350°F/Gas 4 oven for 40 minutes.

Meanwhile, put the muscovado sugar, remaining butter and the cream into a saucepan, stir them together over a low heat, then whack up the heat and bring to a good bubble for a minute or so. Serve the sponge sliced into fat portions and pour over the toffee sauce.

Meringues and custard

Throughout the 1960s and 1970s my mum made pavlovas like they were going out of fashion. They were her party-piece pud. Much to her chagrin, however, they were never quite as spectacular as the confections whipped up by her pal, Diana Crowhurst, the pavlova queen of the Isle of Wight. Along with her themed ikebana floral arrangements, Diana's pavs were the envy of Cowes. They soared, piled and teetering, as did everything then: multi-storey fruit parks, wodged together with whipped vanilla cream. The meringue was sugar crisp on the outside with a wad of silken marshmallowness within. Delicious isles of white.

Eggs and cream make some great puddings. Another is that glorious egg yolk and cream combination, custard: wobbly, unctuous and gloopy; bland, caressing and smooth. You either love it or loathe it. But there's no room for snobbery. Because if you like custard, you like the instant too. And that's the Bird's powder one, that makes the instant bright yellow stuff, excellent for trifles, and slips down without fuss.

Mum visited at the time I baked the custard tart pictured on page 220 (well timed, Mum). I had to put a cage, a lock and a *do not touch, sniff or snick* notice on it. For it had to have its picture taken and she was hovering dangerously near. A proper custard tart is a rare thing of devourable beauty. The just-set eggy milk cuts as smooth as silk: it pierces without pressure and quivers, cracks and slithers. Gone in minutes just after baking in my house.

Custard is at the heart of many a good pud. Just think of all those other great puds that are made of, baked in, sat in or poured with the stuff: sliced bananas and custard, ice-cream, a trifle, and bread and butter pudding with its triangles of oven-crunchy bread sat in a wobbling brandy custard bath. Then there's crème brûlée, a rich vanilla custard under a double-glazing of sugar, and then there's...oh let's get on with it.

Perfect pavlova and meringues

Good meringue is the key to pavlovas and – naturally – to all meringues themselves, and indeed I use my pavlova mix to make meringues. I've been through the mill on this one. I've had the Kenwood spinning for days through vast volumes of glossy white gloop and I've whirled like a dervish alongside it in a cloud of egg white and sugar. I've tried just using caster sugar, a mix of caster and granulated, then caster and icing sugar, and then just icing sugar; I've added cornflour, and left it out; a touch of vinegar, or not; ice-cold water in one lot and a dribble of boiling water in another. And I've baked some batches long and slow – which is not the way to go if you want a soft centre – and others fast to produce marshmallow-soft-centred perfection. The one I give here is the best – you won't fail, I promise.

How should I beat the egg whites? You'll need to use some form of electric gadget as a hand-powered whisk could leave you with repetitive strain injury – or, worse still, a limp wrist. Use an electric mixer or put the whites in a large bowl and beat using an electric hand whisk. A sturdy counter-top mixer is best for the job, as the whites need to be whisked for quite a long time to pump lots of air into them. Make sure the mixing bowl and whisk are spotless. Beat the whites with the caster sugar for about 3 minutes until very firm, then add the icing sugar, vanilla, cornflour and wine vinegar and beat for a further 4 minutes until ultra firm, ultra white and very glossy. Get it stiff and then it won't collapse.

How do I get that classic whirled pavlova shape? There's no need for piping bags, nozzles and all that nonsense, unless of course you're aiming for something retro and Fanny Cradock-like. Using a large metal spoon, scoop the whipped whites on to the greased paper, then, using the back of the spoon and starting from the centre, spread out and flatten slightly in one deft controlled sweep. You want to end up with a vaguely circular-looking cushion that has a slight dip to its middle to hold cream and fruit. Don't touch the sides as this will spoil its fluid and curvaceous looks. To make individual meringues, just take heaped spoonfuls, dollop and swirl in the same fashion.

Doesn't meringue take for ever to cook? No, unless you like yours to be so brittle that it explodes into shards and sugar dust on first bite. I don't. Just before putting the meringue into the oven turn the temperature down to 140°C/275°F/ Gas 1 and then bake for 1 hour and 10 minutes, or 45 minutes for small ones. If you have an electric convection oven, 1 hour should be enough for the pav, and smalls at 35-40 minutes. If you like them less marshmallowy, open the oven door for a few minutes to let out some of the heat, then leave them in the turned-off oven for an hour or two. Once out of the oven leave in a warm place to cool; this will prevent excessive cracking. A few cracks are the norm, although individual ones tend to stay more pristine looking. When cool, carefully detach from the paper and if made in advance, keep in an airtight container. It will keep for up to two days but remember it's soft inside and the moisture will eventually work through.

And on top? Passionfruit is the pav's muse these days: its sharpness, crunchy seeds and exotic perfume make it a classy act. Choose the more shrivelled-looking fruit, as they're riper and their juices are more intense than the perfect-looking ones, or go for sliced peaches, raspberries or strawberries. Double cream is a must, but there's no need to sweeten it, as the meringue adds that. However, if you think excess equals success, you can beat ½ tbsp caster (or vanilla) sugar into the cream. Pile it with what you like but keep it on the sharp side, for it must keep the sweetness of the meringue in check.

What other fruit could I use? Don't go crazy, as some fruit can be too rich or the wrong texture. Kiwi fruit, pineapple, bananas, starfruit and such like are big no-nos for me – but if you must, and love so, then do. After all it's your pav. Poached rhubarb is good: keep the sticks in shape by poaching for just 3 minutes, adding a mere 3 tbsp water, then leave to cool, lid on. There's summer's berries – and raspberries are good with hazelnut-flavoured meringue. Go tropical with sliced mango or papaya. You could make individual pavs – which are just large meringues – and spill each with a chilled mix of berries that have been simmered in sugar. The tumbling fruit and juice will cave, crack and plunge into something baby-doll soft.

One last thing... You'll be left with lots of unused egg yolks. Use them in salad dressings, to make real custard and ice-cream, or combined with more whole eggs in extra-rich omelettes and scrambled eggs.

A glorious pavlova

Looks a million dollars, yet is a cinch to make – see the notes on pages 213-14. They'll be impressed, I tell you. This large pavlova will feed six or make six individual ones if you prefer.

butter or oil for greasing
4 medium egg whites, preferably not too fresh
120g caster sugar
110g icing sugar, sieved
½ tsp vanilla extract
1 tsp cornflour
1 tsp white wine vinegar

To serve:
300ml double cream
4 ripe peaches, sliced, or 5 ripe passionfruit or
    other ripe soft fruit

Turn the oven on to 150°C/300°F/Gas 2. Cover a large baking sheet with greaseproof paper, then lightly grease the paper with the thinnest smear of butter or oil.

Beat the egg whites with the caster sugar until very firm, and then add the icing sugar, vanilla, cornflour and vinegar, and beat for a further 4 minutes. Scoop the meringue mix on to the prepared baking sheet in the shapes you prefer (see page 213). Reduce the temperature of the oven to 140°C/275°F/Gas 1, and bake large pavlovas for 1 hour and 10 minutes, smaller ones for 45 minutes. Remove from the oven, leave to cool, then pack carefully into an airtight container if not using straightaway.

Just before serving, whip the cream until it reaches the stage where when the whisk is lifted from it, it forms very soft and floppy dune-like peaks. Sit the meringue on a large platter, dollop a thick blanket of cream over the top and then cover with fruit slices or the flesh scooped from the passionfruit – juices, seeds and all.

Hazelnut and raspberry pavlova Fresh raspberries, double cream and hazelnut meringue can't be improved upon. The meringue won't turn out quite as puffed as the one above, as the ground hazelnuts release oil into the mixture – but the centre turns out deliciously nougat chewy. Make two and you can then sandwich the lot together to make a meringue cake. Toast 100g whole unskinned hazelnuts, rub in a tea-towel to get rid of their skins, then process the kernels to very fine crumbs. Next, follow the instructions for the above pavlova using 120g golden caster sugar and 110g golden icing sugar instead of the white sugars. Fold the ground hazelnuts thoroughly through the mixture after the egg white and sugar are fully beaten, and complete the recipe following the instructions above. Don't be tempted to beat the ground nuts in, as the mixture will collapse. Top with cream as before and pile with raspberries.

Chocolate chestnut and hazelnut meringues The same hazelnut mixture as above can be used to make six sandwiched meringues – and everyone loves meringues. Prepare the meringue mix as for the hazelnut pavlova. Then, using a large metal spoon, make 12 blobs of the mix across greased greaseproof-paper-lined trays, keeping a good 5cm gap between each, as they'll spread a little. Now turn the oven temperature down to 140°C/275°F/Gas 1, and bake for about 35 minutes. Turn off the oven, open the door for a couple of minutes to release some of the heat, then close and leave the meringues in the cooling oven for a good 2 hours. Then take them out and once cool, carefully detach from the paper. To serve, melt 100g dark chocolate in a bowl set over a pan of simmering water. Beat 250g sweetened chestnut purée with about 4 tbsp double cream to make a smooth thick paste, then stir in the melted chocolate until fully blended, and leave to cool. Whip 450ml double cream to soft peak stage, then spread half of the meringues with the chestnut mixture and the other half with whipped cream, and sandwich together.

Gorgeous lemon meringue pie

Mum still makes this. Thank God she hasn't moved on to caramelised lemon tart and stuff, otherwise there'd be nowhere to turn to for a good quivering lemon meringue pie. Serves about six.

250g sweet shortcrust pastry (bought or see
  page 189)
45g cornflour
juice and finely grated zest of 2 large lemons
80g caster sugar
2 medium egg yolks, lightly beaten

Meringue:
4 medium egg whites
250g granulated sugar

Roll out the pastry to about 3mm thickness and use to line a 20cm tart tin or ring. Prick and chill and then blind-bake as described on page 190, but for 15 minutes. Then remove the lining and rice, and brush the inside with just a touch of the meringue egg white.

Meanwhile, blend the cornflour with 2 tbsp cold water and the lemon juice and zest. Then stir in 300ml boiling water (use the kettle). Pour the mixture into a pan and gently simmer for 3 minutes or so, or until thick. Next,

using a hand whisk, beat the sugar and egg yolks together until pale, then, while still beating, pour the thickened lemon water on to the egg mixture. If it's still very runny, gently heat the curd for a couple more minutes on the stove. Once it has cooled pour it into the baked pastry case and leave to go cold.

To make the meringue, using an electric whisk or mixer, beat the egg whites with half the sugar until stiff, then shake in the remaining sugar and beat until very stiff. Spoon the meringue mixture on to the lemon filling and spread it out using a flat-bladed knife, swirling it a bit. For a retro look, spoon the mix into a poly bag, snip off the tip and pipe dollops, cones, swirls or whatever you want over the lemon filling. Bake in a high 220°C/425°F/Gas 7 oven for about 10-15 minutes, or until the meringue dunes have taken on a touch of colour, are crisp on the outside, yet soft within. Eat with double cream.

Deep custard and nutmeg tart

You will need a 6cm deep x 16cm diameter tart ring – that's a metal ring/band without a base – or use a spring-form tin. If you don't have a deep tart ring, use your favourite tart tin instead. But bear in mind, the shallower and wider the tart ring or tin you use, the shorter the baking time needed. And the shallower the tin, the wider it should be to accommodate the filling. You can always make little custards, using muffin tins – they'll only need a 30-minute bake and are mid-morning coffee material.

350g sweet shortcrust pastry (bought or see
  page 189)
oil or butter for greasing
3 large egg yolks (keep a spoonful of the whites)
900ml full-fat milk
1 large vanilla pod, split
3 large eggs
130g caster sugar
good grating of nutmeg

Roll out the pastry on a lightly floured surface to about 3mm thickness. Lightly grease the tart tin or tart ring (set on a greased baking sheet), then line with the pastry. Flatten out any folds and ruckles, trim off the excess, then press the pastry with your fingers so that it's moulded to the tin and is a similar thickness all over. Now trim it off neatly again. Prick, chill and blind-bake as described on page 190, but for 15 minutes. Once baked, gently ease and lift the lining with its contents out of the pastry case, then brush the hot part-baked pastry immediately with a dash of egg white to seal it.

Meanwhile, heat the milk with the split vanilla pod, without boiling, for about 10 minutes, then turn off the heat and leave to cool a little. Using a wooden spoon, not a whisk, beat the eggs and egg yolks with the sugar until pale, then beat in the hot milk. (The custard filling must be dense – the use of a whisk would create air bubbles.)

Pour the custard through a sieve – to remove any ribbony bits of white – into the tart case, then generously shower the surface with a good grating of nutmeg. It's best to fill the tart case once it's perched on the oven shelf – to avoid any slops from worktop to cooker. Then leave it to bake in a 150°C/ 300°F/Gas 2 oven for about 1½ hours or until set and dappled with a few pale golden blotches. Check up on it a good 10 minutes before the time is up. It's done when it still looks slightly under-set in the centre – the residual heat will firm it up. If you can, eat it while still warm, it's absolutely glorious.

Delicious tinned peach trifle

Okay, this is trailer-trash trifle – everything is instant or comes out of a packet or tin. Seeing as we're into cheating big-time here, you could even buy a jam-filled Swiss roll and use this sliced up instead of having to jam-up the sponge. This trifle may be instant, but not straight to table instant, for all trifles need an overnight sit in the fridge to complete their trifledom. If you want to swap the peaches for sliced bananas, then do so.

3 tbsp Bird's instant custard powder
600ml full-fat milk
8 trifle sponges or 250g plain fatless sponge
strawberry jam
1 x 410g can sliced peaches in syrup
6 tbsp sweet sherry
280ml double cream
1 tbsp caster sugar
handful of toasted flaked almonds or crumbled
  chocolate flake

Make up the custard first according to the tin instructions – using custard powder and milk – then leave to cool. Split open the sponges, spread them thickly with the jam and then sandwich back together again. Arrange the jammed sponges in the base of a large deep bowl. Strain the peach slices, keeping 3 tbsp of their syrup. Mix this reserved syrup with the sherry, and splosh over the sponge. Stick the peach slices, which you have halved, on top, then spoon over the cold custard. Whip the cream with the sugar until it forms soft peaks, then spoon this over too, and sprinkle the top with the toasted flaked almonds (or chocolate flake). Now, you must leave the trifle to stand overnight in the fridge.

No frills crème brûlée

I like crème brûlée as crème brûlée, no farting about. I don't want to find the custard has been flavoured or that there's some fruit skulking around at the bottom of the pot. It's about thick, thick, ultra vanillary custard and brittle shards of sugar. No more and no less. Crunch and cream. Now, I've hesitated putting it in this book, for to be honest it's one of those puds that needs the blow-torch to caramelise the sugar that tops it and blow-torches aren't home cooking. The only other way is to heat the grill until raging hot, then slide the puddings as near to the heat as possible until the sugar has done its thing. I make mine generous, so use four 250ml ovenproof pots, or near that. Alternatively use standard 150ml ramekins and make six.

1 vanilla pod, split
600ml double cream
8 medium egg yolks
1 generous tbsp caster sugar
4 tbsp soft brown sugar

Run the blade of a sharp knife along each opened side of the vanilla pod, scraping out all the seeds – they'll pick up and stick on the blade – then wipe them off into a saucepan and chuck in the pod as well. Pour in the cream, and whisk-stir to mix the seeds through. Put on a gentle heat, and slowly bring to a murmur with a few bubbling blips, then take off the heat and leave on one side, for as long as you can for maximum flavour.

Meanwhile, beat the egg yolks with the caster sugar until pale and creamy. Stir through the infused vanilla cream to rid it of any surface skin and redistribute the vanilla seeds, then fish out and discard the vanilla pod. Pour the infused cream into the egg mixture, beat together, and pour back into the pan. Constantly stirring with the whisk, very gently heat your custard through. It mustn't boil, for the eggs will curdle. If it looks like it's going to bubble, then whip it off the heat and beat through. Once it's thickened, pour it into your ramekin dishes. Sit these in a roasting tin, and pour in enough warm water so that it comes three-quarters of the way up the outside of the pots. Slide into a 160°C/325°F/Gas 3 oven and bake for around 35-40 minutes or until just set in the middle.

Pop the ramekins in the fridge and leave to chill for a few hours (overnight is best). Before you start dinner, sprinkle a tbsp of the brown sugar over each, then blow-torch the sugar or stick under a fierce grill, until the sugar has melted and caramelised. Pop back in the fridge until you're ready for them.

Easy lemon ice-cream

Years back, a friend showed me this easy way to make ice-cream – and you don't need an ice-cream maker. Just plonk the mix in a bowl, put it in the freezer, and forget about it. No stirring. I've been making it ever since.

3 fat juicy lemons
190g icing sugar
450ml double cream

Finely grate the zest of the lemons into a bowl, then squeeze the juice of all the lemons into the bowl too. Stir in the sugar and leave on one side for 30 minutes. Meanwhile, whip the cream with 3 tbsp ice-cold water until it soft peaks, then beat in the lemon juice mixture. Turn into a tub and then shove in the freezer – with no need to stir. Remove 15 minutes before you need to serve it.

Gooseberry fool

You can make gooseberry fool with just the puréed fruit and whipped cream sweetened with a sprinkling of sugar. However, I like mine correct, that's with a very light custard base, so this is the one here. If you don't want to make the custard – and it's only the instant one – then double up on the cream.

500g gooseberries
100g caster sugar
1 tbsp Bird's instant custard powder
150ml full-fat milk
150ml whipping cream

Tumble the gooseberries into a saucepan, pour over the sugar and add 3 tbsp water. Bring to a bubble, turn down to a low murmur, cover and cook – giving a stir through every now and then – for about 20 minutes, or until mushed. Then whizz in a processor until smooth. Meanwhile, put the custard powder in a heatproof bowl, then blend it with 3 tbsp of the milk. Heat the rest of the milk until almost bubbling, then pour this over the blended custard powder, while stirring. Pour the mixture back into the pan and gently heat while stirring to make a custard. Tip in half of the puréed gooseberries and stir, then leave to go completely cold. Whip the cream until it forms soft peaks, then fold this into the gooseberry custard. Fold the remaining gooseberry purée loosely through, spoon into small pots or glasses, and then chill well.

Chocolate, coffee and cake

I started early with cakes, yet I'm sure Dad (yes, Dad...but just this once) was in the kitchen to help. I baked my first one for Mum, who was laid up with a bad back in bed. It was a big cake. Big enough – thinking about it now – to knock Mum back on her back for a few days more. I took it out of a book titled *Talking about Cakes* written by someone called Margaret Bates, pictured on the book jacket with horn-rimmed glasses and bouffant hair. The cake was a real space-age 60s confection. Like the author.

Decades later, and as mother of two prospective little cake makers, my sister's words upon the subject of that first cake could curdle the staunchest of cake mixes. It was a cake that launched praise, love and adoration. I was six (my sister five), and it was made for Mum who, in her state of inertia, was in need of love. 'Sabotage,' said my sister Catherine to me, sounding the perfect little Wednesday Adams, yet now 30 years older, 'was now unfortunately out of the question.' According to her, it appeared from nowhere, immaculately stuck with an almond jacket, its little crown of brandy-snap cones piped perfectly with cream, not a thing out of place, and with me – the icing on the cake – beaming behind it.

My sister, however, went on to become our in-house cake maker, winning best-in-show throughout her school days at numerous village-hall cake-making competitions. She'd send the odd piece of cake to me at boarding school, to remind me she was at home and I was not. Since then I have rung her for a few tips on Victoria sponge making. Her top one is to have everything at room temperature before you begin, and like many sponge makers, she uses margarine (though I've found butter to be the best). I prefer the all-in-one way, where you sling all the sponge ingredients into the mixer bowl and whip the lot up together. Simple. For me this way made the most perfect and easy sponge: light but with a dense buttery crumb, and when spread with red fruit jam and thick cream, it excelled. I'd had to get this sponge thing right. After all, boys must win – and with little effort.

Catherine did the other way, creaming in the butter with the sugar first, laboriously adding things slowly. She'd said no to cream and jam in the filling – it was jam only. I disagreed, for my cake being lighter can take it – and needs it. We just didn't agree on cakes. She may have won prizes, but – I started first. Now though, she has just owned-up to switching to the all-in-one way, and cursing me for being right. So, Catherine... ner-ner-nerner-ner! Now I'm in for it.

Crumbly-soft sweet shop-bought stuff I'm a sucker for too. Take those Fondant Fancies – I'm a big fan. Have been for years too. In case I've lost you, they're those luminous acid-yellow and nightie-pink cubes of cake that come in boxes of six. The love lies in their packet taste: sponge stuck with a bit of jam, a cream squirt, and everything in a blanket of icing. Reminds me of birthday cake: sickly sweet. Aunts fed me these: a Joyce, an Elsie and two Gladyses, whose kitchens were warehouses to boxed tea-time things, where the grill saw only a sultana-sticky bun, and cooking was scissors or a tin-opener. So, at the risk of retiring to burble on in Alan Bennett land – the one of Parker Knolls, lacy curtains and Mr Kipling slices – I must now own up to being rather partial to a Fancy, a slice of Battenburg, a Viennese Whirl or indeed, a macaroon or two. The mere rustle of these and I'm in there, faster than Thora Hird. Hmmm. Imagine that. Enough chat about cakes.

Now to chocolate. Cooking with chocolate is sensual stuff – right from step one. There's the unwrapping of its shiny paper sleeve and the tearing of its thin slip of foil to reveal the first flash of dark square. Then there's the muffled snap and whiff of its bitter musk, followed by shards disappearing into a melt of cocoa-butter darkness, and, finally, a rich plop as it's poured. The pleasure goes on as you emulsify it with other velvety things such as eggs, butter and cream, get the spatula and palette knife behind it, and smack it on thick – getting ribbons, blobs and smudges all over hands, tea-towel and clothes. And then comes the final bit: the eating. Mmmm. The overdoing and undoing of everything.

There are always demands for a replay with chocolate: for more, more – and more. So in here there's an extra-thick slice of the stuff: handsome cakes and profiteroles tidal-waved with it; a mousse and tiramisù made thick with it; a Christmassy fruit-and-nut chunky slab; and an intense tart stacked to the gunwales with the essence of the bean. Enough I think, eh? As if.

PS Just about everything in this chapter is big, as I reckon we don't now cook cakes and things unless it's for a pud or a special something to impress when the hordes descend. So, I've geared it for that.

Perfect sponge

This is easy, as I'm up for the easiest mixing method – the all-in-one-sponge: throw everything into the bowl and switch on. It gives top results. And if you prefer to use margarine instead of butter, please do, but the stuff from the block gives better results than the soft tub marge, as the block contains 10 per cent more fat (and use Stork SB in both cases).

Equipment needed? If you have an electric mixer with a K-beater attachment, use it. If not, use a bowl and an electric whisk or hand whisk. Power tools won't make a better cake but will speed things up.

And the secrets of success? For the perfect sponge, a few things need to be set in order before you start. First, switch the oven to 160-180°C/325-350°F/Gas 3-4, then lightly grease two 20cm diameter cake sandwich tins with butter. Line just the bases of each with circles of greaseproof paper, and grease the paper on top. Next, make sure all your ingredients and equipment are at room temperature. Your eggs must have been removed from the fridge a good 2 hours earlier; the butter (or margarine, if using) must be warm and very soft. Your mixing bowl and K-beater or whisk are best if slightly warm, so dip into hot water, then drain and dry.

Retro coffee cake

This a glam version of the Victoria sponge, and you should follow the detailed instructions above. A dense sponge, not dissimilar to the one Mum made back in the 1960s (though Mum never made it to the walnut bit – her feet were up on the sofa before then). Cuts into about 10 good wedges.

175g unsalted butter, plus extra for greasing
175g self-raising flour
1 tsp baking powder
175g caster sugar
3 medium free-range eggs, lightly beaten
1 tsp vanilla essence
1 tbsp instant coffee mixed with ½ tbsp boiling
  water

Coffee butter icing:
150g unsalted butter, at room temperature
220g icing sugar
1½ tbsp cream
1½ tbsp instant coffee mixed with 1 tbsp boiling
  water
100g shelled walnuts, crumbled

Preheat the oven to the temperature above, and grease and line the sponge tins. Sift the flour and baking powder into the mixing bowl, then plop knobs of the butter on top, shake over the sugar, and add the eggs, vanilla essence and coffee. Then beat everything together until thick and well blended. Spoon into the tins, smooth, bake and test for doneness as above.

Cool in the tins for a few minutes, then loosen the sides of the sponge from the tin with a bendy knife and turn out on to a wire rack. Peel off their greaseproof-papered bases, and leave to go cold.

To make the coffee butter icing, beat the butter with the sugar, then beat in the cream and the coffee. Spread one sponge with a thick swirl of icing and sandwich the two halves together. Next, using a wide bendy knife, spread the icing on the top of the cake first, then around the sides, then stick on the walnuts, if using. The old way was to roll the cake in the walnuts, but things can get messy, so I'd do it by hand.

Classic Victoria sponge with jam and cream

Ideally a sponge should not be stored for longer than two days, for it will start to dry out, even in its tin. So eat it up quick. Cuts into about ten good wedges. I've kept it in 5g denominations for those that like to convert back to ounces.

175g unsalted butter, plus extra for greasing
175g self-raising flour
1 tsp baking powder
175g caster sugar
3 medium eggs, lightly beaten
1 tsp vanilla essence

To finish:
raspberry or strawberry jam
whipped double cream
icing sugar for dusting

Switch the oven to 160-180°C/325-350°F/Gas 3-4, and grease and line the sponge tins. Kick off by sifting the flour with the baking powder into the mixing bowl, then plop knobfuls of softened butter on top, shake over the sugar, crack in the eggs and add the vanilla. Then beat everything together until thick and well blended. It's as easy as that. Spoon an equal amount of the sponge mixture into each lined and greased tin and smooth level with a broad-bladed knife. Bake on the middle shelf of the preheated oven for about 30 minutes or until just springy when prodded in the middle. Some ovens may need 5 minutes longer. Further testing can be done by sticking a skewer or fine-bladed knife in the middle: it should pull out clean. Leave the cooked sponges to sit in their tins for a few minutes, then loosen the sides of the sponge from the tin with a bendy knife and turn out on to a wire rack. Peel off their greaseproof-papered bases, and leave to go cold.

To assemble, spread the base side of one with jam and spread the base side of the other with the whipped double cream, then sandwich the two halves together, so that the cream is on top. Finish it off with a blizzard of icing sugar. Perfection. Now sit down to a cuppa and a well-earned slice.

Deluxe chocolate, coffee and hazelnut gâteau

This cake is more than a cake. It's a gâteau. Not one you would have found on a 70s cream-quivering sweet trolley, but a cappuccino version, tailored with chocolate, hazelnut, espresso and cream. A gâteau of chummy yet grown-up flavours. Perfect for pudding. Tiering up the layers and assembling the whole caboodle is easy. You don't have to be immaculate about it – although artfully constructing something resembling a smart hat is a good approach. Not an Ascot hat mind – completely Mrs Shilling, frivolous and over-the-top – but something that tastes as good as it looks.

You'll need two 16cm diameter loose-bottomed sponge tins, but it doesn't matter if your tins are slightly smaller or bigger. Cuts into eight tall slices. A smaller cake for four can be made by halving the sponge quantities and using 12cm tins. The fatless sponges used in this cake are the same as those used in the strawberry and cream layer cake recipe but with ground nuts added, so look to that one for extra in-depth detail on how to make the sponge (see page 243).

Hazelnut sponge:
butter for greasing
100g shelled hazelnuts, roasted
4 medium eggs
250g caster sugar
250g plain flour
1 tsp vanilla essence

Filling:
1 medium egg
1 tbsp caster sugar
330g mascarpone cheese
130ml double cream, whipped
100ml strong coffee, cold
4 tbsp coffee liqueur, such as Kahlua

Chocolate coating:
125ml double cream
250g dark chocolate (minimum 70% cocoa
   solids), broken into pieces

To make the sponge, grease and base line your tins with greaseproof paper, and then grind the roasted nuts to crumbs in a processor. Using an electric whisk or mixer, whisk the eggs until frothy. Gradually add the sugar and continue to whisk until the mixture is absolutely white and holds its shape. Fold in the flour, ground nuts and vanilla essence and mix. Divide the mixture between your two tins, then bake in a 180°C/350°F/Gas 4 oven for 35-40 minutes, or until firm to the touch. Leave to cool on a rack, then remove the paper and slice off and discard the sugary crust top of each. Then slice each sponge into three rounds or just two – if you're not feeling brave.

To make the filling, beat the egg with the sugar, then beat in the mascarpone. Beat the cream to soft peak stage and fold this into the mascarpone mixture. Then mix the coffee with the coffee liqueur.

To assemble the cake, place a slice of sponge on a serving plate, then sprinkle with some flavoured coffee. Try to avoid sprinkling too near to the edge of the sponge layers. Then cover with a thick layer of mascarpone cream and cover this with another round of sponge and repeat the process until all the sponge is used up – leaving the top layer unsprinkled. Then pop it in the fridge to firm up.

To make the chocolate coating, heat the cream until it almost bubbles, then remove from the heat, add the chocolate and stir until fully melted and mixed. Leave it to cool and thicken, beating through occasionally. You want it spreadable without being too runny.

To keep the plate clean of chocolate, lay four strips of greaseproof paper in a noughts-and-crosses pattern underneath the circumference of the cake; these can then be pulled away after you've been creative. Using a wide knife, apply generous portions of the chocky coating to the sides and top of the cake and swirl over. Take care not to scrape the sponge, as crumbs entering the coat will spoil the effect. Then top with a few extra hazelnuts if you like, and keep in a cool place, enough time for the coffee to work its magic on the sponge. It needs the wait.

Smart double chocolate fudge cake

This is proper chocolate cake. It's the Rolls Royce of chocolate cakes, as it's stuffed, upholstered and trimmed in chocolate. Enough said. There are two chocolate stages involved here – a baking one and a coating one. I'll spell it out, so that you don't get all your chocolate, eggs and butter in a twist. Cake making is the only time I get out the kitchen scales and think about measuring. It's flour free, so anyone with an allergy – no probs. Use the vac-packed cooked and peeled chestnuts you find in supermarkets. Cuts into eight…As smart and tailored as a Prada suit.

120g unsalted butter, plus extra for greasing
100g peeled cooked chestnuts (ready-done vac-packed ones)
200g dark chocolate (minimum 70% cocoa solids), broken into pieces
5 medium eggs, separated
150g caster sugar

Chocolate gloss:
250g dark chocolate (as before)
2 tsp golden syrup
100g unsalted butter

To make the cake, butter the base and sides of a 20cm spring-form tin, then cut a strip of greaseproof paper to fit the sides and a disc to fit the base. Grease the paper as well. Using a processor, blast the chestnuts to fine crumbs. Put a heatproof bowl over a pan of simmering water, making sure the bowl doesn't touch the water, then put the chocolate in the bowl and allow to melt. Stir in the butter and remove the bowl from the pan.

Meanwhile, put the egg yolks in one bowl and the whites in another – bowls large enough to whisk up in. Add the sugar to the yolks and, using an electric whisk or hand whisk, beat until pale and creamy. Then, using a wooden spoon, beat the melted chocolate into this mixture, followed by the ground chestnuts. Whisk the whites until they form soft peaks and fold these into the chocolate and egg mixture too, until there are no traces of white. Pour this mixture into the tin and bake on the middle shelf of a 180°C/350°F/Gas 4 oven for 25-30 minutes. Test it by sticking a skewer through the centre, but remember this is not a sponge cake: the mixture is dense and should remain moist. Once cooked, leave to cool in its tin. Then unclip the tin and lift out the cake, removing the base, then carefully remove the band of paper, tidying off any wayward crumbs. Slide on to a serving plate (or keep in a cake tin).

To make its glossy coat, the day you want to serve the cake, melt the chocolate as on page 231. Stir in the golden syrup, then the butter until thoroughly incorporated. Leave to cool for half an hour, then reheat it again until liquid, then leave to cool again. This twice-heating stops unsightly marks appearing on the cake's jacket once it's set. Once cooled, it should end up spreadable and not too runny – and you may have to wait up to an hour. Meanwhile, cut out four strips of greaseproof paper and slide them under the cake – in a noughts-and-crosses grid arrangement, so that there are no gaps between cake base and plate. Spoon the chocolate mixture into the centre of the cake then, using a wide bendy knife, swirl the glossy chocolate emulsion over the edges, trowel it around the sides and back up on top again, to give it a delicious whipped, whirled and tailored finish. Keep it somewhere cool, but don't refrigerate it.

Chocolate mousse

Easy pud this one. Kids can have it with a bought chocolate flake – and grown-ups too, for that matter.

200g dark chocolate (minimum 70% cocoa solids), broken into pieces
2 tbsp strong black coffee
4 medium eggs, separated
1 tbsp brandy or rum (optional)
whipped double cream to serve

Melt the chocolate with the coffee in a heatproof bowl set over a pan of simmering water. Stir it occasionally, then remove the bowl and leave the mixture to cool just a little. Beat the egg yolks into the chocolate, along with the brandy. Beat the whites until stiff – an electric something or other will help with this – and then fold them thoroughly into the chocolate mixture. It's best to mix in a big spoonful thoroughly first then fold in the rest. Now spoon the mousse into individual pots and chill for several hours, preferably overnight. Eat with whipped cream on top.

Glossy chocolate profiteroles

This was such a posh dessert, which we never saw at home. Heavens, no. It was the one that Dad would quote, just to spark a snarl from Mum. Only the Beverleys or Barbaras of the time delivered this, at their elegant soirées, floating around in bell-sleeved chiffon and charm bracelets. Mum was more bought choc éclairs, Sunday lunches and a rope of amber beads. A profiterole is just the waif version of a chocolate éclair, so you could make éclairs instead with the same set of ingredients – just pipe your pastry out long shaped rather than blob it. Makes 20 to 25.

100g unsalted butter, plus extra for greasing
150g plain flour
1 tsp caster sugar
4 medium eggs, beaten
300ml double cream, whipped

Chocolate sauce:
250g dark chocolate (minimum 70% cocoa
  solids), broken into pieces
50g unsalted butter
3 tsp golden syrup
3 tbsp double cream

Lightly grease two baking sheets with butter and line each with greaseproof paper. Switch the oven to 200°C/ 400°F/Gas 6. Stick the butter and 250ml water in a saucepan, bring to a bubble, then remove from the heat. Tip in the flour, sugar and ½ tsp salt, beating at the same time: it will start looking like a massive glob of roux at this point. Keep beating away until the mixture leaves the sides of the pan and goes into a ball.

Now beat in the eggs, one at a time, until well blended. Then using two teaspoons, form the mixture into walnut-sized balls and place on the prepared baking sheets. Or pipe them for a pointy top effect. Bake the choux balls for about 45 minutes – check up on them after 30. If they're golden, puffed and crisped, then they're ready. Transfer them to a wire rack, then slice them almost halfway through, to allow the steam out. You don't want them chewy. You can store them in a tin for a day or two – but if doing this, pop them back in the oven for a few minutes to make sure they've crisped up and lost all their moisture.

For the sauce, melt the chocolate in a bowl set over a pan of simmering water, then mix in the butter, golden syrup and cream, and remove from the heat. This can be reheated – just put it back over the water pan. Near to when you want to serve, whip the cream until it soft peaks, then stuff or pipe a blob into each profiterole. Serve them doused with the chocolate sauce.

White and dark chocolate tiramisù

Makes six pots, or you could put it all into one dish.

2 medium eggs
caster sugar
500g mascarpone cheese
250ml double cream, plus 2 tbsp
100ml strong, freshly brewed coffee
3 tbsp Kahlua liqueur, or other coffee liqueur
1 packet sponge finger biscuits
1 tbsp shelled hazelnuts, roasted and ground
100g white chocolate, broken into pieces
150g dark bitter chocolate (minimum 70% cocoa solids), broken into pieces

Using a hand whisk, beat the eggs with 2 tbsp of the sugar until pale, then beat in the mascarpone and the 2 tbsp double cream until the mixture is smooth. Mix the coffee with another 2-3 tsp of sugar and the liqueur, then dunk each sponge finger briefly into this. Layer the soaked fingers into the base of each dish or pot, about four per serving. Dribble a tbsp more of the coffee mixture over each, sprinkle with hazelnuts, then spoon the mascarpone on top, gently pushing down to fill any gaps.

Melt the white chocolate in a bowl set over a pan of simmering water, making sure the bottom of the bowl is not touching the water. As soon as it has melted, allow it to cool, just a little. Meanwhile, beat the double cream until it forms soft peaks, then beat the white chocolate into the cream. Spoon on top of the mascarpone, level off and refrigerate until needed.

To serve, melt the dark chocolate (in the same way as the white chocolate), then once cooled a tad, pour over each serving, and take to the table straightaway. Delicious. (See image on page 236.)

5-minute tiramisùs These I used to make when I did a stint as pudding chef at Antonio Carluccio's Neal Street Restaurant in London. Beat 1 egg with 1 tbsp caster sugar, then beat in a 250g tub of mascarpone cheese and 2 tbsp double cream. Mix a cup of strong instant coffee with 3 tbsp coffee liqueur, then dunk in sponge finger biscuits (you'll need around 12 in total) until just soft but not falling apart, and use to line four individual little dishes. Break them up a bit to fill any large gaps. Add a dash of the coffee mix to each pot to saturate the biscuits, then dollop the mascarpone mixture on top. Smooth over with a knife, and dust with cocoa powder. Now just leave them to chill and set for a few hours in the fridge.

Christmas choc 'n' nut slab

What with its nuts, figs and spice, this looks and tastes really Christmassy and feeds loads, so keep this idea for then. It's okay to give it a spell in the fridge to firm it up, but take it out well before you serve, as its true flavour shines at room temperature, and it will cut better. Great with coffee, and no need for any other pud.

vegetable oil for greasing
300g dark cooking chocolate (minimum 70% cocoa solids) and 200g plain (sweeter) chocolate, broken into pieces
1 tbsp Grand Marnier or Cointreau (optional)
10 cloves, finely ground
2 tsp ground cinnamon
¾ tsp freshly grated nutmeg
10 cardamom pods, seeds only, crushed
380ml double cream
12 dried figs, chopped
170g blanched skinned almonds, toasted and chopped
120g shelled and skinned hazelnuts, toasted and chopped
30g candied orange peel, chopped
icing sugar, to dust

Line a very lightly greased tin measuring 4cm deep x 18cm square (or a shallow container of similar volume) with clingfilm. Put the chocolate and liqueur (if using) in a heatproof bowl and place over a pan of simmering water – making sure the base of the bowl isn't in contact with the water. Let the chocolate melt.

Mix the ground cloves, cinnamon, nutmeg and cardamom into the cream and warm through without boiling. Remove the chocolate from the heat and gently stir in the spiced cream but do not beat. Mix together the remaining chopped ingredients, then pack a layer into the lined container. Pour some of the spiced chocolate ganache over until just covered, then add another layer of fruit and nuts and some more of the ganache. Continue until everything is used up, smooth with a palette knife, then refrigerate until set.

When set, use the edges of the clingfilm to lift the chocolate slab from the container. Turn on to a chopping board and peel away the clingfilm. Bring the chocolate to room temperature, dust with a drift of icing sugar and slice into slim rectangles or cubes. Will last a couple of days, unless it's all scoffed. (See image on page 237.)

Lemon syrup cake

Fail-safe and glorious, that's lemon cake. For those that like their cake extra sticky and lemony, make up a double quantity of the syrup and save half for serving – and dollop slices with crème fraîche or double cream. You can dress it up further by topping the cake with lemon icing or lemon curd.

110g unsalted butter, softened, plus extra for
  greasing
175g caster sugar
175g self-raising flour
4 tbsp milk
grated zest of 1 lemon
2 large eggs

Lemon syrup:
juice of 2 fat lemons
75g icing sugar

Lightly grease a 900g loaf tin with butter, then line the sides and base with greaseproof paper and butter again. Put all the cake ingredients, plus a pinch of salt, in a bowl or mixer and beat for about 3 minutes, until well blended. Spoon the cake mix into the lined and buttered cake tin and bake in a 180°C/350°F/Gas 4 oven for about 45 minutes. Then remove and leave in the tin to cool a little.

To make the syrup, gently warm the lemon juice and icing suger in a pan until the sugar has fully dissolved. Prick the cake all over with a fork or skewer – you can stab deep – then pour the hot syrup all over. Leave the cake until it is almost cold before turning out – and if serving as a pud, dollop slices with crème fraîche or pour on cream.

Buttered ginger cake

A tin of this sticky ginger cake came with us on every family camping and caravanning holiday, and lasted the trip. It was stowed under the dining table's fitted seat, so we all had to shove up every time it was needed. Which was often.

It improves with keeping, and each magnificent slice should be buttered. Not sure that sitting on it helps, though. I'm sure you could make it with self-raising flour and then do away with the baking powder and bicarb, but then we've always made it this way and it works. If you don't want a big one, halve the quantities, and use a 900g loaf tin instead.

170g unsalted butter, plus extra for greasing
450g plain flour
1½ tsp ground ginger
2 tsp baking powder
½ tsp bicarbonate of soda
6 fat knobs stem ginger in syrup, chopped
220g soft brown sugar
350g golden syrup
280ml full-fat milk
1 medium egg

Lightly grease and then line a 2.3 litre square or round tin (or something of similar size) with greaseproof paper and then butter the paper on the inside as well. Sift the flour, ground ginger, baking powder, bicarb and ½ tsp salt into a big mixing bowl (or your electric mixer bowl) and then mix well together. Add the stem ginger to the flour mixture. Tip the sugar, butter and golden syrup into a saucepan and warm through, giving it a stir, but don't allow it to get hot – it's just to get the syrup on the run – then remove from the heat. Stir in the milk and lightly beat in the egg, then tip this into the flour and beat well until everything is well mixed – or turn on the mixer. Pour the cake mix into your prepared tin and bake it in a 180°C/350°F/Gas 4 oven for 1½ hours (a smaller one about an hour). If it starts to darken too heavily, then cover loosely with foil. Once cooled in its tin, remove and store in a tightly sealed tin. It will keep for an age – up to a month.

Deluxe chocolate tart

It's deep, it's rich, it cuts into big slices. It's downright everything you want from chocolate. Make it for a crowd – and eat it with cream. You'll have some pastry left over – but too much rather than too little makes the rolling and then the lining of the tin easy. You can use shop-bought sweet shortcrust if you prefer. Make sure all your ingredients are at room temperature. Cuts into 12 slices.

500g sweet shortcrust pastry (see page 191)

Filling:
400g dark bitter chocolate (minimum 70% cocoa solids), broken into pieces
300g unsalted butter
90g caster sugar
4 medium eggs
6 medium egg yolks
3 tbsp brandy (optional)

Roll out the pastry to about 3mm thickness and fit into a 4cm deep x 26-28cm diameter greased tart tin. Prick the base all over with a fork. Trim the sides but leave a 5mm overhang (to combat any shrinkage). Prepare and chill as for blind-baking (see page 190), then bake blind for about 15 minutes in a 190°C/375°F/Gas 5 oven. Remove and carefully trim off the pastry overhang, then lift out the liner with the rice, and return the pastry case to the oven, on a lower shelf, for another 10-15 minutes to bake the inside. Once out of the oven, brush the inside with a very light coating of egg white (you'll have some left over from the filling), which will help keep the pastry crisp once the filling is in.

Meanwhile, prepare the filling. Break the chocolate into a heatproof bowl and place over a simmering pan of water (without it touching), until melted. Then stir the butter into the chocolate and once fully blended, remove the bowl from the pan and leave to cool, just a little. Meanwhile, using an electric whisk beat the sugar with the whole eggs and the yolks until well thickened, then beat in the brandy (if using). Using a wooden spoon, gently beat this into the chocolate mixture, until it looks dark through and through. Pour the chocolate mixture into the baked tart case, level, and pop back in the oven for about 5 minutes, then remove and leave for about 2 hours so that the chocolate sets. It will keep overnight – but don't refrigerate.

Strawberries and cream layer cake

This is high-rise strawberry heaven. It's a gâteau, one of the best homes for strawberries and cream, and it's got white chocolate in. Eat for a summer tea or as pud. This cuts into six generous wedges. If white chocolate scares you, leave it out – it will still be gorgeous.

butter for greasing
2 medium eggs
125g caster sugar
½ tsp vanilla essence
125g plain flour

Filling:
500g strawberries
2 tbsp caster sugar
150g white chocolate (optional), broken into pieces
450ml double cream, at room temperature
100ml Kirsch or a strawberry liqueur

Dig out a 16cm diameter loose-bottomed cake tin, or something near in diameter, then cut out a circle of greaseproof paper to fit the base. Grease the inside of the tin with butter, then stick the paper in to base-line, then grease the top side of the paper.

To make the sponge, you'll need to go electric, as it involves a lot of beating. So, using a hand-held electric whisk or, better still, a mixer with whisk attachment, whisk the eggs until frothy. Gradually add the sugar and continue to whisk until the mixture is absolutely white and holds its shape – this could take a good 4 minutes or so. Then beat in the vanilla essence, then fold in the flour and mix together by hand – but don't over-do it. You don't want to lose the air that's been beaten into the whites. Spoon the mixture into the prepared tin, level, then bake in a 180°C/350°F/Gas 4 oven for 30-40 minutes, or until firm to the touch.

Once cooled a little, remove the sponge from its tin, peel off the paper, and leave to cool on a rack. Then, using a serrated bread knife, slice the sponge into three rounds. The best way to do this is to hold the sponge flat on the work surface with the flat of your hand, then to saw through parallel with the work surface. It's a lot easier than it sounds. Promise.

To make the filling, slice each strawberry in half lengthways, then toss the slices with the sugar. (Any juices that collect from the sugared strawberries can be mixed with the liqueur just before assembly.) Melt the white chocolate (if using) in a bowl set over a pan of simmering water – making sure the bottom of the bowl is not touching the water. As soon as it has melted, remove from the heat and allow it to cool just a little. Meanwhile, beat the double cream until it forms soft peaks, then, if using the chocolate, beat it into the whipped cream.

To assemble the cake, take one sponge slice and place it on your chosen cake plate, then sprinkle it with a good few drops of the liqueur. Spread with white chocolate cream, and cover with a layer of sliced strawberries and then a touch more cream. Lay another sponge slice on top and do the same, repeating with the final slice, then lightly press together until the whole caboodle gently bulges at the seams. Top the cake with the remaining cream and strawberries. Leave somewhere cool for a good 2 hours to allow the delicious juices to work their magic into the sponge. Fantastic.

Index